Sakya Paṇḍita: Three Biographies

Sakya Paṇḍita: Three Biographies

Chosen and introduced by His Holiness the Sakya Trichen

Written by
Drogön Chögyal Phakpa (Lodrö Gyaltsen)
Gorampa Sönam Sengé
Jamgön Ameshab (Ngawang Kunga Sönam)

Translated by Khenpo Kalsang Gyaltsen and
Chodrungma Kunga Chodron

Wisdom

Wisdom Publications
132 Perry Street
New York, NY 10014 USA
wisdom.org

Library of Congress Cataloging-in-Publication Data
Names: 'Phags-pa Blo-gros-rgyal-mtshan, 1235-1280, author. | Go-rams-pa Bsod-nams-seng-ge, 1429–1489, author. | Ngag-dbang-kun-dga'-bsod-nams, 'Jam-mgon A-myes-zhabs, 1597– approximately 1662, author. | Kalsang Gyaltsen, Khenpo, translator. | Peak, Lois, translator.
Title: Sakya paṇḍita: three biographies: chosen and introduced by his holiness the Sakya Trichen / by Drogön Chögyal Phakpa (Lodrö Gyaltsen), Gorampa Sönam Sengé, Jamgön Ameshab (Ngawang Kunga Sönam); translated by Khenpo Kalsang Gyaltsen and Chodrungma Kunga Chodron.
Description: New York, NY, USA: Wisdom, [2025] | Includes bibliographical references and index. | Text in English. Translation from Tibetan.
Identifiers: LCCN 2024048194 (print) | LCCN 2024048195 (ebook) | ISBN 9781614297574 (paperback) | ISBN 9781614297734 (ebook)
Subjects: LCSH: Sa-skya Paṇḍi-ta Kun-dga'-rgyal-mtshan, 1182–1251. | Sa-skya-pa lamas—China—Tibet Autonomous Region—Biography. | LCGFT: Biographies.
Classification: LCC BQ7950.S347 P43 2025 (print) | LCC BQ7950.S347 (ebook) | DDC 294.3092 [B]—dc23/eng/20241209
LC record available at https://lccn.loc.gov/2024048194
LC ebook record available at https://lccn.loc.gov/2024048195

ISBN 978-1-61429-757-4 ebook ISBN 978-1-61429-773-4

29 28 27 26 25
5 4 3 2 1

Cover design by Gopa & Ted2, Inc. Interior design by PerfecType.

Printed on acid-free paper that meets the guidelines for permanence and durability of the Production Guidelines for Book Longevity of the Council on Library Resources.

Printed in Canada.

Contents

Introduction

By His Holiness the Forty-First Sakya Trichen

THE BIOGRAPHIES OF great masters are a powerful source of inspiration for practitioners. From biographies we can learn how the earlier gurus proceeded on the spiritual path; how they studied and practiced; what helped them develop their experience; and how they attained realization. In this way, we can then try to follow in their footsteps. For me personally, biographies are a very, very important source of inspiration, especially the biography of Sakya Paṇḍita.

I am, of course, not only a practitioner in the same religious tradition as Sakya Paṇḍita, but am also a descendant of the same Khön Sakypa family lineage. From a very young age, I received Sakya Paṇḍita's blessing rituals and initiations, learned his biography, heard stories of his great wisdom and knowledge, and tried to emulate how he practiced. Not only members of the Khön family, but members of all Sakya monasteries and nunneries honor his anniversary days, perform his guru yoga practice, and, of course, study his writings.

This book contains three biographies of Sakya Paṇḍita (1182–1251) by Drogön Chögyal Phakpa (1235–80), Gorampa Sönam Sengé (1429–89), and Jamgön Ameshab (1597–1659). They each have their own way of understanding how the great master cultivated his good qualities, and they wrote primarily to inspire themselves. They also drew on different historical sources or, in the case of Chögyal Phakpa, personal memories. Although each of the biographers provides a similar account of the major events of his life, each highlights different aspects and inner qualities. Taken together, an amazing and inspiring account of this great master arises.

Sakya Paṇḍita was the fourth of the five great founders of the Sakya order. Sakya Paṇḍita's great-grandfather, Khön Könchok Gyalpo, established a monastery in the Sakya region of Tibet in 1073. Khön Könchok Gyalpo's son, Sachen Kunga Nyingpo, is considered the first of the five founders of the Sakya order. Sachen Kunga Nyingpo's sons, Sönam Tsemo and Jetsun Drakpa Gyaltsen, were the second and third founders; they were pure lay-vow holders and did not marry or take a consort. Sakya Paṇḍita was the son of their brother, Palchen Öpo, and was tutored from childhood by his uncle, Jetsun Drakpa Gyaltsen. Sakya Paṇḍita's own nephew and student, Drogön Chögyal Phakpa, became the fifth of the five founders. They were all very learned scholars and realized masters.

Sakya Paṇḍita's life was inspiring, and we can learn from virtually every aspect of it. He was a such a great master that his influence still shapes Tibetan Buddhism today. His thoughts, words, and deeds were influential not only to the Sakyapa. He also made important contributions to the religious and political landscape of Tibet, Mongolia, and now also the West.

There are many logical reasons, prophecies, and quotations that make us believe that Sakya Paṇḍita was no ordinary human being, but a true emanation of Mañjuśrī, and that his mind fully possessed every type of wisdom. We believe that he was already enlightened, and like the Buddha, came to this world in the form of a human being in order to show us how to follow the path from suffering to liberation. As Mañjuśrī incarnate, his life demonstrates to us that if we study, even ordinary humans can gain great knowledge and wisdom. And he was not only a scholar with great wisdom, he was also very highly realized, a true mahāsiddha who fully combined great wisdom and great realization.

Sakya Paṇḍita lived during a very tumultuous time. To the south of Tibet, invading armies were destroying the great Buddhist universities and monasteries in India, such as Nalanda and Vikramaśīla, and to the north and east, much of Eurasia was being overtaken by Mongol conquest. Despite the difficult political situation of his time, Sakya Paṇḍita devoted his life to the study, teaching, and preservation of the Dharma. He became a truly great scholar.

In fact, Sakya Paṇḍita was the first Tibetan to be awarded the exalted Indian title of paṇḍita, which was reserved for the greatest scholars who had achieved outstanding mastery in each of the classical disciplines and then-known sciences. Before him, there were no other Tibetan paṇḍitas. In addition to his native Tibetan, Sakya Paṇḍita was fully fluent in both spoken and written Sanskrit, which was the language of the Dharma at the time. It was very difficult to learn and even then was little known among ordinary Tibetans. In fact, he wrote several treatises on various aspects of Sanskrit linguistics and could fluently discuss and debate in that language.

There is a story about Sakya Paṇḍita's great mastery of Sanskrit that is recounted by his nephew and spiritual heir, Chögyal Phakpa, in this book. When Sakya Paṇḍita was a youth he studied extensively and received full ordination from the great Kashmiri master, Śākyaśrībhadra. Once, as his teacher expounded the teachings in Sanskrit, Sakya Paṇḍita followed along reading from a Tibetan text. Seeing this, other students laughed at him. Śākyaśrībhadra asked Sakya Paṇḍita, "What use is that Tibetan text?" Sakya Paṇḍita said, "It may not be of use to others, but it is of use to me," and then, looking at the Tibetan text, Sakya Paṇḍita back-translated it perfectly into Sanskrit. Then Śākyaśrībhadra admonished the students, "Why do you laugh at him? He understands the teaching perfectly." Later, Śākyaśrībhadra was the one who bestowed upon him the title of Paṇḍita.

One of the stories from Sakya Paṇḍita's life that is personally very inspiring to me also occurred during his youth, when he was still studying with his primary guru and paternal uncle, Jetsun Drakpa Gyaltsen. Sakya Paṇḍita requested him to bestow the profound guru yoga blessing, but Jetsun Drakpa Gyaltsen refused, saying, "You don't see me as a buddha, you see me as your uncle." Sometime after that, Jetsun Drakpa Gyaltsen became ill, and Sakya Paṇḍita served his guru day and night without regard for his own health or comfort. By that merit, any small obscurations Sakya Paṇḍita may have had were purified, and he perceived his guru as Mañjuśrī. At that moment, Sakya Paṇḍita's inner wisdom opened, and he attained comprehensive and detailed understanding of all knowable things. This event in Sakya Paṇḍita's life shows that although through study one can gain outer knowledge, it is only through devotion that one can gain inner awakening. The experience of inner awakening brings definitive certainty of all knowable things in a single moment, such that one no longer needs to study.

Another remarkable episode that occurred during his youth is recounted in these biographies. One night, Sakya Paṇḍita dreamed that the Indian paṇḍita Vasubandhu, who was the author of the *Treasury of Abhidharma* (*Abhidharmakośa*), gave him teachings for a month. When Sakya Paṇḍita awoke from that dream, he had comprehensive and precise knowledge of the Abhidharma. This is truly extraordinary. Ordinary people don't dream that a great master gives them extensive teachings on Buddhist philosophy, or even if a few of them might, they barely remember the content of the teachings when they awaken. But in Sakya Paṇḍita's case, his dream experience was both transformational and effective. He not only remembered the teachings entirely and precisely, but he instantly became a great knowledge holder of the Abhidharma.

At Sakya, there are some holy relics related to Sakya Paṇḍita's life that have become pilgrimage destinations. One is known as Tamnyen Shuktri, or Good News Throne. This is the throne upon which Sakya Paṇḍita was sitting upon when he was informed that his brother had given birth to a son. That son became his successor, Drogön Chögyal Phakpa. That throne is also the same one upon which Śākyaśrībhadra had long ago sat when he bestowed upon Sakya Paṇḍita the vows of a fully ordained monk. When we go to these holy places and make offerings and aspirations, it deepens our devotion.

As his teacher, Jetsun Drakpa Gyaltsen, had earlier prophesied, Sakya Paṇḍita was summoned in his later life to the court of the Mongol khan near what is now Lanzhou, China. At that time, the Mongol khans were very powerful. They had conquered a huge part of the world, and they possessed everything imaginable. Perhaps because of this, they realized the importance of religion and searched everywhere for great religious teachers. They sent messengers to Tibet to learn who were the greatest Tibetan religious masters. The messengers returned saying this lama is very dramatic, this one has a large following, that one is very lenient, and so on—but as far as knowledge of the Buddhadharma is concerned, Sakya Paṇḍita is the greatest. So the khan summoned Sakya Paṇḍita to his court in Mongolia.

After receiving the khan's summons, Sakya Paṇḍita journeyed slowly from Sakya to the khan's court near Lanzhou together with a large retinue, which included his young nephew, Chögyal Phakpa. When they met, the khan asked Sakya Paṇḍita to cure him of a skin disease from which he had suffered for a long time. Many doctors had tried, but none could cure the khan. But with his unimpeded wisdom and clairvoyance, Sakya Paṇḍita had a prophetic dream that correctly identified the ailment as a naga disease arising from previous negative karma, and he then performed rituals that completely cured the disease. The khan was impressed and grateful. The dream and the curing of the khan are recounted in fascinating detail in this book.

The khan's appreciation of Sakya Paṇḍita's great wisdom and growing interest in Buddhism made Sakya Paṇḍita the object of the jealousy for spiritual teachers of other traditions. This jealousy grew as the khan became Sakya Pandita's disciple, receiving the Hevajra empowerment from him and bestowing upon him many great offerings. In an attempt to discredit and embarrass Sakya Pandita before the khan, these jealous teachers magically created an illusory shrine in the middle of a lake and then invited the khan and Sakya Paṇḍita to consecrate it. They had planned to dismantle the magical illusion as soon as Sakya Paṇḍita set foot upon it, but everyone was amazed because as Sakya Paṇḍita consecrated the shrine, the magical illusion became a real, habitable shrine. In fact, after that, Sakya Paṇḍita resided there for some years. That was one of his many amazing miracles witnessed by his Dharma heir and nephew, Chögyal Phakpa, and is also recounted in this book.

As I have said, Sakya Paṇḍita was one of Tibet's greatest scholars. He was a scholar in all fields of knowledge, and after extensively studying all fields of knowledge in Sanskrit, he wrote a book in the Tibetan language explaining each of the major and minor Indian sciences of the day. This was an important milestone in introducing Indian scholarship to Tibet.

Sakya Paṇḍita was a tremendously accomplished author of a wide variety of works. His writings are extremely special—they are authoritative, precise, clear, profound, and elegantly composed, yet easy to understand. And there are so many of them! A good number are still studied today. The profundity and elegance of Sakya Paṇḍita's writings is one of the reasons that he is considered to be a genuine emanation of Mañjuśrī.

One of Sakya Paṇḍita's many famous works is known in English as *The Treasury of Logic on Valid Cognition*, or *Pramanyuktanyiti* in Sanskrit. It condenses the entire field of Buddhist logic. This work was translated from Tibetan into Sanskrit, which was something very special. At that time, there were so many Dharma texts, especially texts on Buddhist logic, that were translated from Sanskrit into Tibetan and studied by Tibetan scholars, but Sakya Paṇḍita's *Treasury of Logic on Valid Cognition* was the only text translated from Tibetan into Sanskrit and studied by Indian scholars! Since that time, scholars from all four schools of Tibetan Buddhism have written many commentaries on it over the years; this is also quite special because in Tibet, it is not common for scholars in one school to write commentaries on texts from another tradition.

Additionally, *The Treasury of Logic on Valid Cognition* continues to be widely studied.

In Sakya Paṇḍita's day, of course, there were no radios, telephones, or newspapers, and all news had to spread by word of mouth, so for the fame of a Tibetan scholar to spread all the way to India and for his writings to be studied there was something extremely special. As Sakya Paṇḍita's fame spread in India, a Vedic scholar named Harinanda and his retinue became jealous and sent a challenge to Sakya Paṇḍita in Tibet, inviting him to engage in debate. They traveled to meet each other half way at Kyirong Monastery in Nepal. Before the debate began, they each staked their faith; whichever scholar lost the debate would convert to the other's religion and follow the other scholar. The debate was conducted in the Sanskrit language and went on for many days, but in the end Sakya Paṇḍita was victorious. He beat them in philosophical argument in their own language! Then Harinanda and the other scholars shaved their dreadlocks and converted to Buddhism. One of the biographies of Sakya Paṇḍita, the longest one, written in verse, by the Tibetan king Rinpungpa Ngawang Jikdrak Gyaltsen describes this debate and even the topics that were argued and some of the points that were made.

Another of Sakya Paṇḍita's famous works is *Classification of the Three Vows*. It clearly describes the correct way to observe the vinaya, bodhisattva, and Vajrayana vows, and points out incorrect observances and how to rectify them. This book is still studied and discussed today.

Sakya Paṇḍita is also famous for *Illumination of the Sage's Intent*, which he wrote while he was at the Mongol court and sent back to his followers in Tibet. It explains how to practice the entire Buddhist path from the first development of faith all the way to buddhahood, according to the Paramitayana tradition. It is a wonderful book—practical, scholarly, and inspiring.

Although Sakya Paṇḍita lived nearly a thousand years ago, his teachings and writings on how to follow the Buddhist path from our current state of suffering to perfect enlightenment are ever more relevant today. Human defilements, obstacles, and shortcomings have changed very little over the years, and the only way to truly uproot them is through the study and practice of the Dharma. To encourage us in our efforts, we need a source of inspiration to demonstrate how we should study and practice. By studying the biographies of this great master, we can see how and what he studied in order to become a great scholar. We can also learn how and what he practiced in order to become a great mahāsiddha. We always say, "For the sake of all sentient beings, I must achieve enlightenment." Sakya Paṇḍita actually became an enlightened buddha. These biographies teach us how to study and practice in order to follow in his footsteps in order to achieve enlightenment ourselves.

How do we follow in Sakya Paṇḍita's footsteps? First, we must study, especially his biographies, through which we develop devotion based on admiration for his great wisdom and vast holy activities. After we have developed devotion to Sakya Paṇḍita, praying to him will bring great blessings. Then we merge our devotion to Sakya Paṇḍita with devotion to Mañjuśrī, because Mañjuśrī is the manifestation of all the buddhas' wisdom. Mañjuśrī is sometimes referred to as the "father" of the Buddha because buddhas are born from wisdom. For most people, it is easier to start with developing devotion to Sakya Paṇḍita, because Sakya Paṇḍita is in human form, and a human-to-human relationship may be easier than a relationship to one who is beyond the human realm.

By merging our devotion to Sakya Paṇḍita with devotion to Mañjuśrī, we become certain that Sakya Paṇḍita is a true emanation of Mañjuśrī, who is the embodiment of all of the buddhas' wisdom. By praying to the two as indivisible, the benefit is doubled, and we can receive great blessings. But of course, we must study as well. Some people with extraordinarily good karma may receive blessings instantly, but most people must first study, and then by praying to Sakya Paṇḍita as inseparable from Mañjuśrī, their ability to learn gradually increases. Through diligence, they will achieve wisdom and the spiritual attainments.

Many thanks to Venerable Khenpo Kalsang Gyaltsen, abbot of Tsechen Kunchab Ling, which is my temple seat in the Americas, and to Chodrungma Kunga Chodron, who accepted my request that they translate these biographies of Sakya Paṇḍita in order that this great master may become more widely known in the English-speaking world.

1

Holy Biography of the Glorious Sakya Paṇḍita Based on His Own Words

By Drogön Chögyal Phakpa (Lodrö Gyaltsen)[1]

Prostrations to the Guru and Mañjuśrī!

> Your immaculately pure nature is completely beyond description,
> Accomplishes aspirations for others' benefit, and emanates a multitude of forms;
> Protector, Lord of Existence and Peace, your body's unchangeable nature is the three suchnesses,
> I prostrate with pure devotion to you, holy lama, and describe a part of your holy biography.

My lama, the Lord of Dharma, is the real Vajradhāra, but some beings perceive him as and believe him to be a common Dharma teacher. However, I have seen some truly amazing holy events, which follow.

When the Lord of Dharma entered the womb of his mother, Nyitri Yum, a sign appeared in his mother's dream that a bodhisattva had entered her womb. She dreamed that a beautifully dazzling king of the nāgas, with a precious crown and other jewels, asked her to give him accommodation. While he resided in the womb, his mother's body felt light, she moved about easily, felt healthy and blissful, and excellent samādhi arose in her mind. At the time of his birth, a multitude of auspicious signs appeared that a bodhisattva had been born.

When my Lord of Dharma had developed to the stage where he could crawl, he spoke to his mother in Sanskrit, which was a sign of the ripening of the habitual tendencies of his previous lives. But because his mother did not understand his words, she was afraid that his speech was abnormal. She told Jetsun Drakpa Gyaltsen that her son spoke words she could not understand, and asked him if there might be a problem with her son. Drakpa Gyaltsen understood that the child was speaking Sanskrit, and replied that she should not be afraid that her son was abnormal.

The child drew the Indian alphabet in the dust on the ground with his fingers, with the complete vowels and consonants in both Nāgarī and Lanydza scripts. Then, afraid that others may step on it, he erased it. My Lord said that he had learned to read both Sanskrit and Tibetan without being taught so long ago that he did not recall which he had learned first.

When he grew a bit older, he learned without difficulty further studies in Tibetan and Sanskrit, astrology, medicine, arts such as drawing and design, and other subjects. While he was still a youth, he had already become a treasury of wisdom and good qualities. Because of this, many learned masters, including those who were his own teachers, unanimously stated that he was not ordinary, and undoubtedly an emanation of an enlightened one, or a greatly blessed being. All were amazed at his abilities.

While still a youth, he received empowerment from his father,[2] and studied the *Lotus-Born Hevajra Sādhana*, including the six-limbed sādhana, the empowerment ritual, the consecration ritual, and the fire puja ritual. From the *Cakrasaṃvara Tantra*, he studied the teachings of the masters Luipa, Kṛṣṇapa, and Vajra Gantipa and the practical instructions of the offering ritual.

Every day he performed the practices of Ārya Acala, Mañjuśrī, Avalokiteśvara, Uṣṇīṣavijayā, Mārīcī, Vajravidāraṇa, and others. He also received and thoroughly studied *Explanation of the Fourteen Root Vows*, *Fifty Verses on Guru Devotion*, the explanation of the bodhisattva vow known as *Twenty Vows*, the analytic cycle of Vajrapāṇi in the sutric tradition, and many theoretical and practical medical texts. He comprehensively learned all of these. He also gradually received empowerments, blessings, tantric explanations, and pith instructions on the Dharma of the Sakya forefathers and ancestral masters.

At the age of eight, he gave a commentary on the *Lotus-Born Hevajra Sādhana*. At the age of twelve, he gave a commentary on the second chapter of the *Hevajra Root Tantra*. At the age of fourteen, he explained the common commentary *Sāmputa Tantra*. By the age of fifteen, he had completely mastered all of the Dharmas belonging to his father and the founders of the Sakya tradition.

One night, when he was eighteen, my Lord dreamed that he received teachings on the *Treasury of Abhidharma* (*Abhidharmakośa*) directly from Vasubandhu in front of Achi stupa behind Sakya Monastery. He experienced that night as an entire month. In front of the stupa, his master Vasubandhu faced the east. The master's complexion was slightly blue and he was not too young, of middle age. In his dream, Sakya Paṇḍita received the complete Abhidharma teachings over a single thirty-day period, each morning for thirty mornings. My Lord of Dharma sat to the right of Master Vasubandhu facing the north, reading the text while receiving the teachings.

When he awoke early the next morning, he had the entire *Treasury of Abhidharma* in his memory, both the words and their meaning. My master said that later, when he actually received teachings on the *Treasury of Abhidharma* from the Kashmiri paṇḍita Śākyaśrībhadra, it was identical.

Another time, he dreamed of someone who said, "I want to give you the throne of Master Dignāga. Please follow me." He then led him to a cave in India that faced east and said, "This is Master Dignāga's cave." When the door of the cave opened, my master saw that one side of the cave was filled with texts. He opened the texts and read them. While he was reading, someone came and pulled the hem of his Dharma robe, and he awoke while he had not yet had enough time to read all of the texts. My Lord said that this might have been an indication that in those days he had many distractions and had to give teachings to people from far away, which somewhat interrupted his genuine study of the Dharma. He also said that after this dream, special wisdom arose in him, through which he could unmistakably understand the meaning of logic texts.

At the age of nineteen, he received teachings on logic and the Five Treatises of Maitreya from Master Shuhrul at Trang. When he was twenty, he traveled to meet Master Tsurtön Shönu Sengé at Nyangtö Kyangdul. From him he received a teaching on pramāṇa. After hearing it only one time, he completely and unmistakably knew every word of the teaching and its meaning, and he asked the master for permission to give that teaching to others.

Based on his own experience with study, Master Shuhrul feared that Sakya Paṇḍita had not yet studied enough. Therefore, he said, "You should still study more." Then my Lord received the first part of the *Ascertainment of Valid Cognition* (*Pramāṇaviniścaya*) four times, followed by the latter part of the text twice. Then the master Shuhrul said, "In Tsur, the teachings are as complex as the filaments under the cap of a mushroom. However, I do not feel that these are truly according to the explanations as given in India."

About this time, my Lord heard that his father and spiritual master was ill and he returned to Sakya, where his father passed away. Intending to perform the appropriate activities on his father's behalf, he wrote to his master, "Because I need to give a teaching here, I request you to postpone for a time the Dharma teachings."

His teacher planned to postpone the teachings for a while due to this request, but the other students did not concur. Because the teacher cared greatly about my Lord, the other students could not bear it, especially one student named Yamatak Thengjuk. Yamatak told the master, "If you care so much about the son of the Sakya, that's okay, we can disperse. But if you need us, too, you must continue without postponement." Because of this, the master continued the teachings.

My Lord of Dharma soon returned, bringing many material offerings. He also brought Jarchöpa as an attendant. Together they made extensive material offerings, in addition to long, middle-length, and abbreviated sets of the Buddha's sermons. Then the master Shuhrul said, "Although I could not wait for you, I will go back and teach again from where we left off." Sakya Paṇḍita told the master that this was not necessary for his sake, so they continued the teachings.

Sakya Paṇḍita also began to teach the master's students the *Ascertainment of Valid Cognition* and a commentary on that text, giving two sessions per day based on the teachings of the master. In this way, within a month, he gave both the root and commentary on the *Ascertainment of Valid Cognition* from memory. The entire assembly was amazed at his ability.

Sakya Paṇḍita received the teaching of the *Collection of Madhyamaka Reasoning* (*Madhyamaka Yuktikāya*) from the same master, Tsurtön Shönu Sengé. After that, he returned to Sakya and performed the appropriate rituals of dedication for the departure of his father and spiritual master. Having completed these, he collected a large quantity of gold and other material to offer his master, and set out to see him.

On the way, when my Lord reached Tsang, at Chumik Ringmo, he met Śākyaśrībhadra, who was giving Dharmottara's teachings on pramāṇa logic. My Lord sent his attendant with all of the material offerings to his teacher Tsurtön Shönu Sengé, and remained to receive teachings from Śākyaśrībhadra.

When Śākyaśrībhadra gave teachings in Sanskrit using a Sanskrit text, Sakya Paṇḍita read from the Tibetan text. Seeing this, the young scholars among Śākyaśrībhadra's students laughed derisively at Sakya Paṇḍita. The abbot asked them why they laughed, and they explained, "We are laughing because while you give the teaching in Sanskrit, he reads from a text in Tibetan."

Śākyaśrībhadra asked Sakya Paṇḍita, "Is that text of any use to anyone?" Sakya Paṇḍita replied, "Although it is not of use to others, it is of use to me." Saying thus, he back-translated the teachings and commentaries he had received from the Tibetan text into Sanskrit. Śākyaśrībhadra realized that his translations were identical, and scolded the young scholars, "Why do you laugh at him? The Sakyapa exactly understands what I taught."

Sakya Paṇḍita told me that he asked Śākyaśrībhadra, "What Tibetan masters teach is said to be barely bluish, but not blue itself. What does this mean?" The Kashmiri paṇḍita answered, "Blue itself exists as it is. But I don't know what 'barely bluish' means." Through this answer, Sakya Paṇḍita realized the essential point of the entire discipline of logic.

My Lord also received many teachings on logic from the paṇḍita Dānaśilā, as well as teachings on other practices, such as Kurukullā, yoginīs, Mañjuśrī, Rakta Yamāri, White Acala, and others. From Paṇḍita Saṃghaśrī from Nepal, my Lord also studied a cycle of works on the Sanskrit language, and works on logic such as the *Commentary on Valid Cognition* and others. Sakya Paṇḍita told me in his own holy words, "I am a fortunate person because these days there is no one more learned in Sanskrit than the Nepali master Saṃghaśrī in either the east or west of India, and he came to where I lived so that I could study from him."

The Kashmiri paṇḍita Śākyaśrībhadra went to Central Tibet. While he was gone, Sakya Paṇḍita invited Paṇḍita Sugataśri to Sakya, and intensively studied Sanskrit, logic, poetry, composition, rhetoric, and other subjects from him for two years.

Later, when Śākyaśrībhadra returned to the region of Tsang, while he was residing at Nyung Chung, Sakya Paṇḍita went to pay his respects and requested the bestowal of full ordination. Śākyaśrībhadra accepted, and at the age of twenty-five, Sakya Paṇḍita shaved his hair at the temple of Nyangmé Gyen, the seat of the great master Lotön, and received ordination at Nyung Chung. At the ceremony, the Kashmiri abbot Śākyaśrībhadra was the principal abbot, Chiwo Lhepa Jangchup Ö served as master of activities, and Master Shuhrul served as master who shows the secrets. The ceremony was also witnessed by other realized and venerated beings among an ocean-like gathering of the sangha.

Śākyaśrībhadra advised him, "Since you have now received full ordination, it is important to be diligent in observing the vows that are to be preserved." He appointed Venerable Joden as vinaya instructor to Sakya Paṇḍita. This instructor was extremely strict in all observances, and constantly corrected even the most minor infractions.

Next, Sakya Paṇḍita studied the Seven Treatises on Valid Cognition[3] from Śākyaśrībhadra, and this teaching was repeated three times. From him, he also studied the commentary on that teaching, as well as supplementary texts such as *Ornament for Clear Realization* (*Abhisamayālaṃkāra*), works by Dharmottara, the *Treasury of Abhidharma*, *Vinaya Mūlasūtra*, *Prātimokṣa Sūtra*, *Bhikṣukārikā*, and other minor teachings on the vinaya. He also studied the commentary on the *Kalacakra Tantra*, *Immaculate Light*, and supplementary texts, and the *Cakrasaṃvara Tantra* and the *Guhyasamāja Tantra*, with their commentaries and supplementary texts such as those of Nāgārjuna and the tradition of Jñānapada. He received empowerments in these tantras and learned all of them thoroughly.

From Chiwo Lhepa Jangchup Ö, he received the commentary on the *Perfection of Wisdom in Eight Thousand Verses* (*Aṣṭasāhasrikā Prajñāpāramitā*) known as "*Twenty Thousand*," teachings on the *Compendium of Abhidharma* (*Abhidharmasamuccaya*), as well as teaching cycles in the Kadam tradition and some minor teachings on Mantrayāna oral instructions.

Because his meditation had given rise to inconceivably steady samādhi, he was able to realize the relationship between outer and inner interdependence and to prophesy future events. He said that when he meditated or concentrated, nothing whatsoever could disturb him, even amid a crowd of people.

Through the power of receiving the lamas' blessings, inconceivable knowledge of the good qualities of scripture and realization arose in his mind. This is clear because my Lord himself stated:

> When I was young, I asked my lama to bestow the guru yoga blessing but he refused, saying, "You do not regard me as the Buddha, and instead regard me as your uncle. You are yet unable to dedicate your body and all possessions to the lama." Later, fearful signs of my death arose, and my health was indisposed. At the same time, my Dharma Lord manifested some discomfort for a few days. At that time, I served him day and night without rest, thought of sleep, or food. This seems to have purified some of my negativities.
>
> Then my Dharma Lord bestowed upon me the guru yoga blessing. At that time, the attitude arose in my mind that my lama was the genuine Buddha, and I saw him as Mañjuśrī, the embodiment of all the buddhas. Uncommon devotion arose in my mind, and through this, I was completely liberated from my signs of death. My health was completely restored, and from that time on, I began to realize the unmistaken essential points of scripture and reasoning, such as the meanings of Sanskrit words, logic, poetry, rhetoric, composition, secret Mantrayāna, Pāramitāyāna, abhidharma, vinaya, sūtra, and others. I attained fearless courage concerning the meaning of the entire Tripiṭaka, and received the kind consideration of deities, spirits, and human beings. Even self-conceited ones such as kings of India desired to receive Dharma teachings from me. Some genuine realization arose inwardly in my mind.
>
> My Lord of Dharma's manifestation of discomfort at that time did not arise from his body, but he manifested it to give rise to an auspicious interdependent connection on my behalf. If others also practice in this way, without doubt similar unmistaken auspicious signs of interdependence will arise.

Sakya Paṇḍita also directly perceived many deities such as Mañjuśrī, Acala, Tārā, and others, and they directly bestowed a multitude of doors of Dharma upon him. Based on this, countless good qualities of meditation arose in his mind.

My Lord Teacher told me:

> One night, I dreamed I was seated upon a high throne made of stone, giving Dharma teachings to an ocean-like gathering. I began speaking in Sanskrit with the first verses of the *Commentary on Valid Cognition* (*Pramāṇavārttika*):
>
> > Prostrations to you who have
> > thrown off the net of conceptual thought and
> > possess a profound and vast body, from which
> > shine ever-noble rays of light in all directions.
>
> At that moment, the sun and moon arose from my right and left shoulders. The next morning, I related the dream to my Lord of Dharma Jetsun Drakpa Gyaltsen. He replied, "This is a rarely occurring dream. We must celebrate it fully, by making offerings."

Sakya Paṇḍita told me of another dream:

> A creek to the west of Sakya became a huge river. On the bank of the river, my Lord of Dharma Jetsun Rinpoché Drakpa Gyaltsen sat where the bank steps down to the water, listening to the secret songs of the Mantrayāna Dharma sung by Lopön Sönam Tsemo, who held his head high. While I listened, I climbed the steps of the bank toward Sönam Tsemo. I heard that a similar dream had occurred to Śākyaśrībhadra, and when I asked him about it later, the dream had occurred to both of us on the same night.

It is said that my Lord received teachings directly, not in dreams, in Sakya Monastery itself, from the space in front of him. He also clearly heard a voice that seemed to arise from his heart, saying, "In your twenty-seven previous lives, without interruption you were born as a paṇḍita, greatly learned in the *Commentary on Valid Cognition*. Later, he again heard the same voice, but instead of "twenty-seven," it said "thirty-seven." He related these things to me himself.

On numerous occasions my Lord said, "It seems that I have habitual tendencies from previous lives to study Sanskrit and logic. Because I need no effort whatsoever to learn these subjects."

Another time, when he gave Dharma teachings, a voice in space or in his heart said, "You are the emanation of Lord Drakpa Gyaltsen and will be able to tame a multitude of sentient beings, including those who were unable to be tamed even by buddhas as numerous as the sands of the Ganges."

My Lord told me, "Later, while I was teaching in the holy shrine of Khadang in Yeru, another voice spoke, 'This is your spiritual master from many previous lives,' and I instantly remembered the previous voices."

Once, when Sakya Paṇḍita manifested slight discomfort, Mañjuśrī, Nāgārjuna, Śāntideva, and other holy beings manifested to comfort him.

Some disciples with pure perception, such as Podon Rinpoché and others, perceived him as inseparable from Mañjuśrī.

My Lord was also clairvoyant. Evidence of this occurred once when my Lord visited the north. While he was there, in the middle autumn month of the Female Wood Snake year (1246), and again in the last autumn month of the Male Iron Dog year (1250), he declared that he would depart for another realm in the Iron Pig year (1251). Some of his close disciples heard and recorded this, and it later occurred just as he had predicted.

Concerning his holy activities, his Dharma teaching was just as described in *Well-Explained Reasoning* (*Vyākhyāyukti*). No matter what subject he taught, his explanation was precisely and accurately suited to the students' needs. His explication included an overview of the topics to be covered, an outline, transitions between topics, refutation of criticisms, and other features. His responses to questions were immediate, effortless, and always precisely according to Dharma. Whenever he taught any of the five major sciences, his teaching was fascinating, delightful to the learned, and cut the net of doubts for both humans and non-humans.

To give an example of this, when my Lord went to Samyé Monastery, the leaders of Samyé invited him to turn the wheel of Dharma. There, he gave most of the Lamdré teachings, and most of an explanation of the *Hevajra Root Tantra*. When he reached the fifth section of the last chapter of the tantra, he was invited to a celebration by Sinpori, who had a long connection with the hosts, and seated at the head of the assembly. Customarily, in central Tibet, important masters were invited to such ceremonies and given large material offerings. They had a responsibility to participate.

Sakya Paṇḍita continued the remainder of the reading transmission of the tantra. Following this, at the request of the assembly, he gave another Dharma teaching, advice, and blessings, which lasted until late at night. One of the leaders told the gathering, "Our requests are endless. Let's stop at this point and disperse. The lama's health may suffer if we make too many requests." With this they concluded the teachings.

One of the attendants locked the door. Then my Lord napped a bit while seated in meditation posture. He dreamed that a group of ordinary people arrived. They did prostrations, made offerings, and sat in a row. The one who sat at the head of the row asked my Lord, "Doesn't every mother sentient being experience the suffering of the four major torrents of birth, old age, illness, and death?" My Lord responded, "Yes, it is exactly so." "In that case, is there any supplication prayer that is of benefit in those situations?" Sakya Paṇḍita responded, "In those situations, you may recite the following prayer:

> Despite understanding birth as birthless,
> I am still not freed from the cage of birth;
> in every birth, in whatever birth I take birth,
> protect me from birth in an inferior birth.

"Thus you should pray."

Then the people asked, "In that case, is it permissible to replace 'illness,' 'aging,' and 'death,' with 'birth' in this prayer?" My Lord responded, "Yes, you are allowed to do so." He felt that the people understood the meaning of the verse. The people did prostrations and requested, "Please keep us in your holy mind." Thus my Lord dreamed, and he told me that when he awoke and contemplated the meaning of the verse, he realized that it was suitable.

Regarding Sakya Paṇḍita's composition, it is said that texts can be composed for two purposes: primarily to benefit others, and primarily to demonstrate elegant composition. When composed primarily to benefit others, the words and meaning of his texts are flawless, logical, clear, in harmony with the sūtras and tantras, and beyond criticism, even by the most learned. Indeed, all of his writing is amazingly beautiful.

Some of his works were composed primarily to demonstrate elegance in composition, such as *Homage to the Sugātas [in Lhasa]*, *Beseeching the Compassion of the Sugatas*, and *Jewel Treasury of Elegant Sayings*. All of these works are beautifully composed, the words and meaning are in balance, and the metaphors do not contradict the meaning behind them. Clear distinctions are made between the types of prose, heavy and light accents, and long and short sounds. The words and punctuation beautify and ornament the compositions.

Although they are elegantly written, their meaning is clear, and the poetry is easy to recite and pleasant to hear. All of his writings are as works of pure gold, ornamented by jeweled tassels of precious stones such as rubies. It could also be said that they are like a garland of perfect pearls, extremely beautiful and elegantly composed. When his compositions are read or heard by others, they delight the learned, are suitable for quotation by the intelligent, and are the object of admiration by the wise.

Concerning Sakya Paṇḍita's skill in debate, because he possessed peerless intelligence and had attained fearless courage through realizing the meaning of every scripture exactly and correctly, all of his speech was flawless, and his statements faultless. His words were beyond criticism, and therefore, the courage of every challenger quailed. He defeated many Tibetan masters who were known as great scholars and outshone many Buddhist paṇḍitas of India.

He also defeated masters of other religions. For instance, the Indian Brahmanical scholar Harinanda was famous throughout India for his learning. When he heard of the fame of Sakya Paṇḍita, he came to Tibet to challenge him to debate, together with six other learned Hindu masters. Sakya Paṇḍita thoroughly defeated all of them with his wisdom and placed them in the right view.

In this way, my Lord's entire life passed with his mind resting in the profound samādhi of the two stages. Until the age of sixty-three, he engaged in study, contemplation, meditation, teaching, composition, and debate in Tibet. In this way he served the Buddhadharma, and like the ascent of the morning sun, his fame pervaded the world.

Once, Sakya Paṇḍita's teacher Jetsun Rinpoché Drakpa Gyaltsen told him of his future, saying, "Later in your life, people from the northern lands will come to you speaking a foreign tongue, wearing hats like flying hawks and shoes with toes like the nose of a pig. They will invite you to their homeland. At that time, do not decline their invitation, and go without hesitation. This will be of great benefit for the Buddha's doctrine and many sentient beings."

In the latter part of my Lord's life, his fame reached the ears of Godan Khan.[4] The khan said, "I have heard that in Tibet there is a famous Buddhist teacher known as 'Sakyapa.' I wish him to be invited here." Thus, he sent his general Dorta to invite my Lord. When Dorta arrived in Sakya and offered an invitation letter from the khan, my Lord remembered the prophecy of Jetsun Drakpa Gyaltsen and gladly accepted the invitation.

In the Male Wood Dragon year (1245), at the age of sixty-three, my Lord set out from Sakya with two nephews. On his journey, many famous learned masters and other fortunate disciples with great faith requested empowerments, blessings, explanations of tantra, and pith instructions. He fulfilled each person's request according to their needs, and turned the wheel of Dharma in many places. Traveling thus, the journey took three years.

On the way, a Kadam master known as Namkha Bum asked him, "Is there any reason that you can benefit the land of Hor[5] by your presence?" Sakya Paṇḍita responded, "They said, 'You must come to Hor be our spiritual teacher, for if you refuse I will send an army to Tibet.' As he has written thus, I fear that if war were to start, great harm would befall Tibet. Therefore, I have embarked, hoping to benefit beings, but I have no certain evidence that I can be of benefit. Generally, if it is of benefit to other beings, I have not the slightest resistance to giving up everything, even my body and life, which is all that I have."

Once, when Sakya Paṇḍita was traveling in Drosang, someone offered him a quantity of black fabric with a pattern of golden dots. He gave the fabric to one of his followers, a physician named Biji, saying, "Keep this fabric. In the future, our Sakya teachings will become like stars shining in a cloudless sky. Although some say that the Sakyapa reject *ringsel* relics, concerning this, it is said:

> Most *ringsel* arise from spirits,
> or possibly from wholesomeness,
> or arise from the four elements.
>
> *Ringsel* of the three enlightened ones
> are produced by the power of good qualities.

Such *ringsel* arise from an authentic source;
their number is uncountable
and increases without decline.

"If I produce *ringsel*, an uncountable number will arise. You should cherish them and wrap them in this fabric. Of course, I am only jesting, so do not tell others, as it will create unwholesomeness."

When Sakya Paṇḍita was sixty-five, in the eighth month of the year of the Male Fire Horse (1247), he reached the khan's palace in Lanzhou. At that time, Godan Khan had gone to the land of Hor for the celebration of the enthronement of Guyuk Khan. He returned to Lanzhou in the beginning of the next year, the year of the sheep (1248), and had an audience with Sakya Paṇḍita in the palace. The khan was delighted to meet Sakya Paṇḍita and they had a relaxed discussion of Dharma and ordinary affairs.

Before Sakya Paṇḍita arrived in Lanzhou, there were already some Tibetan monks at the palace. However, they had been unable to demonstrate any special activities to evidence the good qualities of the Buddhadharma. Because of this, at gatherings in the palace to perform aspirations and prayers, the Mongolian folk practitioner Erkawun and the oracles of Hor were seated at the head of the assembly and led the chanting of aspiration prayers.

The Lord of Dharma, Sakya Paṇḍita, and Godan Khan engaged in extended intensive discussions of Dharma. When the khan could not understand various important points, scholars and practitioners from Uyghur assisted him. Through this, the khan came to have a good understanding of the meaning of the Dharma, and he was delighted to receive teachings from Sakya Paṇḍita.

Soon, the khan decreed to his subjects that the Mongolian practitioner Erkawun and the oracles should not sit ahead of the Buddhist monks and that the Lord of Dharma, Sakya Paṇḍita, should preside at the head of the assembly. He also decreed that throughout the land, Buddhist monks should lead the chanting of aspirations and prayers, and that their position should be venerated.

Godan Khan had a skin disease, and Sakya Paṇḍita performed many healing rituals for him, including making water and torma offerings. Early one morning during the period in which these rituals were being performed, on the eleventh day of the third month of the Year of the Sheep

(1247), Sakya Paṇḍita dreamed that a crippled being with a body covered in sores and spots came to visit him. Sakya Paṇḍita asked his identity, and he replied, "My leader has been summoned by the Sakyapa, but his body is too weak from illness to travel, so he sent me in his place to respond to your summons."

In his dream, Sakya Paṇḍita replied, "Godan Khan sent a messenger to Tibet and invited me from that distant land. I am residing in his palace in response to his invitation and therefore wish to benefit him. What is the cause of his illness? What will cure his disease?"

The crippled one replied:

> Before anyone lived here, my leader was the owner of this entire area. In a previous life, Godan Khan was born a king who accumulated vast merit from virtuous deeds directed toward Buddha Śākyamuni. After departing from that life, he was born the king of Minyak, and wished to build a palace on the place where my leader resided.
>
> The king of Minyak advised a Buddhist monk, "Now I will build my palace here. Please perform any necessary preparatory rituals to request use of this place from the land-owning spirits." Buddhist monks came to perform rituals on my land, chanted prayers with melodious tunes, played musical instruments, and performed *torma* rituals. However, they did not know how to perform the earth-blessing ritual correctly, so my leader did not give permission for them to build the palace.
>
> The king began construction anyway, which was tremendously destructive for my leader and myself, and caused us to feel as if we were being crushed. We were unable to overcome the power of the humans and so we moved north, and took up residence here. Now the king has come again, burned the land, plowed fields, and created much harm for us. We didn't know where to go, and my leader was extremely angry at the king. My leader gathered the local spirits and told them, "This king has twice kicked us off our land, and now I wish to retaliate." He requested the local spirits' assistance, but they said, "This king is powerful and has accumulated merit through Buddha Śākyamuni, so we dare not challenge him. It is better not to dwell on the arable

land. We recommend that you move to the springs and swamps." My leader took their advice and moved to the wetlands.

The king examined the records of previous Buddhist monks and found that they had been exaggerated. He also saw a golden statue of the Buddha Śākyamuni and dug at its base with a chisel, to see if it was gold, wood, or stone. Seeing this, all the spirits gathered together, thinking, "Now we will be able to harm him, because his merit has declined through this nonvirtuous act." Despite their efforts, they were unable to harm him because his merit was still too strong. The spirits tried to harm the king by other means, and caused a disagreement between the king and his prime minister.

Eventually, the minister assassinated the king. As the king drew his last breath, he made an aspiration, "May I be able to take birth as a powerful king in my next life, and be able to retaliate against all of you and subjugate you as my servants."

As a result of this aspiration, that king took birth as the grandson of Genghis Khan, and became known as Godan Khan. Later, when he grew up, he came here, bringing many horses and people who trampled the swamp where my leader lived. He also killed many horses in the swamp, and wherever the blood of the horses fell, some spirits died, some spirits became sick, and some spirits developed skin diseases. All of the creatures who live in the swamp, such as frogs and others, are barely clinging to life. I have tried to save them with the heat of my body.

Indeed, many weak and nearly dead frogs and tadpoles hung from the crippled being's body. He said:

Before you arrived, some Buddhist monks at the palace performed aspirations and rituals for Godan Khan, but they neglected to offer any effective benefit to the nagas and land-owning spirits, like us. After you arrived, Lord of Dharma, you gave us medicine and food to eat. This has helped us tremendously and is curing our disease. Before, I was unable to move due to my illness, but your healing has made it possible for me to come. However, my leader is close to death. If he dies, Godan

> Khan will also die. If he is cured, the Godan Khan will also be cured. Minor rituals will not be sufficient to keep him alive. Please perform major rituals on behalf of the khan and my leader. Healing him will ensure the healing of the khan, and healing the khan will benefit you as well.

My Lord intended to ask what rituals would benefit the leader, but due to a small hindrance, the crippled being disappeared. My Lord recounted this story to me.

To heal the khan's disease, Sakya Paṇḍita performed the ritual of Siṃhanāda. This completely cured his skin disease, and the khan became extremely devoted to Sakya Paṇḍita. He received profound and vast Dharma teachings, beginning with the bodhisattva vow from the Mahāyāna tradition, as well as teachings on many texts. He venerated Sakya Paṇḍita highly, and from that time on Sakya Paṇḍita bestowed many Dharma teachings in a multitude of languages for different ethnic groups. Through this, those who were not previously devoted to Buddhism were placed in the path of the Buddha, and those who were devoted were placed on the path of the Mahāyāna. In short, he placed countless sentient beings on the stage of maturation and liberation and caused the Buddhist doctrine to flourish throughout the land.

After remaining in the palace and teaching the Dharma for some time, the Lord of Dharma set out with the intention to return to Tibet. However, in his transcendent wisdom, he realized that remaining in the north would be of much greater benefit to the doctrine and to beings. Therefore, he remained there at leisure, sending generous material gifts to his students in Tibet. As a gift of Dharma, he composed and sent them *Illumination the Sage's Intent* (*Thub pa'i dgongs pa rab tu gsal ba*), which explains the stages of the path. With it, he sent the instructions, "I have bestowed this teaching throughout Tibet, including Utsang and Kham. All of my students have already received reading transmission of this text. Therefore, all of you exert yourself in its study and explanation, and practice accordingly."

This great teacher, the second omniscient one in our eon, remained in this world until the age of seventy, causing the doctrine to flourish and aiding countless sentient beings by maturing them and placing them in the state of liberation. Yet ultimately, the holy one rested his intent in the realm of reality. The manner in which this occurred was described in the following way by the physician Biji:

> In the month of Thakar in the Female Pig Year (1251), when the Lord of Dharma intended to depart for the benefit of other beings, eighteen great signs occurred. On the eighth day of the month of Thakar the earth trembled greatly, and I asked him what this sign could mean. The Lord of Dharma replied, "Generally, such a sign indicates that a great bodhisattva intends to depart for the benefit of other beings. We may be in this category."
>
> At midnight on the twenty-ninth of that month, Tathāgata King Proclaimer of Inexhaustible Melodies, in saṃbhogakāya form, clearly manifested in the sky. He was white in color, with one face and two hands. My Lord of Dharma told me, "Offer incense," and accordingly I arranged offerings and burned incense. The next day, he said that early that morning Eleven-Headed Avalokiteśvara had manifested and blessed him.
>
> On the sixth day of the month of Mindruk, all of the disciples who were abiding with the Lord clearly heard the sound of celestial musical instruments. We thought that the music was performed by the monks who were preparing for the Uṣṇīṣavijayā ritual in the shrine room. My Lord said, "It may be. Why don't you go see if they are playing music." We checked and asked them, but they said, "We heard the melody, but were not playing."
>
> We returned to the Lord and asked what this might indicate. My Lord said, "The music was performed by celestial beings who have come to escort me. Arrange offerings, as I must go for the benefit of others." At that time, a shower of flowers fell from the sky, such as had never been seen before.
>
> On the thirteenth of the month, while we were sitting in the sun, a long white cloud stretched toward us from the direction of the sun. My Lord of Dharma pointed to the sky and smiled, asking me, "Did you see that?" I said, "No, I didn't see anything, but for some reason, my mind is filled with joy." My Lord said, "You have fewer negative karmic tendencies, however, you still possess negativities. You should perform practices to purify your

negative deeds. I have seen Lord Buddha Śākyamuni sitting on a lion throne, surrounded by his retinue of arhats. Now light incense." This I did.

On the fourteenth, while we were sitting in the afternoon sun, a similar white cloud again extended toward us from the direction of the sun. That day, the Lord of Dharma told me that he clearly perceived Śrī Hevajra with mandala, and again asked me to light incense, which I did.

On the fifteenth, in the morning, while staying outside, I again saw a similar cloud, and that day he thrice told me that he perceived Mañjuśrī, and asked me to light incense, which I did three times. Once after lighting it, my Lord gazed upon me and smiled. I asked him why, and he replied, "The bodhisattvas Mañjuśrī and Maitreya are conversing." He told me what they were saying, but I have forgotten.

The next day, we circumambulated the temple, and Chokjin Pal was walking ahead of us carrying a table and cushion. I was assisting the Lord of Dharma by serving as a support, his left hand resting on my right shoulder. When we reached the main shrine, he was seated upon the cushion carried by Chokjin Pal, and he told Chokjin Pal, "Go make tea for us." He told me, "Light incense for Ayuh Tārā," so he seems to have perceived Tārā.

On the seventeenth, about midnight, while he was sitting in his room, he suddenly stirred from his rest and stood up, saying, "Didn't you see something? Didn't you hear the sound of music?" Master Joden was also there, and I replied, "Yes, we heard the sound of music, but did not see anything." My Lord gazed at me and said, "I saw the mandalas of thirteen deities, with Cakrasaṃvara and others at the head. All the viras and yoginis were singing and dancing." Following these words, he spoke many verses, but I could not catch them. However, Master Joden recalled some of them, but they are not quoted here. He also told us, "Do not mention this to others, as it may cause them to accumulate unwholesome karma."

About that time, at Jugur Memar, a geshé known as Dorang became severely ill. I sent my student Rinchen Gyaltsen to examine the patient. He returned with the report that the geshé was seriously ill. He could not move and his bed was completely covered with feces and urine. Because there was no one to help him, the situation was critical. My Lord and many others heard this report. My Lord said, "Since the buddhas and bodhisattvas know this, in their compassion why do they not gaze upon him?"

Well after midnight, before dawn, my Lord's lama Jetsun Drakpa Gyaltsen appeared in the sky in front of him, together with the mahāsiddhas Virūpa and Kṛṣṇapa. Jetsun Rinpoché Drakpa Gyaltsen spoke to Sakya Paṇḍita, saying, "Don't feel disappointed. This contaminated body must experience the four rivers of birth, old age, illness, and death." Then Mahāsiddha Virūpa smiled at my Lord, and Kṛṣṇapa said, "That is right."

My Lord told me that Mahāsiddha Virūpa dipped his ring finger into the nectar in the skull cup he was holding and asked me to extend my tongue. He put a droplet of nectar on my tongue, and at that moment, I experienced realization of nonconceptual bliss and clarity. I thought, "There is no higher or more exalted experience than this, not even the primordial wisdom of the buddhas, which is completely beyond conceptual and nonconceptual experience."

Then Jetsun Rinpoché Drakpa Gyaltsen said, "When you depart from this place to perform the benefit of others, you will be born as a vidyādhara who dwells in the east, beyond many worlds of existence. During that life, you will please a multitude of tathagatas and purify your buddha realm. You will also mature a multitude of sentient beings and accomplish most of the paths and stages. In your third life, you will be reborn as the prince of King Nyimai Tophel. At that time, even during your youth, you will be able to compose and explain a multitude of Dharmas, be able to gaze upon every world of existence through your clairvoyance, and be able to liberate hundreds of thousands of devoted disciples."

Sakya Paṇḍita told me, "Any disciples who in this life receive empowerment or have even the smallest Dharma connection to me will take birth as my disciples at that time." He also mentioned the length of that life, but I cannot recall it.

Jetsun Drakpa Gyaltsen said, "When he departs that life, he will be born as Buddha Vimalāśrī and perform the benefit of countless beings." Having said this, Jetsun Drakpa Gyaltsen gazed back at the mahāsiddhas Virūpa and Kṛṣṇapa, saying, "Isn't that true?" Both affirmed this, each saying, "That is so."

My Lord asked me to arrange a *tsok* offering, which I did. Then he performed the practice of Profound Guru Yoga. As a result, his secret organ became completely concealed and no longer visible. An uṣṇīṣa clearly appeared on the top of his head, and a white circular hair appeared between his two eyebrows like the curl of a conch shell. These and many other perfect physical qualities manifested on his holy body.

On the seventh day of the eleventh month, all those who were in the Emanation Temple heard the sound of many musical instruments. I asked my Lord, "What does this indicate?" He replied, "All of you should be diligent in supplication. Even one moment of devoted service to the guru from whom one received excellent Vajrayāna empowerments is of much more merit than giving all one's possessions, including one's head, legs, or arms in the Pāramitāyāna tradition."

Whatever I had received I had offered to my guru, so when he said this, I had nothing to offer, except one newly made red *chamtsé*, which I had been given by Neten in appreciation for healing his legs. I thought that I wanted to offer it to my Dharma Lord, who had already worn it. When I thought this, he smiled and said:

> You do not need to give that to me. I have already worn it, so that is sufficient. It is the same as if you had offered it to me. When I reach excellent enlightenment, I will be able to see everything as clearly as an *amalaki* fruit in my palm. I will be able to see every act of service without exception that you disciples have done. I will also be able to see the service of all those who hold the bodhisattva vow and empowerments. Any recollection of me, physical touch, conversation, or other connection will not be meaningless,

> and will liberate from lower rebirth. Therefore you, too, should feel joy that you performed so much service for me.

One night, from evening until early in the morning, I spent the entire night serving him, sometimes supporting him from behind, and sometimes from the side. He called Dulwa Gyaltsen to come, and when he arrived, he asked him to bring the beautiful *chamtsé* that had been offered to him by Lady Sorokta. He told me:

> Now you should wear this *chamtsé*. We have many connections from our previous lives. First, you served me as tea server, then I sent you to Jobum Gukshri in Minyak. Then, through the devotion of the Mongol emperor, we have met again here, and you have served me in many ways in this life. In the next life, there is no way that you will not take rebirth as my attendant.

On the fourteenth of the eleventh month of Malpo, early in the morning, there occurred a multitude of celestial offerings: victory banners, together with the music of celestial instruments, song, and a multitude of offerings appeared. The earth trembled greatly. At that time, my Lord of Dharma departed into peace.

On the twenty-fifth of that month, when the holy body was cremated, the smoke manifested in the colors of the rainbow, and all who gathered heard celestial music. All of the relics produced *ringsel*.

> Perceiving a great Lord Vajradhāra
> as an ordinary being is a great delusion,
> like seeing a conch shell as yellow.
> Bless us by your holy deeds.

Colophon

This holy biography of Sakya Paṇḍita, Lord of Dharma, describes in a few words a small part of his great qualities, including the prophecies that he would become a tathagata. Written by the vajra holder Lodrö Gyaltsen Palsangpo, a disciple who respects Sakya Paṇḍita's holy feet upon his crown. Later edited and some important parts condensed and inserted according to the descriptions of Lama Martön Chökyi Gyalpo, the scholar Gyalwapal, Biji Rinchen Drak, Dampa Kunga Drak, and Bartön Dorjé Gyaltsen, without exaggeration or understatement.

This was written just as the words were uttered from the mouth of Sakya Paṇḍita himself. Those who wish to learn in more detail, particularly about his studies and great learning, should consult the biography by Lopön Rinchen Pal, who attained high accomplishment.

2

Sakya Paṇḍita: A Holy Biography

By Gorampa Sönam Sengé[6]

Gorampa's commentary on the *Classification of the Three Vows* begins in the following way:

> Herein is the fourth compilation of the Buddha's scriptures, a treatise that thoroughly evaluates what is and is not the Dharma, a lamp to illuminate the entire sūtra and tantra, a jewel that is the font of every wish of the faithful, a sun that burns the underbrush of misleading teachers, and an ocean into which all elegant words converge, a treatise known as *Classification of the Three Vows.*

This explanation has three topics: the great good qualities of the author of that treatise, how that treatise was composed, and the contents of the treatise so composed.

I. The Great Good Qualities of the Author of that Treatise

This has ten topics:

A. The good quality of having been born into a special family clan
B. The good quality of abiding in morality as a spiritual basis

C. The good quality of training the mind through study, contemplation, and meditation
D. The good quality of spreading the Buddha's doctrine through teaching, debate, and composition
E. The good quality of being accepted by lamas and tutelary deities
F. The good quality of possessing unimpeded clairvoyance and detachment
G. The good quality of being venerated by great worldly beings
H. The good quality of receiving a genuine prophecy
I. The good quality of emanating exalted objects of the holy body, speech, and mind
J. The good quality of producing disciples who were illuminators of the Buddha's doctrine

IA. The Good Quality of Having Been Born into a Special Family Clan

This has five subtopics:

1. How the lineage of celestial gods arose
2. How from that the Khön clan arose
3. How from that the Sakyapa arose
4. How Sakya Paṇḍita Took Birth
5. How Sakya Paṇḍita Transcended Worldly Behavior after Taking Birth

IA1. How the Lineage of Celestial Gods Arose

This precious family clan was initially descended from celestial gods. In the beginning, there were three celestial beings known as Chiring, Yuring, and Usé. The people requested them to be their lords, and the younger one accepted the headship. He had four sons, who were known as the four Sijili brothers. They engaged in battle against the eighteen Dong clans, during which their uncle Namlha Yuring assisted them. Thus, they were able to defeat the eighteen clans, who became their subjects.

Yuring married a daughter of the Mu family named Dembu. They had seven sons who were known as the seven Masang brothers. The six older brothers and the father were said to have ascended to the celestial realm.

The youngest brother married a daughter of Thokla Öchen named Thokcham Urma. They had a son named Thoktsa Pawo. Thoktsa Pawo married Lucham Drama, who was the daughter of a nāga. They a son named Taso Öchen, who was the nāga's grandson. He married a girl named Tsomo Gyal from the Mön family. Their son was known as Yapang Kyé, which means "Born at the Border of the Meadows and the Rocks."

1A2. How from That the Khön Clan Arose

Yapang Kyé engaged in battle with the demon Kyaring Trakmé. He killed him and married Yadruk Silima. They had one son whom they named Khön Barkyé, which means "Born between Those Raging against the Demons." This is how the name Khön first appeared.

Khön Barkyé married Chambu, a daughter of the Tsen family. Their son was powerful, able to perform miracles, and extremely handsome. He was captivating to behold and people used to say, "It is rare for such a one to appear in the human realm," so they named him Könpa Lhajé Gungtak, which means "Rare Lord Gungtag."

His father asked him to find a place for them to reside, so, while he was still a youth, he found Nyen Tsathar Gyi Yachang, a location with eight positive qualities: a lake known as Jetso, which was good for drinking and irrigation; large and small meadows known as Shing Thangchen Thangchung, which were helpful as a location for a house and fields; the valley known as Yachang, which was good for nomads with fine grazing ranges both nearby and distant; woodlands known as the Gunbu Gunmuk Forest, which was good for house building and firewood. On the basis of these observations and explanations, his father decided to take up residence in that area.

During this time, King Trisong Detsen ruled Tibet, and because Könpa Lhajé Gungtak was skilled in worldly activities and had a reputation for great courage, the king appointed him *nang jewa*, or "inner lord." During this period, he was known as Khön Pawoché, which means "Greatly Courageous Khön."

Khön Pawoché had two sons. The elder was Yeshé Wangpo who became a monk and was known as Khön Lui Wangpo Sungwa. He was one of the most learned among the first seven Tibetans to receive monastic ordination. The fame of the Khön family spread widely due to this father and son.

Lhopa Thamché Khyenpa and Yeshé Gon from Dewachen both state that the younger brother was Khön Dorjé Rinpoché. Lama Dampa Sönam Gyaltsen states that Khön Pawoché had four sons: Trizé Lhalek, Tsela Wangchuk, Lui Wangpo Sungwa, and Tsezin. The son of the youngest, Tsezin, was Dorjé Rinpoché.

Khön Dorjé Rinpoché had seven sons. The second-youngest son went to Dronpa and was known as Khön Sherab Yönten. He had a son known as Yönten Jungné who had two sons, the eldest of whom was Khön Tsultrim Gyalpo. The younger took up residence in Khabso Takthok. From there, many Khön descendants spread. One of these Khön descendants took up residence in northern Yeru. From there, too, many descendants spread.

Khön Tsultrim Gyalpo had three sons. The middle one went to Gangla Cha while the eldest and youngest stayed in Yarlung. The elder son was known as Khön Tsuktor Sherab and he had seven sons. Including them and a younger uncle, there were eight Khön families in the Yalung Valley.

The fifth of the seven brothers was known as Khön Gekyab. He took up residence in Shab and had two sons, the eldest of whom was known as Gethong. The younger son remained in the upper valley of Shab, and some Khön family spread in that area.

Gethong's son was known as Khöntön Balpo. His son's name was Khöntön Shākya Lodrö. He had two sons, the eldest of whom was Khönrok Sherab Tsultrim, and the younger was Khön Könchok Gyalpo. Until Sherab Tsultrim, the family were practitioners of the Dharma that spread during the first propagation period. Within the family were many great scholars and many practitioners who attained the stage of a mahāsiddha based on the practice of Vajrakīlaya. Their Dharma protectors were known as the Brother and Sister Karmo Nyida.

Around that time, a great festival took place in the Dro Valley. Many people gathered for the festival, especially to see Mantrayāna practitioners perform ritual dances wearing the masks of twenty-eight female Īśvaras, each holding their individual hand objects. There were also witches with dreadlocks. People thought that the dances were the greatest show of the festival.

Khön Könchok Gyalpo was among the spectators. When he returned home, he described it to his elder brother, who was not pleased. His elder brother responded, "Now this is what is known as corrupt mantra practice. From this time forward great mahāsiddhas will not arise. Whatever texts and tantric instruments we have should be buried in a hidden burial. I am too old, but you are still young. You must go to Mangkhar to see Drokmi Lotsāwa. He is known to be a great scholar of the profound teachings of the new tantra. You must study from him."

With these words, Khönrok Sherab Tsultrim buried all the texts from the earlier propagation period. After doing so, the Dharma protectors caused various miraculous events to occur. In particular, the Dharma protector Karmo actually manifested her face to Khönrok Sherab Tsultrim, and so Khönrok recited a brief sādhana of Vajrakīlaya and a complete torma ritual, and then offered two sets of fifteen phurbas made of teak wood and the Brother and Sister Karmo Nyida torma ritual to Könchok Gyalpo. Thenceforth without interruption, the descendants of this lineage have performed these torma offering rituals.

Khön Könchok Gyalpo set forth for the Yalung cemetery. There he met Khyin Lotsāwa, who was one of Drokmi Lotsāwa's disciples, and received from him an explanation of the second chapter of the *Hevajra Tantra*. When the teaching was nearly complete, the teacher passed away, after instructing him to receive the remainder of the teaching from Drokmi Lotsāwa in Mangkhar.

According to these instructions he went to Mangkhar, where he met Drokmi Lotsāwa. From him he received the three Hevajra tantras and the remainder of the supplementary teachings. Realizing that Drokmi Lotsāwa was very learned, Khön Könchok Gyalpo intended to request further teachings. He returned to Yalung, where he sold some property and offered the remainder of his land to the monastic community. From the sale of the property, Khön Könchok Gyalpo received seventeen horses and their loads. He offered all of these to Drokmi Lotsāwa and requested bestowal of the Lamdré pith instructions. Drokmi refused to give the Lamdré pith instructions, but instead completely gave all of the explanations relating to the *Hevajra Tantra* as well as twenty-four different techniques of practicing tummo beyond thought.

Khön Könchok Gyalpo also received Guhyasamāja from Master Gö Khukpa. He also received *Five Droplets* from Master Sherab Sangwa, who was a paṇḍita from Oḍḍiyāna. From Mal Lotsāwa he received the Cakrasaṃvara root tantra and *Essence of Attainment*. He also received many other teachings from Bari Lotsāwa, Lama Gyechupa, Puhrang Lotsāwa, the Nam Khaupa brothers, and Kyura Akyab. Thus he became a great owner of Dharma.

Later, Khön Könchok Gyalpo built stupas for his father and brother in Jakshong. He placed one set of blessed phurbas inside the stupa for his brother. The other set of phurbas he carried everywhere he went as holy objects. Later, these phurbas were still kept in Sakya.

Khön Könchok Gyalpo remained for some time in Yalung Chukyar. He built a small monastery in Drawo Valley and lived there for several years.

IA3. How from That the Sakyapa Arose

This section has four topics:

a. How the foundation of Sakya was established
b. How an emanation of Avalokiteśvara appeared
c. How an emanation of Mañjuśrī appeared
d. How an emanation of Vajrapāṇi appeared

IA3a. How the Foundation of Sakya Was Established

When Khön Könchok Gyalpo was residing in Drawo Valley, at one point he looked from the top of a mountain and saw that Pönpo Ri Mountain had many auspicious signs, such as soil of whitish color, lush abundance, and a river flowing toward the right. He thought, "If I build a monastery here, it will be of great benefit to the Buddha's doctrine and sentient beings."

With this intent, he held discussions with leaders of the valley, and they gave permission to construct a monastery. When he spoke with the land owners, the four Sang Shungwa families, he asked, "Would it be against your wishes if I were to build a small monastery here? I will be happy to pay the appropriate price." They replied, "Please do build a shrine here, although we won't accept any payment." However, knowing that it would be better for future stability, Khön Könchok Gyalpo offered a white mare, a fine silk curtain, one fine set of women's clothing, a jewel necklace, and one set of armor in exchange for the land. The agreement stated that all of the land from Mongo Creek to Balmo Creek now belonged to the Khön family and would be inherited by their descendants.

Lama Khön Könchok Gyalpo was born in the Male Wood Mouse Year (1034). When he was forty years of age, in the Year of the Female Ox, he took up residence in Sakya and devoted himself for the next thirty years to the holy work of the Buddha's doctrine through meditation, teaching, and study. At the age of sixty-nine, in the Male Water Horse Year (1103), on the fourteenth day of the month of Yugu, he passed away.

IA3b. How an Emanation of Avalokiteśvara Appeared

When Lama Khön Könchok Gyalpo reached the age of fifty-nine in the Male Water Monkey Year (1093), his consort, Machik Shangmo, gave birth to a son who became Lama Kunga Nyingpo. From the beginning, the child was very handsome, attractive, and enticing to everyone, and he had many positive qualities, such as calm, good behavior, honesty, wisdom, natural compassion, and others. When he was a youth, he trained in a various types of worldly knowledge, such as how to evaluate jewels, horses, men, and women; poetry; composition; medicine; and many other arts and sciences.

Concerning his study and practice of the Dharma, in the very beginning, Kunga Nyingpo received the Hevajra initiation from his own father, and later received many related teachings from him.

When Kunga Nyingpo was eleven years old, his father, Könchok Gyalpo, passed away. An astrologer was consulted who recommended that, for the future to be filled with success, the laying of the temple's foundation, the farewell ceremonies for the recently departed, and the appointment of a throne holder should all take place on the same day, if possible. According to this recommendation, the monks from two temples in Trang Drakmarwa were invited to perform the farewell ceremonies and, on the same day, the foundation of an additional temple was laid and Lama Bari was appointed Khön Könchok Gyalpo's successor. Bari Lotsāwa held the responsibility of throne holder for eight years.

Kunga Nyingpo received instructions on the sādhana of Mañjuśrī from Bari Lotsāwa and entered retreat for six months. At the end, he directly perceived Mañjuśrī and directly received profound teachings on topics such as *Parting from the Four Attachments* and other vast inconceivable doors of Dharma. Through this, he attained the state of *dhāraṇī*, which means the state of perpetual memory, as well as peerless intellectual analysis.

At the age of twelve, Kunga Nyingpo set out for Ngurmik. There he met Drangti Darma Nyingpo, from whom he received the *Compendium of Abhidharma*. During this time he left a handprint upon the surface of a rock, which can still be clearly seen.

After the passing of Drangti, he received the *Treatise on the Foundation of Yoga Practitioners* (*Yogācārabhūmiśāstra*) and Asaṇga's two compendia from some of the Dharma masters who were tutors. He also studied valid cognition (Skt. *pramāṇa*) and other topics from Khyung Rinchen Drak from Nyangtö and tutor Medikpa.

Then Kunga Nyingpo returned to Sakya. He completely received all of the teachings that Bari Lotsāwa possessed, such as explanations of the Pāramitāyāna including the *Ratnakūṭa* and *Avataṃsaka Sūtra*; two hundred different teachings related to the kriyātantra and caryātantra; relating to anuyogatantra teachings, two traditions of Guhyasamāja, the *Yamāntaka Tantra*, three Hevajra tantras, and an explanation of the Cakrasaṃvara root and commentary tantras as well as their supplements and an explanation of the sādhana. He completely received and understood all of these.

From Master Mé Lhangtser at Drompa Yutsé he received teachings on the *Ascertainment of Valid Cognition*, the *Droplet of Reasoning* (*Nyāyabindu*), and three explanations of the Svātantrika Madhyamaka school. After that, he intended to receive the teachings held by his father and set off to meet Khön Gyichuwa and request teachings from him.

The night that Kunga Nyingpo received the preliminary empowerment, he dreamed of a large muddy river that was said to be the ocean of existence. Many people were waiting to cross the river and were calling out to him, "Please rescue me!" He rescued three people by the last bridge, seven people by the middle bridge, and many people by the closest bridge.

After receiving the initiation, he also received the explanation of the three Hevajra tantras in the Dronbi tradition and many other teachings relating to the tantra, such as the eighteen categories of attainment.

Around that time, Lama Sé was giving teachings in Doktö. One day, Kunga Nyingpo went there with some young monks who were disciples of Khön Gyichuwa. Upon meeting Lama Sé, they had a detailed conversation and Lama Sé realized that Kunga Nyingpo was the son of Khön Könchok Gyalpo. He hugged him tightly, saying, "Now it is possible for the living to meet the deceased! Inside the body of this decaying old man are precious Dharma teachings. I will give them to you, but you must return quickly. If you think that you will come slowly, next year I will depart from this world."

After this conversation, Kunga Nyingpo remained there for one night.

That night, Lama Sé taught him clearly what titles are included in the main Lamdré teachings and what titles are included in the supplementary teachings.

Kunga Nyingpo went home with the intention to return to receive the teachings from Lama Sé and asked permission to do so from Khön Gyichuwa. But Khön Gyichuwa did not grant it. Then, Kunga Nyingpo thought, "Maybe I will go next year." Next year Lama Sé's words came true, as he passed away that year.

After that, Kunga Nyingpo went to study from Lama Nam Khaupa. From him, he received inconceivable teachings concerning the four classes of tantra, pith instructions, and many sādhanas, including *Practical Instructions on Performing Activities*. In particular, he received complete teachings on yoga tantra.

From Master Ngok, he received an explanation of the *Illumination of the Twenty Thousand Stanzas*, the *Prajñāpāramitā in Eight Thousand Verses*, and teachings on the *Ornament of Clear Realization* (*Abhisamayālaṃkāra*) root text and commentary.

Not long after that, he received a message that Lama Gyichuwa was ill and he must come quickly. Kunga Nyingpo set out immediately but was unable to arrive before he passed away. Khön Gyichuwa had left final instructions for Kunga Nyingpo: "You must take full ordination and become the leader of the Khön assembly."

Kunga Nyingpo concluded the activities associated with Khön Gyichuwa's passing and acquired the necessities for ordination. Lama Nam Khaupa heard of this and prevented him from taking ordination, saying, "Not taking ordination will be of greater benefit." Still, Kunga Nyingpo took leadership of the Khön assembly.

Because Lama Gyichuwa was also a disciple of Mal Lotsāwa, Kunga Nyingpo took one of Lama Gyichuwa's Cakrasaṃvara texts and set off to see Mal Lotsāwa in Gungthang Nalatsé Nesar. There he received from Mal Lotsāwa the *Cakrasaṃvara Tantra* and supplementary teachings, three teachings on *Yamāntaka Kṛṣṇaśaturā Tantra*, and the pith instructions of Paṇḍita Nāropā. After receiving these, Kunga Nyingpo went to Yeru. From there, he sent seventeen gold coins to Lama Mal Lotsāwa in appreciation for the teachings.

Mal Lotsāwa was pleased and realized that Kunga Nyingpo was a great samaya holder. He sent a message saying, "Please return. I have more teachings that I would like to give you." Kunga Nyingpo returned and received many teachings, especially those related to caryātantra and the Dharma protector Segön Wish-Fulfilling Mahākāla.

As holy objects of that Mahākāla, he received a mask of Segön Mahākāla, a black cloth, and an iron vajra with nine prongs. Mal Lotsāwa told Segön Mahākāla, "From now onward, you must follow the Sakyapas."

After that, Kunga Nyingpo left the monastery. At Latö, he met Jetsun Puhrang Lochung and from him received teachings related to Cakrasaṃvara. He also received many Dharma teachings from other masters such as Kyura Akyab, the Nepali paṇḍita Padmaśrī, the Indian yogi Bhota Rāhula, and the Nepali paṇḍita Jñana Vajra. Then, with the intent of receiving the Lamdré teachings, he traveled toward Sakthang Ding. There he met Jetsun Shang Gönpawa, and from him received the complete Lamdré pith instructions as well as supplementary teachings. He practiced these as he received them. At the end, as a summary of the teachings, Shang Gönpawa gave him prophetic advice: "You must seal this teaching and practice for eighteen years. After that you will become the owner of these teachings." Shang Gönpawa thus empowered him.

Shang Gönpawa also told him, "Generally, if you emphasize the practice of these teachings, you will be able to attain the stage of excellence in this single life. However, if you emphasize explanation of these teachings, you will meet an inconceivable number of disciples and benefit them. In particular, you will find three disciples who will attain the stage of mahāmudrā without abandoning their physical body. You will have seven disciples who will attain the stage of patience, and about eighty yogis who will attain high realization."

Then Shang Gönpawa passed away, and Kunga Nyingpo performed all of the activities associated with his passing. After completing these he embarked for Gungthang.

In Gungthang, Kunga Nyingpo got food poisoning. Later a relapse occurred and he was seriously ill for nearly two months. As a result, he forgot all of the Dharma teachings that he had received. He entered retreat at Drangkhang Nyingpa and performed supplications to the lama; as a result, he was able to remember some of the teachings. Still, he continued to supplicate and practice. One night, Lord Shang Gönpawa appeared in his dream and gave him Dharma teachings, after which his memory was completely restored. He continued to practice and as a result, Mahāsiddha

Virūpa directly appeared and remained there for a month. During this time he received teachings both day and night from Mahāsiddha Virūpa, such as seventy-two different tantras and four teachings so profound that they are never to go beyond the fence of the Sakya, as well as many other teachings and blessings.

The great lama Sakyapa Kunga Nyingpo had inconceivable and extraordinary good qualities. One of these was simultaneously manifesting six different configurations of his holy body: leading thirty meditators in Tsarkha, giving Lamdré teachings in Sakya Monastery, receiving Dharma teachings from Mal Lotsāwa in Gungthang, performing the consecration of a mandala which was built by Namkha Drimé at Cham Lhakhang, giving Dharma teachings to the nomadic villagers of Sangdong, and turning the wheel of Dharma at Shab Gongar.

Thus the great lama Sakyapa Kunga Nyingpo was never distracted for even a moment from the profound practice of creation and completion, and he acted for the benefit of other sentient beings through the four social gatherings[7] until the age of sixty-seven.

In the Male Earth Tiger Year (1158), on the fourteenth day of the ninth month of Thakar, in northern Yeru at Kyawo Khadang, he passed into parinirvāṇa. At the time of his passing, the great master manifested four different physical manifestations: one departed for Sukhāvatī, the second for Potala, the third for Oḍḍiyāna, and the fourth for the Golden-Colored Realm in a northern world of existence. These things were clearly seen by most of the people in that area. When the holy body was cremated, none of the local sangha experienced any discomfort, and most even experienced a state of profound meditation. The majority of people perceived four faces and some saw eight faces.

How disciples of the great lama appeared

Just according to Khön Könchok Gyalpo's dream during the preliminary initiation from Lama Khön Gyichuwa, and also according to the similar prophecy by Shang Gönpawa, the three disciples who attained a stage of high attainment without abandoning their bodies were an acārya from Singala, Bodhisattva Tak, and Gompa Kyibar. The seven who attained the state of patience were Jetsun Drakpa Gyaltsen, Shujé Ngodrup, Gatön

Dorjé Drak, Nakgom Sönam Gyaltsen, Tsarkhai Naljorpa, Gompa Ödrak, and Aché Mangchungma.

According to Lama Chagen's statement, however, there were eleven disciples who attained the state of patience. They were Jetsun Drakpa Gyaltsen, Shujé Ngodrup, Gomchen Tagen, Jangsem Ngagyal, Ajo Phaktön, Jomo Mangchungma, Mangjo Jangyen, Danpa Joden, Deshek Khampa Dorgyal, Shang Sumthokpa, and Shengom Dorjé Sengé.

Fifteen are listed as dwelling in a state of great heat, such as Jetsun Sönam Tsemo and others. Thirty-one are listed as dwelling in moderate heat, such as Kyura Akyab and Jomo Shangmo from Drilchen. Those dwelling in small heat were Khampa Aseng, Netso Baltön, Ngari Drakseng, Jomo Mangchungma, and many others. Additionally, there were many other scholars who reached high attainment, such as Palchen Öpo, Nyen Tsuktor Gyalpo, Gyagom Tsultrim Drak, Minyak Prajnā Dzala, Khampa Galo, and many others.

IA3c. How an Emanation of Mañjuśrī Appeared

The great lama Sakyapa had four sons. The first was named Kunga Bar. His mother was named Jocham Phurmo and she was the youngest queen. When Kunga Bar was young, he went to India to study. He became renowned for being well trained in all five sciences, however, he became ill with a fever shortly before he returned to Tibet, and this took his life in Magadha, India.

Machik Ödrön from Tsamorong, who was the eldest queen, had three sons. The eldest was Lopön Rinpoché Sönam Tsemo.

Lopön Sönam Tsemo was born in the Male Water Dog Year (1142). At that time his father, Kunga Nyingpo, was fifty-one years old. Soon after he took birth, Sönam Tsemo spoke to his mother, saying, "I have transcended childish behavior." He repeated this twice.

He always sat in full meditation posture. Seeing this, everyone was greatly amazed. At the age of three he saw Hevajra, Mañjuśrī, Tārā, and Ārya Acala and taught the three tantras, the *Chakrasaṃvara Root Tantra*, and the *Compendium* from memory. He also remembered that he had taken eleven successive births as a paṇḍita in India, including a life as Mithup Dawa.

When he reached the age of seventeen, he taught forty different tantras from memory. He was famous in both India and Tibet for being well trained in every aspect of Vajrayāna.

Above the door of the stupa in Bodhgaya, a ḍākinī wrote the words, "An emanation of Mañjuśrī, Sönam Tsemo, excellent and noble, well trained in every aspect of Vajrayāna, has taken birth in Sakya." It is said that Paṇḍita Deva Mati from Kauśāmbī searched everywhere and finally found Sönam Tsemo in Tibet.

In short, until the age of seventeen, Sönam Tsemo was trained by his father in Vajrayāna studies, such as in commentaries on *Condensation of Vajrayāna* (*Dorjé Thekdü*), methods of peforming mandala rituals, sādhanas, blessings, pith instructions, practical instructions, and many other explanations. In that year his father passed into parinirvāṇa.

The following year, Sönam Tsemo asked his younger brother to take the responsibility of holding the throne of the Sakya, and set out for Sangphu to meet the great Master Chapa Chökyi Sengé. From him he learned Sanskrit, logic, the pāramitās, Vinaya, Abhidharma, and many other teachings based on the Tripiṭaka. There he spent eleven years in study. As a token of appreciation for having received these teachings, he made elaborate offerings of Dharma and material objects, such as Prajñāpāramitā texts, a pagoda with a golden roof, and many other things.

After returning to Sakya, on one occasion Lopön Sönam Tsemo was giving Lamdré teachings at Utsé Nyingma. While explaining the section on the view, amid enormous offerings in the sky, there appeared three emanations: Mañjuśrī, Virūpa, and Avalokiteśvara. These were visible by Jetsun Drakpa Gyaltsen, Shujé, and Moktön. Nine other disciples also attained the state of pure vision.

Another perspective on this was written by Sönam Tsemo's brother Drakpa Gyaltsen in his *Homage*:

> Prostrations to you who has completely accomplished the five
> sciences;
> who during sleep, rests in the equipoise of clear light;
> whose doubts are cut by Mahāsiddha Virūpa
> and any other deity at any time of day or night.
>
> Prostrations to you whose fame is proclaimed throughout the
> three realms,

whose conduct is completely free from the stain of flaws,
who has discarded the extremes of misleading speech and is a speaker of true meaning,
and whose mind is free of elaborations and possesses the essence of emptiness.

Prostrations to you who has clear eyes that perceive knowledge
of language, logic, paramita, mantrayāna, and the rest,
well understanding the words and meaning at a glance,
who voluntarily strives to benefit others.

Prostrations to you who satisfies others through the four types of giving,
who engages in teaching, debate, and composition without distraction
who continuously meditates on the two processes, and
who understands all post-meditation perceptions as illusion.

Prostrations to you whose fame is proclaimed throughout Jambudvīpa,
who at the age of twenty-seven is renowned as the life-pillar of the Buddha's doctrine,
who has received teachings from the great lama and all tutelary deities, and
yet still appears to study with great scholars from U and Tsang.

Prostrations to you who inspired your disciples with a multitude of emanations,
and who in a half day, traveled to Potala, Palri, and Oḍḍiyāna
and returned with an assembly of ḍākinīs and viras
to tame and engage others.

Prostrations to you who opened many doors of samādhi in my mind,
who during empowerment is undifferentiated from the Lord of the Mandala,

who explains the profound meaning of Dharma, and who produced
the sound of celestial music together with rays of light pervading earth and sky.

One should understand his good qualities to be just as this describes.

This great lama wrote many important texts, such as a commentary on the *Saṃpuṭa Tantra*, a commentary on *Engaging in the Conduct of the Bodhisattva* (*Bodhisattvacaryāvatāra*), *How to Enter the Door of Dharma*, and many other texts. He placed a multitude of disciples in the stage of maturation and liberation.

At the age of forty-one, in the Male Water Tiger Year (1182), on the eleventh day of the month of Malpo, Sönam Tsemo passed into parinirvāṇa without abandoning his body.

Most of his disciples were shared in common with Kunga Nyingpo, so they are not listed separately here.

The middle son, Jetsun Rinpoché Drakpa Gyaltsen

Drakpa Gyaltsen took birth in the Female Fire Rabbit Year (1147) amid many auspicious signs when his father, Kunga Nyingpo, had reached his fifty-sixth year. He had already transcended the behavior of a child. Even when he was barely able to speak, he enjoyed remaining in solitude and was not attached to food and objects. He delighted in the diligence of acquiring good qualities.

Drakpa Gyaltsen received upasīkā vows at the age of eight from the bodhisattva Dawa Gyaltsen. After receiving the vows, he maintained pure conduct even more strictly than the fully ordained. It is said that meat and alcohol never touched his mouth except as a samaya substance during tsok offerings. He taught the *Twenty Vows* and the *Lotus-Born Hevajra Sādhana*.

At the age of twelve, he dreamed that he swallowed the three Hevajra tantras, which caused him to comprehensively understand the suchness of all phenomena.

Around that time Sachen Kunga Nyingpo passed away, and Drakpa Gyaltsen held a large gathering to make offerings to the departed. During this gathering, he taught the second chapter of the *Hevajra Tantra* to the disciples, and everyone was amazed at his ability. Before his father's passing, Drakpa Gyaltsen had received from him myriad Vajrayāna teachings.

Beginning at the age of thirteen, Drakpa Gyaltsen took the responsibility of becoming throne holder of the Sakyapa. While holding these responsibilities, he also studied inconceivable Dharma teachings. In summary, these were the Tripiṭaka and the four classes of tantra, received from his older brother Lopön Sönam Tsemo and from Nyen Tsuktor Gyalpo, Shang Tsultrim Drak, Nyak Wangyal, Dzayasena from Nepal, and Lotsāwa Palchok Dangpoi Dorjé. All of these teachings he understood comprehensively.

Also, inwardly, he continuously meditated without interruption on the two processes.[8] For example, when he set out to give Dharma teachings, he meditated the Hevajra sādhana while on the way. By the time he sat upon the throne, he had completed the sādhana up to the section on visualizing the master of the race as his crown ornament. When he gave torma offerings at the beginning of Dharma teachings, he would substitute this for his daily torma offerings. Teaching the Dharma substituted for the recitation of the mantra. In the same way, he meditated on Cakrasaṃvara as he returned to his residence. In short, he performed the mandalas of seventy different deities within one cycle of day and night.

The Lamdré teaching had been sealed for nine years by his lama, however he exceeded that and did not teach it for thirteen years. After that he widely taught the Lamdré and brought many fortunate disciples to the stage of complete maturation.

Drakpa Gyaltsen also greatly illuminated the Buddha's doctrine through teaching, debate, and composition, and was an excellent protector for the protectorless.

There are also amazing biographical stories, such his memories of his previous lives in a dream and how he obtained a prophecy.

When he was eighteen, he dreamed that he read half of the *Litany of the Names of Mañjuśrī* (*Mañjuśrīnāmasaṃgīti*), which he had memorized in a previous life but had not yet studied in this life. At the age of nineteen, he dreamed that he completely recited the entire text.

At the age of twenty, he dreamed of his previous life as an upasika who practiced Mantrayāna Dharma in eastern India, at a place known as Bhalendra. He also dreamed of another life as a pure paṇḍita living north of Vulture's Peak. After that, he took another birth as a pure paṇḍita in the north of Oḍḍiyāna. After that, he took birth as Doktön Chugupa in Chungpa, Tibet, and taught the *Litany of the Names of Mañjuśrī* to his disciples. During this time, the great Lachen was his disciple.

At the age of thirty-seven, when he was napping in the early morning not long after his older brother, Lopön Sönam Tsemo, passed into parinirvāṇa, he heard a very clear sound like the buzzing of a bee emitting from his holy body. From that sound he received a prophecy: "From here you will embark for a life in the Golden-Colored Realm in the north, beyond many worlds of existence. You will take birth as Yönten Thayé, the crown prince of a universal emperor known as Sönam Thayé, a disciple of the tathāgata buddha known as Serö Nampar Tsenpai Gyalpo." These were the words of the prophecy.

One day, at the age of forty-nine, while Drakpa Gyaltsen was at Rutsam, he saw in a dream both of his teachers, Sachen Kunga Nyingpo and his brother Sönam Tsemo, teaching the path of the fourth initiation. He also dreamed that he gave initiations and Dharma teachings to a multitude of beings.

His disciples who put even a little effort into the path attained signs of having reached the heat of the path of liberation. About seventy disciples achieved even more exalted realizations than that. About thirty disciples attained high realization. Five or six of his disciples attained the stage of patience that is described in the Pāramitāyāna. He himself attained a level equal to those who achieved the stage of patience.

When Jetsun Drakpa Gyaltsen reached the age of fifty-six, one night in a dream he saw Sachen Kunga Nyingpo and a symbol on a stone with a smooth white surface that summarized all of the Lamdré teachings that he had previously received, including the pith instructions.

At the age of sixty-one, Drakpa Gyaltsen received an invitation from ḍākinīs to travel to the Kechari realm. He refused to go, saying, "It will be more benefit if I remain here." Another day he received a sign: a golden wheel the size of a chariot wheel appeared in a beautiful meadow. He was invited to sit upon it and was told, "We will elevate you to the Kechari Realm." As before, he refused.

At the age of sixty-seven, he saw the great lama Sakyapa himself, who cut through many of his doubts concerning the Dharma. For example, once he saw the Lama Sakyapa in the center with Hevajra and a retinue of nine to his right and the Buddha Śākyamuni and a retinue of eight great śrāvakas to his left. He was asked, "If you take vows, from whom would you take the vows? If you take initiation, from whom would you take initiation?" Jetsun Drakpa Gyaltsen responded, "If I were to become a monk, the abbot who would bestow the vows, and if I were to take initiation, the lama who would bestow the initiation would be you yourself, Great Lama Sakyapa."

The Lama Sakyapa responded, "That's how it should be." With these words, the Buddha and his eight close bodhisattva sons and Hevajra and his nine deities in saṃbhogakāya form were all absorbed into nine emanation bodies, and these were all absorbed into the great lama Sakyapa himself. The great lama answered many other Dharma questions and then finally said, "Noble son, you should regard the nature of all phenomena just like this," and with those words, he became invisible. Then Jetsun Drakpa Gyaltsen awoke.

At the age of sixty-eight, he received an invitation from a messenger from the pure realm of Sukhāvati, which he also refused.

At the age of sixty-nine, many celestial beings appeared, praising the pure realm of Sukhāvati and denigrating this realm of suffering. He responded, "I do not take particular joy in superior pure realms or displeasure in inferior realms. In fact, for the purpose of purification, inferior realms are more exalted. There are a multitude of beings who lack protection and who are dependent on me. Therefore I will not go yet." With these words, he refused them.

Seventy days passed, and again the celestial beings appeared, begging, "Please, you must go to Sukhāvati." He also perceived the configuration of Sukhāvati in his vision. On the morning of the seventieth day, Jetsun Drakpa Gyaltsen was sitting straight up and took a short nap. During the nap, he saw the sky filled with countless celestial beings, a beautifully-ornamented throne lifted by lions, and countless offerings.

The celestial beings supplicated the Lord of Dharma, saying, "We are the ones who have invited you." The Lord of Dharma remained for a while without saying anything. They realized that the Lord would be happy to accept their request. They pointed with their hands and said, "Behold the configuration of Sukhāvati." He perceived a very beautiful configuration, enticing to the mind.

Someone said, "Doesn't this contradict the previous prophecy that Jetsun Drakpa Gyaltsen would depart for the Golden-Colored Realm?" He responded, "Through the power of my aspirations, I prayed to be born in the presence of the holy father and son [Sachen Kunga Nyingpo and Sönam Tsemo]. Therefore, for a short time I will take birth in Sukhāvati, where they are dwelling. Not long after that, I will take birth in the Golden-Colored Realm in the form of a universal monarch and purify that realm into a buddha realm. I hope that after that, in my third life, I will be able to achieve the excellent attainment of mahāmudrā without abandoning that body." Saying thus, he remained in deep single-pointed meditative absorption.

Thus he performed activities for the benefit of countless disciples until the age of seventy. In the year of the Male Fire Rabbit (1216), on the twelfth day of the month of Tra, he passed into parinirvāṇa.

Listing of his disciples

Most of Sachen Kunga Nyingpo and Sönam Tsemo's disciples were also disciples of Dharma Lord Drakpa Gyaltsen, especially his four great spiritual sons with the last name of Drag: Kar Shākya Drak, Nupa Rikzin Drak, Salwa Wangchuk Drak, and Detön Könchok Drak. His two heart-sons were Sakya Paṇḍita and his brother. The four disciples who received the commentary on the *Ornament of Saṃpuṭa* were Mutsu Jangchup Drak, Changtön Tsöndrü Drak, Lhathok Yönten Sung, and Rikden Sherab Rinchen. The other well-known disciples were José Chakyi Dorjé, Dratön Yeshé Sengé, Shang Gyalwa Palsangpo, Lhopa Rinchen Palsangpo, and many others.

Palchen Öpo, the youngest son of Sachen Kunga Nyingpo

Palchen Öpo was born in year of the Male Iron Horse (1206) when his father was fifty-nine years old. He was well trained in all of the Dharmas of his father and grandfather. He was especially learned in medical science and many pith instructions. With great compassion, Palchen Öpo acted for the benefit of many sentient beings. He passed into parinirvāṇa when he was fifty-four years of age in the Female Pig Year (1260).

Palchen Öpo had two sons. The oldest was the Lord of Dharma, Sakya Paṇḍita, whose biography will be explained later.

Palchen Öpo's younger son's name was Sönam Gyaltsen. He was born in the Male Wood Dragon Year (1241), when his father was thirty-five years of age. He received countless pith instructions and teachings on scripture and logic from Jetsun Drakpa Gyaltsen and from Sakya Paṇḍita. He became well trained in these and understood them all comprehensively.

Sönam Gyaltsen's main practices were Hevajra and Vajrakīlaya. Especially, he was able to bring Vajra Mahākāla, Mahākālī, and other Dharma protectors as his retinue. He benefitted countless beings. Many deities appeared to him in his pure perception shortly before he departed.

He always respected his teachers as inseparable from the tutelary deities. He gave advice to his disciples: "Your teachers are none other than the Buddha. Do not allow any doubts about this to arise. Develop devotion toward them. As for me, I will take the life of a hidden yogi who will practice the profound path and give initiations to disciples in the south." Thus he said and exerted himself in single-pointed meditation on profound samādhi.

He departed on the twenty-second day of the month of Jal, in the year of the Female Earth Pig (1027). That year he had reached the age of fifty-six.

Palchen Öpo had five consorts and eight children. Drogön Chögyal Phakpa was born to Machik Kunkyi in the Male Wood Sheep Year (1235), when his father was fifty-two years old.

Chögyal Phakpa

Chögyal Phakpa was born the Male Wood Sheep Year (1235) amid auspicious signs. His mother's name was Machik Kunkyi. His father was fifty-two years old at that time of his birth.

Even as an infant, he was remarkable. As a child he knew how to read and write without needing to be taught by others. He was able to remember his previous lives, such as his birth as Master Satön Ripa, who was said to be able to communicate directly with Avalokiteśvara, and also his life as Langriwa.

When he was three years old he taught the *Lotus-Born Hevajra Sādhana*. At the age of eight he taught the *Jātaka* tales. At the age of nine, when the Lord of Dharma [Sakya Paṇḍita] was turning the wheel of the preliminaries, he gave a teaching on the second chapter of the *Hevajra Tantra* and a public talk. Everyone was greatly amazed at his ability, and his learning crushed the pride of many scholars. It was unanimously agreed that he must certainly be a holy person (Tib. *phakpa*) because such an intellect would be impossible in an ordinary person. These words were proclaimed everywhere, and as a result he became known as "Phakpa."

At the age of ten he traveled with Sakya Paṇḍita to Central Tibet, where he received the vows of novice ordination with the Lord of Dharma Sakya Paṇḍita as abbot, and the abbot from Sulphu serving as the master who offers the Dharma robes. He learned the precepts and instructions for the novice vows from Master Sherab Pal from Kyormolung.

From this time forward, he gradually began to receive teachings from Sakya Paṇḍita related to the Tripiṭaka, as well as many Vajrayāna teachings. He comprehensively understood whatever teachings he received.

The Lord of Dharma Sakya Paṇḍita happily promoted Chögyal Phakpa to the position of teacher at the age of seventeen because he possessed all of the Dharma knowledge that he himself had transmitted. Sakya Paṇḍita gave him a conch shell for gathering the Dharma, an alms bowl, and the responsibility to lead his disciples, saying, "This is the time to recall your prior commitment and act for the benefit of Lord Buddha's doctrine for a multitude of sentient beings." Speaking thus, he transferred the responsibility for teaching the Buddha's doctrine to him.

At the age of nineteen, Chögyal Phakpa bestowed the Hevajra initiation at the request of Kublai Khan to twenty-five disciples headed by the khan and his queen. Thus, the Vajrayāna teachings were introduced to the Land of Hor.

The next year, the emperor embarked for the Land of Jang [Lijiang in Yunan Province] for military activities. During this time, Chögyal Phakpa went to the north of China to consecrate the Lord of Dharma Sakya Paṇḍita's stupa. Following that, as Sakya Paṇḍita had advised, Chögyal Phakpa intended to receive full ordination from Uyukpa and to receive many other Dharma teachings that he had not received before. While he was traveling to the west, he received the news that Uyukpa had passed away, so he returned to China. At the same time, the emperor returned to China, and they were reunited at the khan's court.

At the age of twenty-one, in the year of the Female Wood Rabbit (1256), Chögyal Phakpa invited Khenpo Drakpa Sengé to China and received ordination on the border between China and Hor. Drakpa Sengé served as abbot, Sönam Gyaltsen from Joden Jangthang as *lelop* ("master of activities"), and Jangchup Gyaltsen from Yarlung as *sangté tönpa* ("master of secret instructions"). Many of the Lord of Dharma's disciples served as venerable Sangha.

Chögyal Phakpa then received teachings on the Prajñāpāramitā from Drakpa Sengé, who had served as his ordination abbot. He also received complete instruction in the Vinaya from many masters.

At the age of twenty-three, Chögyal Phakpa traveled on a pilgrimage to Five-Peak Mountain at the invitation of Dongtön. There, he gave the Yamāntaka initiation and many other Dharma teachings. While he was giving Dharma teachings, the Lord of Dharma Sakya Paṇḍita clearly appeared in his vision and taught many essential Dharma points. Also, Sakya Paṇḍita prophesized, "One hundred and one thousand years from now, you will achieve the excellent attainment of mahāmudrā." Thus he prophesized and encouraged. At that time, Chögyal Phakpa composed this verse:

> Long wearied by many sufferings in existence,
> receiving breath from the excellent voice,
> the Lord of Wisdom and Embodiment of Compassion:
> Prostrations to the Lord of Dharma.

Thus he paid homage to the Lord of Dharma.

He returned to the emperor's palace and, while he was turning the wheel of Dharma there, engaged in debate with seventeen masters of Sinshing. They were all completely defeated through his logical reasoning, and he caused them to hold the correct view.

At the age of thirty he returned to Sakya Monastery, where he also extensively turned the wheel of Dharma. At the same time, he received a multitude of Dharma teachings from many great masters, such as Nyen Ösung, Drupthop Yönten Palsangpo, Chim Namkha Drak, Tsokgom Kunga Pal, Kashmiri paṇḍita Tathāgata Bhadra, Dorjé Öser from Shangshung, Lo Lotsāwa, Kyopa Pal Rinpoché, Öser Sherab from Taktön, Rinchen Dorjé from Ngönpa, Öser Sherab from Bumpa, Draksang from Thangpé, Shākya Jangchup from Doklo, Khenpo Sengé Silnon, José from Chiwolhé, Wangchuk Tsöndrü from Ngönpa, Chögön from Rilung Phukpa, Lopön Lhatsun, the physician Darma Sengé, and Sangyé Bum from Central Tibet. From these masters, he received an ocean-like number of teachings, pith instructions, and other outer and inner sciences. Thus he became a Dharma master.

At the age of thirty-three, he again received an invitation from the emperor and embarked for China, where he spent many years. At the age of forty-two, he returned home to Sakya with an enormous amount of material offerings from the emperor comparable to that of Vaiśravaṇa, the Lord of Wealth. However, he did not use even the smallest part of these offerings for his own purpose. It was all spent for the purpose of turning the wheel of Dharma; setting the foundations of Dharma schools; building shrines to the Buddha's holy body, speech, and mind; and generously providing resources for those in need. Thus, his only actions were for the benefit of the Buddha's doctrine and sentient beings.

Chögyal Phakpa also made elaborate Dharma gifts to countless people in the lands of China, Hor, and Tibet. He also served as abbot in bestowing full ordination and novice ordination vows for 1,450 people. One of his disciples, a vinaya vow holder known as Chökyi Gönpo, was also said to have served as abbot for full ordination and novice ordination vows in China for 1,447 people within a year. Thus, many were established on a firm foundation of the moral precepts.

Chögyal Phakpa also gave Vajrayāna initiations, blessings, and pith instructions for countless people in fourteen different languages. Thus many were established on the stage of maturation and liberation.

Chögyal Phakpa composed many texts, all of which are easy to understand and excellent in content. His wonderful skill in composition is evident in his many commentaries on the Buddha's sermons and treatises, homages, supplications, and written advice on how to practice both the greater and lesser vehicles, as well as his many sādhanas, mandala rituals, pith instructions, indexes of the Buddha's scriptures, responses to questions, dedications, and benedictions.

In these ways he acted for the benefit of sentient beings until the age of forty-six. Beginning from the first day of the tenth month of the Dragon Year (1280), on the occasion of the birthday of Lord of Dharma Sakya Paṇḍita, Chögyal Phakpa prepared elaborate offerings and diligently practiced meditation. On the evening of the third day of the month he received a multitude of Mahayana Dharma teachings, such as the *Collection of Madhyamaka Reasoning* (*Yuktikāya*), directly from Ārya Nāgārjuna, who was sitting under the Bodhi tree at Śrīparvata. At that time, in his pure vision, he also perceived that elaborate celestial offerings had been arranged.

Next, Chögyal Phakpa gave advice to his nephew Dharmapāla, saying,

"The biographies of previous lamas such as Sachen Kunga Nyingpo and others, including myself, tell how they dedicated their lives to the Dharma. It is also important for you to make a commitment to follow those biographies."

He continued to preside over the performance of rituals and to bestow Dharma teachings until the eighteenth of that month. After that he remained in his private residence for four nights. On the morning of the twenty-second, he peacefully departed, seated in full meditation posture, holding vajra and bell in his hands. At that time, many auspicious omens occurred, such as showers of flowers and celestial music and lights. Celestial perfume pervaded the area.

Among the disciples of the great master Chögyal Phagpa were his own nephew Dharmapāla, and his younger male relatives Lopön Yeshé Jungné and Rinchen Gyaltsen. His students also included Sharpa Jamyang Rinchen Gyaltsen, Kunga Sengé, Yegen Phakshi, and Kunga Mönlam from Nyithok, Kunmön from Sulung, Kunsö from Ganden, Tashi Pal from Ganden, and Shang Könchok Pal. He also produced countless other learned and realized masters who spread the Buddha's doctrine.

Thus, the four sons of Sachen Kunga Nyingpo, Sakya Paṇḍita and his brother, and Chögyal Phakpa are known as the seven emanations of Mañjuśrī.

IA3d. How an Emanation of Vajrapāṇi Appeared

When Lopön Sangtsa Sönam Gyaltsen reached the age of fifty-six, he had a son named Drogön Chakna. He was born in the Female Earth Pig Year (1239). From birth, Drogön Chakna was naturally very intelligent. He benefitted a multitude of beings through his great compassion, primarily through powerful activities. He lived until the age of twenty-nine. Drogön Chakna had a son known as Dharmapāla Rakṣita who also passed away at the age of twenty-nine.

Sangtsa had a consort named Machik Jondro, and together they had a son named Lopön Rinchen Gyaltsen, who was born when his father was fifty-five years old.

Sangtsa had another consort whose name was Machik Dorjé Den. They had a son named Lopön Yeshé Jungné who was born in the same year.

Lopön Yeshé Jungné's son was the great master Sangpo Pal. He was born in Bodong in the Male Water Dog Year (1262). Sangpo Pal had twelve sons, including Tishri Kunlo, and through him the lineage of pure Khön lamas has continued without interruption to the present to benefit the Buddha's doctrine.

IA4. How Sakya Paṇḍita Took Birth

When the Lord of Dharma Sakya Paṇḍita was preparing to take birth as the son of Palchen Öpo and Nyitri Cham from Mangkhar, auspicious signs occurred for Nyitri Cham. She dreamed that the king of the nāgas came and requested she provide accommodation. Since that time, she felt uncontaminated bliss and joy of both body and mind.

On the twenty-sixth day of the month of Kyitdarawa (the middle month of spring) in the Male Water Tiger Year (1182), Sakya Paṇḍita took birth amid extremely auspicious omens. For example, there was a shower of flowers, a great gathering of celestial ḍākinīs appeared, and light pervaded the entire valley.

IA5. How Sakya Paṇḍita Transcended Worldly Behavior after Taking Birth

While he was still crawling, one day Sakya Paṇḍita's mother saw that he was writing in Sanskrit upon the surface of the earth. He would then erase his writing so that others would not step on it.

His mother invited his uncle, Jetsun Drakpa Gyaltsen, to see what Sakya Paṇḍita was doing. He was writing all of the consonants and vowels of both the Lanydza and Bhatu scripts and was able to read them aloud. Again, afraid that some may step upon it, he erased the writing completely.

Jetsun Drakpa Gyaltsen was greatly delighted to see this. Later the Lord of Dharma Sakya Paṇḍita himself stated, "I have known both Sanskrit and Tibetan scripts from the beginning, and I do not remember which was first."

IB. The Good Quality of Abiding in Morality as a Spiritual Basis

When Sakya Paṇḍita was young he received full lay vows from Jetsun Drakpa Gyaltsen, at which time Drakpa Gyaltsen named him Kunga

Gyaltsen. After that he received two traditions of the bodhisattva vow and all four empowerments of anuyogatantra. He also received the initiation of Śrī Hevajra from his own father. Thus he became a holder of the three vows.

When he reached the age of twenty-seven, he received full ordination at the holy shrine of Nyangmé Gyengong that was built by Lotön Dorjé Wangchuk. Sakya Paṇḍita's abbot was the great Kashmiri master Śākyaśrībhadra, and Jangchup Ö from Chiwolhé served as master of activities. Dönmori from Shu served as the master of secrets, and there were other sangha who attended as objects of veneration. At that time, the abbot added the name "Palsangpo" to his prior name, Kunga Gyaltsen.

IC. The Good Quality of Training the Mind through Study, Contemplation, and Meditation

Level of skill in the science of art among the five sciences

The golden statue of Mañjuśrī, which Sakya Paṇḍita built for the holy shrine of his master Jetsun Drakpa Gyaltsen, and his skill in drawing images and symbols of Mañjuśrī on the walls of Samyé Monastery cannot be compared even to the most skillful contemporary artists.

Level of skill in the science of medicine

Sakya Paṇḍita learned all of the root and commentary texts in *The Eight Branches of Medicine*, the medical treatise composed by Ārya Nāgārjuna, *The Ten Different Medical Treatments*, and the pith instructions of Ācara. All of these he thoroughly learned and comprehensively understood. As a result he composed the text *Medical Science: Summary in Eight Branches*.

Level of skill in linguistics

From the Nepali paṇḍita Saṃghaśrī, Sakya Paṇḍita received teachings on the following treatises on Sanskrit: *Kalāpa*; *Candapa*, which is a system for composing Sanskrit sentences also known as *Prātiya*; a treatise on poetry known as *Shönu Jungwa*; a four-thousand-verse treatise on poetry known as *Yangchen Gulgyen*; *Dāndri*; and a treatise on composition known as *Bhi-*

tam, which was primarily composed as an homage to Mañjuśrī. He learned all of these and comprehensively understood them well.

He also studied the thesaurus *Amarakośa* and a commentary on the first chapter from Paṇḍita Dānaśila. From Paṇḍita Sugātaśrī, he received teachings on a six-thousand-verse commentary on *Kalāpa*, focusing on word composition; *Suwinta*, which is a collection of nouns; *Tidenti*; three major treatises on poetry; three minor treatises on poetry; a treatise on composition known as *Rinchen Jungné*; a commentary on *Yangchen Gulgyen* in eight thousand verses; the complete root text of *Amarakośa*; more than half of the treatise *Natsok Salwa*; and a treatise on opera known as *Sugkyi Nyima*.

From the Kashimiri abbot Śākyaśribhadra, he also received a summary of a Sanskrit treatise. He not only learned these but comprehensively understood them.

Although poetry and synonymics are among the minor sciences, they are mentioned here because they are part of the science of language.

Level of skill in logic

First, Sakya Paṇḍita studied the *Ascertainment of Valid Cognition* from Shönu Sengé, who was from Kyangdurwa.

Then from the Kashmiri paṇḍita, Śākyaśribhadra, he received three chapters of the *Commentary on Valid Cognition*, according to the commentary *Yitkyi Shingta* by Lhawang Lo; a commentary on the *Compendium of Valid Cognition* (*Pramāṇasamuccaya*); *Droplet of Reasoning* (*Nyāyabindu*); a summary of views of the opponents of the *Droplet of Reasoning* by Kamalaśīla; *Proof of Other Minds* (*Saṃtānāntarasiddhi*); a subcommentary on the *Commentary on Valid Cognition* known as *Eighteen Thousand*; a chapter on establishing validity by Dharmottara; the chapter "Proving the Validity of the Brahmin"; the root text and commentary of *Treatise on the Objects of Cognition* (*Ālambanaparīkṣā*) by Dignāga; the root and commentary of the chapter on *lung*.

From the Paṇḍita Danaśila, he received a commentary on the *Analysis of Commentary*, a commentary on *Reasoning of Debate* (*Vādanyāya*), the chapter "Engaging Youth" by Lopön Dralé Namgyal; and *Ascertaining the Simultaneity of the Object*.

From the paṇḍita Saṃghaśrī, he received a commentary on the first chapter, and a commentary on *Yitkyi Shingta* according to the *Compendium of Valid Cognition*, and a commentary on *Proving the Validity of the Brahmin*. He received all of these and translated them into Tibetan and also received the branch treatises *Reasoning of Debate* and *Drops of Logic* (*Hetubindu*) and their commentaries.

From Paṇḍita Sugataśrī, he received a commentary on the first chapter of the *Commentary on Valid Cognition* in four and a half thousand verses; *Speech of Reasoning* (*Tarkabhāṣā*) by Mokṣākaragupta; and a text by Kaṇāda. He received all of these and understood them well.

Level of skill in inner science

From the great Mañjuśrī of the Sakya lineage, Jetsun Drakpa Gyaltsen, Sakya Paṇḍita received all the teachings relating to the Tripiṭaka, such as the pāramitās, and relating to tantra, he received all the teachings on kriyātantra, caryātantra, and also yogatantra.

Within the anuyogatantra, he received the Guhyasamāja in the Ārya tradition, including supplements, and in the Jñānapada tradition, three commentaries, *Handfuls of Flowers from the Ornamental Tree of Paradise (Gyen Jönshing Nyimpai Metok)*, with supplementary texts; three Yamāntaka tantras; and the *Cakrasaṃvara Root Tantra*. He also received the commentary tantras *Vajra Ḍākinīs* (*Dorjé Khandro*), *Ocean of Ḍākinīs* (*Khandro Gyatso*), *Description of the Lama* (*Ngönjö Lama*), *Origin of Heruka* (*Heruka Ngönjung*), *Comprehensive Conduct* (*Kuntu Jöpa*), *Unification of the Four Yoginis* (*Naljorma Shi Khajor*), *Origin of Vajravārāhī* (*Dorjé Phakmo Ngönjong*), three Hevajra tantras (Kyé Dorjé gyüsum), *Mahāmudrā Droplet* (*Chakgya Chenpoi Thiklé*) and other tantras relating to *tigle* droplets; three *Arali* tantras, including *Nonconceptualization* (*Tokpamepa*) and *Origin of the Protector* (*Gönpo Ngönpar Jungwa*); and also Kālacakra supplements.

Concerning pith instructions, he received the Lamdré teaching that possesses the four authenticities and four ear-whispered teachings, which originated with Virūpa and was transmitted through Shang Gönpawa directly to the great lama Sachen Kunga Nyingpo. He also received both the long and short lineages of these pith instructions.

He also received complete instructions on the Cakrasaṃvara creation and completion processes in the highest secret tradition, which originated with the mahāsiddha Nāropā and continued through the Phamthing brothers; the complete instructions of Vajrabhairava, which also originated with the mahāsiddha Nāropā; and the pith instructions of the *Sarvadurgatipariśodhana Tantra*, which was transmitted through Lord Rinchen Sangpo, including the root mandala.

From Khenpo Chöjé, he received the *Bright Lamp* (*Drönma Salwa*) commentary on the *Guhyasamāja Tantra*; *Five Stages of Completion* (*Dzokrim Rinba Nga*); two mandala ritual texts; *Guhyasamāja* in the Jñānapada tradition, including the sādhana *Complete Nobility* (*Kunsang*); many teachings relating to the *Cakrasaṃvara Tantra*; a commentary by Dorjé Nyingpo on the second chapter of the *Hevajra*; and many other teachings. Sakya Paṇḍita also received many sūtras, tantras, commentaries, and supplements from various masters, including from his own father, Palchen Öpo; Bodhisattva Chiwolhé; Paṇḍita Dānaśīla; Saṃghaśrī; Sugataśrī; and others. If one wishes to know more, one should consult his list of teachings received.

A list of teachings in dreams

One night above Sakya Monastery, in front of the Achi stupa, Sakya Paṇḍita received teaching on the *Compendium of Abhidharma* from a not-too-slim bluish-looking paṇḍita who said that he was Vasubandhu for an entire month. When he awoke, he comprehensively understood both the words and meaning of the *Compendium of Abhidharma*, and later when he received the same teaching from the Kashmiri paṇḍita, he said that there was no discrepancy whatsoever.

Another night, he dreamed that someone asked him, "Please come forward, we are going to appoint you the holder of the seat of the great master Dignāga." This person handed him a key to open a cave door. The entire cave was filled with scripture. The master gave him instructions and pith instructions through which he understood logical reasoning without any effort.

All the Dharma teachings that he received he correctly analyzed through contemplation and practiced through reasoning that arose from meditation. As a result, a sign of his achievement was that he possessed unimpeded clairvoyance, had no wrinkles on his face and no white hair, and possessed inconceivable good qualities, such as stable samādhi. The Lord of

Dharma himself stated, "I possess meditative samādhi that is undistracted even in the midst of public gatherings."

ID. The Good Quality of Spreading the Buddha's Doctrine through Teaching, Debate, and Composition

This section has three parts:

1. How the Buddha's doctrine was spread through Sakya Paṇḍita's teaching
2. How the Buddha's doctrine was promoted through his debate
3. How the Buddha's doctrine was spread through his composition

ID1. How the Buddha's Doctrine Was Spread through Sakya Paṇḍita's Teaching

The words of all of his teachings encompassed the entire doctrine of the Tathāgata, both esoteric and exoteric, as summarized in the five major sciences. His method of expressing these teachings was easy to understand and suited to the intellect of individual disciples. The subjects contained in his writings are without error. How these were explained to individual disciples will be elaborated later. As a brief example, at the age of nine, he taught the *Lotus-Born Hevajra Sādhana*, and at the age of eleven, the second chapter of the *Hevajra Root Tantra*, and *Unification of the Buddha* (*Sangyé Nyamjor*). At the age of twelve, he taught the *Vajrapañjara* and *Saṃpuṭa* tantras. From this time until the age of seventy, he taught continuously without interruption.

ID2. How the Buddha's Doctrine Was Promoted through His Debate

When the glorious renown of the great lama, who was the teacher of all beings, was proclaimed throughout all of India, both east and west, six heretic logicians led by Harinanda and his retinue from the south of India wanted to challenge him in debate and came to Tibet. When our Lord Lama was residing in Kyirong at the Wati temple, there was a great gathering, and at that time the six teachers approached. They did not respect the Lord Lama or the shrine of the Sugāta. Beginning with a few auspicious words, they remained in their seats, saying, "In our tradition, from the time of the Guru Brahma until the present, none of our masters have relied upon Gautama's doctrine, and we never take refuge in the Triple Gem. We are an extremely pure tradition of rishis."

The Lord of Dharma responded, "You must be oppressed by the sleep of great ignorance, because Brahma himself was extremely devoted to the Buddha Śākyamuni. For a verse states: 'Extremely exalted, with four hands and faces . . .'"

The Vedic logicians were greatly displeased and entered into debate. All of the inferior challengers were defeated word by word and rendered speechless. Furthermore, Sakya Paṇḍita was able to influence them to give up their inferior views and to enter the flawless path. They took Buddhist vows, shaved their heavy load of dreadlocks, and entered the path of renunciation that contains the wealth of the precious jewels of the doctrine of the Buddha Śākyamuni.

Understanding that any future challengers of the Buddhist doctrine might act in a similar way, in order to establish them on the path of liberation, Sakya Paṇḍita wrote the following poem:

Hari and his retinue believed their god (Mahadev) to be
the greatest god on this great earth, which is dressed in oceans
  and girdled with waters.
The followers of the sages Kargā, Vyāsa, Vālmīki, Kaṇāda,
  Akśapāda, and Kapila
came with topknots, dressed in bark and leaves, bearing sticks
  and *kusha* grass,
daubed in ashes, bearing loads of dreadlocks, well wrapped in
  muza grass, wearing deerskin upper robes,
worshipping tridents with a symbolic design of three lines, and
  wearing Brahmin threads and sacred raiment made of silk.
Thus came the well-trained Vedics, skilled in reciting the *Veda*,
  complete masters of linguistics and prosody,
holding the view that the self is existent,
proud of their performance of austerity.
The attitude of these heretics was like drunken elephants.
The crusher of their brains with a glorious lion's roar, possessed
  of a powerful intellect with sharp fangs of logic,

with robust limbs of grammatical treatises, dignified by the
mane of the Sugāta's doctrine,
with eyes glaring, roaring in Sanskrit proclamations of proof
and refutations through evidence:
Such a king of mountain lions
dwelt in Sakya in the Land of Snows.
Protector of other wise lions,
he conquered those inferior opponents
like a pack of foxes.
In the future, too, may the holy Dharma
defeat all those with mistaken views,
and may the Doctrine of the Sugātas,
the victory banner of infinite joy, be upheld.

With this proclamation, the Vedic logicians shaved their dreadlocks and became renunciates. Their hair can still be seen in the holy shrine of Sakya Monastery.

ID3. How the Buddha's Doctrine Was Spread through His Composition

Having trained in previous lives,
relying upon many learned ones,
and through detailed intellectual analysis,
I am fearless with respect to all knowable things.

As Sakya Paṇḍita states above, he attained the stage of fearless courage with respect to all knowable things. For the purpose of teaching the path of liberation to future practitioners, he composed a multitude of treatises that were commentaries on the intent of the Sugāta's holy scripture. These included treatises on language, such as the *Entry Door for Scholars*, *Summary of Sanskrit,* and many other works in this field; *A Bouquet of Various Flowers of Prosody*; a treatise on synonymics titled *A Treasury of Words*; a treatise on drama titled *Engaging in Greatly Joyous Theatrical Performances*; many treatises on inner sciences, including *Illumination of the Sage's Intent*, which details the practice of the Mahāyāna perfections; and many treatises on the Vajrayāna, including *Homage to Nairātmyā* with commentary.

To remove the stains of general misunderstanding of the scriptures, he composed *Classification of the Three Vows* and a multitude of responses to questions on essential points asked by various masters. As a summary of the essence of all of these, he wrote the *Articles of Petition to the Buddhas and Bodhisattvas of the Ten Directions*. He composed these and many other amazing texts.

IE. The Good Quality of Being Accepted by Lamas and Tutelary Deities

When Sakya Paṇḍita received the profound path guru yoga from Jetsun Rinpoché Drakpa Gyaltsen, he perceived his guru as none other than Mañjuśrī himself, the embodiment of all buddhas. He stated that as a result, he "unmistakenly understood the essential point of all dharmas, attained inconceivable samādhi and realization, was reverently respected by the arrogant leaders of both China and Tibet, and spontaneously accomplished many other excellent qualities and virtues of both Dharma and worldly affairs."

Well-known scholars in both eastern and western India, such as the great Kashmiri paṇḍita Śakyaśribhadra and his retinue, Dānaśīla, Saṃghaśrī, Sugataśrī, and others, arrived in his presence as if invited and offered to impart knowledge of a variety of sciences.

How he was accepted by tutelary deities

When for the purpose of his disciples the Lord of Dharma manifested an appearance of illness, Śāntideva appeared and taught Dharma teachings on the causes and results of saṃsāra. Nāgārjuna taught four summaries of Dharma and eight examples of illusion. Mañjuśrī promised that he would be Sakya Paṇḍita's tutelary deity in every future life. Avalokiteśvara appeared and gently touched him. Ārya Tārā appeared and promised liberation from saṃsāra. Maitreya appeared and opened the doors of hundreds of samādhis. Ārya Acala appeared and promised to dispel the hindrances of the four māras.

At midnight on the twenty-ninth day of the month of Thakar, the Tathāgata King Proclaimer of Inexhaustible Melodies directly appeared and Sakya Paṇḍita received from him the hidden meaning of elaborate, moderate, and condensed scriptures. In the morning, Sakya Paṇḍita took the Mahāyāna bodhisattva vow from Avalokiteśvara. Just before the sun arose, in the presence of Mañjuśrī, Sakya Paṇḍita cut the web of doubt.

On the thirteenth day of the tenth month of Mindruk, Sakya Paṇḍita saw the Buddha Śākyamuni with a retinue of śrāvaka arhats turning the wheel of Dharma and teaching the four noble truths, at which time he recited the Samantabadhra's Aspiration to Noble Conduct in the Sanskrit language. On the fourteenth day, Sakya Paṇḍita received empowerment in the mandala of Hevajra, and on the fifteenth, he saw Tārā three times. Additionally, he saw thirteen other mandalas, such as Cakrasaṃvara mandala.

IF. The Good Quality of Possessing Unimpeded Clairvoyance and Detachment

One day, when the Lord of Dharma was traveling in the city, someone offered him a black cloth with many golden spots as a token. He gave it to the physician Biji, saying, "Keep this well, for our Doctrine will become like stars in a clear sky. Some may say that the Sakya reject holy relics." He uttered a verse:

> Most relics are produced by spirits,
> Some are created by those inclined to virtue.
> Some are also produced by the four elements.
> Holy relics from the three noble ones
> Arise from the power of good qualities,
> Like a precious jewel from an authentic source.
> Such relics increase beyond numbering
> Without decline.

"This is a fact. If any relics arise from me they will beyond number. Keep them, and use this cloth to cover them."

Also, Sakya Paṇḍita predicted his own passing, as is stated in the homage to him written by one of his disciples:

> In the mid-summer month of the Wood Female Snake Year
> and in the last autumn month of Iron Male Dog Year,
> you declared you would depart in the Iron Female Pig Year . . .

It occurred exactly as prophesized.

IG. The Good Quality of Being Venerated by Great Worldly Beings

This has three parts:

1. How human kings bowed at his feet
2. How nāga kings bowed at his feet
3. How spirit kings bowed at his feet

IG1. How Human Kings Bowed at His Feet

When the Lord of Dharma's renown had spread throughout Jambudvīpa, a bodhisattva emanation known as Godan Khan offered an invitation to Sakya Paṇḍita. When Sakya Paṇḍita received the invitation, he remembered Jetsun Drakpa Gyaltsen's earlier prophecy: "In the latter part of your life you will receive an invitation from people wearing a certain costume," and he described their hats and shoes. "At that time, you must go without second thought. It will be of great benefit for the Buddha's doctrine and many sentient beings."

In response, Sakya Paṇḍita embarked from Sakya in the Male Wood Dragon Year (1245), at the age of sixty-three, with two nephews and other members of his retinue. He arrived at the palace in Lanzhou in the Male Fire Horse Year.

At that time, Godan had gone to the land of Hor for the enthronement of Guyuk as Great Khan. Once he returned, he met Sakya Paṇḍita in the first month of the Year of the Sheep (1249). When they met, they had detailed discussions regarding both religious and worldly concerns. The emperor was extremely pleased and said, "Previously, the Erkawun and oracles sat above the monks. From now on, the Lord of Dharma, Sakya Paṇḍita, must be honored at the head of everyone, and the chanting of prayers and aspirations must be led by the Lord of Dharma." Having announced such a decree, the crown of Buddhism was elevated in the land of Hor.

Godan Khan himself received many Dharma teachings, such as about the bodhisattva vow and other profound and vast topics. He brought the people of the land of Hor to the Buddhist doctrine and they also made offerings to and venerated the Triple Gem, acted for the benefit of other sentient beings, and abandoned some aspects of nonvirtuous actions and paths.

IG2. How Nāga Kings Bowed at His Feet

Early one morning on the eleventh day of the third month of the Year of the Sheep, Sakya Paṇḍita dreamed that a crippled being, whose body was covered with sores and spots, came to visit him. The crippled one said:

> Before anyone lived here, my leader was the owner of this entire area. In a previous life, the emperor Godan Khan was born a king and accumulated vast merit based on Buddha Śākyamuni. After departing from that life, he was born as the king of Minyak and built a palace on top of the place where my leader resided. The king began construction, and this caused tremendous destruction to my leader and myself, and caused us to feel oppressed. We were unable to stay in that place, so we moved north and took up residence here.
>
> Now the emperor has come again and caused many different kinds of harm to us. We didn't know where to go, and my leader was extremely angry at the emperor. My leader gathered the local spirits and told them, "This king has twice invaded my land and now I wish to retaliate." He requested the local spirits' assistance, but they said, "This king is powerful and has accumulated merit based on the Buddha Śākyamuni, so we dare not challenge him. It is better not to dwell on the arable land. We recommend that you move to the springs and swamps." My leader took their advice and moved to the wetlands.
>
> The king examined the records of previous Buddhist monks and found that they had been exaggerated. He also saw a golden statue of the Buddha Śākyamuni and dug at its base with a chisel with the intention to test whether it was made of solid gold or filled inside with wood or ceramic. With this, all the spirits gathered together, thinking, "Now we will be able to harm him because his merit has declined through these nonvirtuous actions." They caused disagreement between the king and his prime minister until, finally, the minister assassinated the king.

> As the king drew his last breath, he made an aspiration, "May I be able to take birth as a powerful king in my next life, be able to retaliate against all of you, and subjugate you as my servants."
>
> As a result of this aspiration, he was born the nephew of Genghis Khan and became Godan Khan. Later, when he had grown up, he came here, bringing many horses and people who trampled the swamp where my leader lived. He killed many horses in the swamp, and wherever the blood of the horses fell, some spirits died, became sick, or developed skin diseases. All of the creatures who live in the swamp, such as frogs and others, are barely clinging to life. I have tried to save them with the heat of my body.

Indeed, many weak and nearly dead frogs and tadpoles hung from the crippled one's body. He continued on to say:

> Earlier, the Buddhist monks at the palace performed aspirations and rituals for the emperor Godan Khan, but they neglected to offer any effective benefit to the nāgas and landowning spirits like us. After you arrived, Lord of Dharma, you gave us medicine and food to eat. This helped us tremendously and is curing our diseases. Before I was unable to move due to my disease, but your healing has made it possible for me to come here. However, my leader is close to death. If he dies, the Emperor Godan will also die. If he is cured, the Emperor Godan will also be cured. Minor rituals will not be sufficient to keep him alive. Please perform major rituals on behalf of the emperor and my leader.

For their benefit, the Lord of Dharma performed the ritual of the bodhisattva Siṃhanāda, and through this the emperor was completely freed from illness.

IG3. How Spirit Kings Bowed at His Feet

When the Lord of Dharma was residing in Sinpori, early in the morning he dreamed that some laypeople appeared. They made prostrations and offerings to him, saying, "Don't all sentient beings experience the sufferings of the four torrents of birth, illness, old age, and death?" He replied, "Yes, they do." They said, "We would like to request from you a prayer that they may be freed from these." Sakya Paṇḍita said,

> Despite understanding birth as birthless,
> I am still not freed from the cage of birth;
> in every birth, in whatever birth I take birth,
> protect me from birth in an inferior birth.

Thus the Lord of Dharma spoke.

Then the people asked, "In that case, is it permissible to replace 'illness,' 'aging,' and 'death,' with 'birth' in this prayer? My Lord responded, "Yes, it is permissible." The people replied:

> Glorious Lama, Lord of Dharma, Omniscient Teacher:
> lama, through your kindness, accept us!
> In this birth and in every existence,
> protect us from the suffering of birth, illness, aging, and death.

With these words, they offered prostrations and thanked him. When he awoke, Sakya Paṇḍita thought, "These were the kings of the Dharma protectors of that shrine."

IH. The Good Quality of Receiving a Genuine Prophecy

Once while Sakya Paṇḍita was giving Dharma teachings at Sakya Monastery, Jetsun Drakpa Gyaltsen appeared in the sky in front of him. He proclaimed, "I have been your teacher in twenty-seven previous lives. None other than me were suitable to tame you."

When Sakya Paṇḍita was staying in Kyawo Khadang, he again heard the words, "I have been your lama for twenty-five previous lives," and was reminded of the previous proclamation.

When he was at Lanzhou, a patient told Sakya Paṇḍita that he was suffering due to not having a helper. Enormous compassion arose in Sakya Paṇḍita, and he even thought, "The buddhas and bodhisattvas are lacking compassion because they didn't notice this situation."

The next morning, Jetsun Drakpa Gyaltsen appeared to him with

Virūpa on the right and Kṛṣṇapa on the left. They said, "You must not be disappointed by this. The nature of this contaminated body is that it must cross the torrent of birth, aging, illness, and death."

Mahāsiddha Virūpa asked Sakya Paṇḍita to extend his tongue and then put a droplet of nectar from his skull cup on it, touching the tongue with his ring finger. The Lord of Dharma stated that his mind completely transcended conceptual and nonconceptual thought and experienced bliss, luminosity, and nonconceptualization. He thought that nothing more exalted than this could arise, even in the minds of the buddhas.

Then Jetsun Rinpoché Drakpa Gyaltsen said, "When you depart from this place, to act for the benefit of others, you will be born as a vidyādhara who dwells in the east, beyond many worlds of existence. During that lifetime you will please a multitude of tathāgatas and most of your journey on the paths and stages will be accomplished. In your next life you will take birth as the prince of King Nyimai Tophel of eastern India, in a land known as Mumuni. There, you will be able to liberate hundreds of thousands of devoted disciples. In your third life, you will become a fully enlightened Buddha known as Vimalāśrī."

Jetsun Drakpa Gyaltsen asked Virūpa, "Isn't that true?" He said, "That is so." Kṛṣṇapa also smiled and rejoiced at that.

At that time, his secret organ became completely recessed and no longer visible. An uṣṇīṣa clearly appeared on the top of his head, and a white circular hair appeared between his two eyebrows. These and many other perfect physical qualities manifested on his holy body.

II. The Good Quality of Emanating Exalted Objects of the Holy Body, Speech, and Mind

Thus, until the age of seventy, he performed inconceivable activities for the welfare of sentient beings.

On the morning of the thirteenth day of the eleventh month of Malpo in the Female Iron Pig Year (1251), he extended his hand and blessed the head of Chögyal Phakpa. He advised him, "You must practice profound guru yoga, which is the single path of all the buddhas." He then remained in full mediation posture, holding the vajra and bell in front of his heart, and manifested the appearance of entering into mahāparinirvāṇa.

His holy body remained in the same position, without loss of dignity or radiance of complexion, until the third day. On the morning of the eighteenth, his precious holy body was encased.

On the twenty-fifth, when the cremation was offered, many celestial offerings pervaded the earth and sky, such as a shower of flowers and the fragrance of sandalwood. The smoke was rainbow colored and shaped like a tent, within which many youthful celestial beings held offering substances such umbrellas and victory banners while singing beautiful songs of auspiciousness and playing celestial music. At the tip of the smoke were many artistic designs, such as a vajra, sword, and utpala flower, all of which were clearly perceived by the people who had gathered there.

At that time, for three nights, two Chinese practitioners and one practitioner from Minyak remained in inconceivable deep samādhi, including the samādhi of *śūraṁgama* ("going to heroism").

The next morning, the holy relics were put in a precious box by the disciple Biji Rinchen Drak. Later he displayed them before Godan Khan and Sakya Paṇḍita's disciples.

How the exalted objects of the holy body, speech, and mind appeared on his relics

In the middle of your exalted crown, Hevajra's image and
a stainless image of Mañjuśrī clearly appeared;
on your forehead, Cakrasaṃvara;
on the back of your head, the Blessed Buddha;
on your shoulder, Kasarpaṇi;
on your marrow bone, Avalokiteśvara;
on your spine, the four secret mothers;
on your kneecaps, Tārā and Acala;
on the nāga tree of the right arm bone, Maitreya with the wheel-turning mudra.
These ten emanation appearances arose on your holy physical base.

As a symbol of the lion's roar of emptiness, the pleasant melody of Brahma,
a raised letter *A* clearly appeared, symbolizing birthlessness;
a victory stupa above each ear;
and a samaya vajra marked with a *hūṃ* in the center,

symbolizing the dharmakāya, the natural purification of the
holy mind.

This should be understood as explained.

IJ. The Good Quality of Producing Disciples Who Were Illuminators of the Buddha's Doctrine

This great master began to teach at the age of nine, beginning with the *Lotus-Born Hevajra Sādhana*. He taught continuously until the age of seventy in the lands of Tibet, Hor, and China. The sunlight of his teachings opened the lotus of profound meaning and produced countless intelligent disciples; like a great number of bees, the buzzing of whose teaching spread the doctrine of the Buddha in every direction.

Chief among all of the disciples were his younger brother, Lopön Sönam Gyaltsen, and his nephews, Chögyal Phakpa and his half-brother (Rinchen Gyaltsen). Among the disciples who were able to uphold the lineage of realization, the chief were two known as Drup and Tsok. Among those able to uphold the lineage of pith instructions, chief were two known as Lho and Mar. Among those able to uphold the lineage of practice, chief was Gyalwa Yangönpa. Among those able to uphold the lineage of explication, chief were those from the three directions, known as East, West, and Center; "East" refers to Sharpa Sherab Jungné and his younger brother Dorjé Öser, "Center" refers to Kyotön Drimé, and "West" refers to Uyukpa Rikpai Sengé and his successor Jamyang Nyithokpa. Jamyang Nyithokpas had four pillar-disciples. The first three were Khangtön Öser Gyaltsen, Nyen Darma Sengé, and Shang Dodé Palsangpo, who were known as Khang, Nyen, and Shang. The fourth was Surkhang Shākya Drak.

There were thirteen senior disciples whose names ended with "Palsangpo." They were Tsokgom Kunga Palsangpo, Drupthop Yönten Palsangpo, Rinchen Kyopa Palsangpo, Lhopa Kunkhyen Rinchen Palsangpo, Shang Gyalwa Palsangpo, Shang Dodé Palsangpo, Charup Sengé Palsangpo, Drup Nyingpo Dorjé Palsangpo, Dongtön Sherab Palsangpo, Joden Jangchup Palsangpo, Khaupa Öden Palsangpo, and Kyotön Drimé Palsangpo.[9]

There were seven junior disciples whose name ended with "Gyaltsen." They were Sharpa Yeshé Gyaltsen, Khangtön Öser Gyaltsen, Gandenpa

Chökyi Gyaltsen, Sölchawa Dulwa Gyaltsen, Uyukpa Palgyi Gyaltsen, Yarlungpa Shakya Gyaltsen, and Yarlungpa Jangchup Gyaltsen.

There were many other great beings who were fortunate disciples of this great lama, such as Jamyang Sherab Öser from Tsangnak Phukpa, Terawa Jamgön, the physician Biji, Lotsāwa Sherab Rinchen from Mustang, Khenpo Drakpa Sengé, Lama Öser Shākya, and others.

Your holy body was dignified by glorious auspicious signs and exemplary marks;
your roar of elegant speech subjugated heretical teachers;
you were venerated by powerful rulers of the earth—
prostrations to you, O Sakyapa, the second Buddha.

The exalted disciples born from your holy speech
upheld the victory banner of teaching, practice, and pith instructions without decline.
Reverent prostrations to all of you, amazing upholders;
bestow upon me an intellect that understands profound meaning.

This concludes the good qualities and greatness of the author of the *Classification of the Three Vows.*

3

Sakya Paṇḍita Kunga Gyaltsen: A Sacred Biography

By Jamgön Ameshab (Ngawang Kunga Sönam)[10]

JETSUN DRAKPA GYALTSEN'S younger brother, Palchen Öpo, took as consort Machik Nyitri Cham of Garpu. They had two sons, the eldest of whom was named Kunga Gyaltsen and came to be known as Dharma Lord Sakya Paṇḍita.

Sakya Paṇḍita took birth in the Water Male Tiger Year (1182), on the twenty-sixth day of the month of Tra, when his father, Palchen Öpo, was thirty-three years old.

After Sakya Paṇḍita had been conceived and dwelt his mother's womb, great meditative experience arose in his mother's mind. On the day that he was born, light pervaded the entire area, both day and night.

After he was born, when he could barely crawl, Sakya Paṇḍita spoke some Sanskrit words, which was an awakening of previous habitual tendencies. Yet his mother was worried. She asked Jetsun Rinpoché Drakpa Gyaltsen, "This child is speaking words I cannot understand. Is there any sign of a speech impediment?" Drakpa Gyaltsen observed the child and realized that he was speaking Sanskrit. He answered her, "You do not need to worry that your son will have a speech impediment."

Around that time, Sakya Paṇḍita wrote the complete Sanskrit alphabet with his finger in the dirt, both vowels and consonants, in both Nāgarī and Lanydza scripts. When people came near, he was afraid that they may step on the letters, so he erased them.

Thus Sakya Paṇḍita demonstrated that he possessed a good understanding of both Sanskrit and Tibetan scripts, even without being taught.

How Sakya Paṇḍita's Mind Was Well Trained in Study and Contemplation

This has three sections:

1. How Sakya Paṇḍita acquired knowledge of various things as a foundation
2. How as a result of study Sakya Paṇḍita's mind reached the stage of liberation and comprehension of the five major sciences
3. How he acted for the benefit of the Buddha's doctrine and the welfare of sentient beings by reaching the stage of a fully accomplished great paṇḍita

1. How Sakya Paṇḍita Acquired Knowledge of Various Things as a Foundation

Other sources contain a detailed explanation of the masters from whom Sakya Paṇḍita learned various subjects. Here, in response to a question by Chak Lotsāwa, Dharma Lord Sakya Paṇḍita himself explained in easy-to-understand metered verse:

> Prosody: *Crimson Rishi* (*Drangsong Marser*), and a commentary on it by Jayadeva I received from Sugataśrī.
> Rhetoric: *Ornament of Rhetoric* (*Kāvyādarśa*) by Daṇḍin and *Garland of Melodies* (*Sarasvatikaṇṭhābharaṇa*) and others were completely received from Saṃghaśrī.
> Synonymics: *Amarakośa (Immortal Treasury of Synonymy)* and an extensive commentary on it was fully studied from three scholars.
> Three poems by Kālidāsa were taught by Sugataśrī. *Collection of the Bodhisattva's Previous Lives* was learned from the two great masters.
> Guhyasamāja: The Ārya tradition and also the Jñānapada tra-

dition and supplements were received from the two great masters.

The three commentaries on the *Sarvatathāgatasaṃgraha Tantra* and a short commentary on the *Cakrasaṃvara*; *Ocean of Ḍākinīs* and seven others; the three Hevajra tantras and their supplements in the Drokmi tradition; the *Three Unsullied Arali*; *Protectors' Enlightenment Tantra*; *Summary of Suchness* and commentary; both the *Excellent Glorious Diamond Pinnacle Tantra* and *Secret of Everything Equal to the Limit of Space* as well as commentaries on both of these; the *Sarvadurgatipariśodana Tantra* and supplements; *Wrathful King*; *Great Secret* and others; *Auspicious Power Tantra Requested by Susiddhi* (*Subahuparipṛccha Susiddhi Tantra*) and others; *Secret General Tantra*; four commentaries on the *Litany of the Names of Mañjuśrī*; and commentaries on *Hevajra Mūlatantra Raja*, including a commentary on difficult points known as *Kumudi*, *Lotus with a Garland of Pearls*, and *Jewel Garland*, were learned from Jetsun Drakpa Gyaltsen, the Mañjuśrī of the Sakya.

Kālacakra and supplements; *Hevajra Mūlatantra Raja* and the short *Cakrasaṃvara* with commentaries on these written by the two noble ones; *Mahāvairocana Abhisaṃbodhi*; two additional traditions of commentary on the *Litany of the Names of Mañjuśrī*; and many others were received repeatedly from the two great masters Sugataśrī and Saṃghaśrī.

The *Secret Jewel Droplet*, *Vajra Beneath the Earth*, *Secret Ornament*, and *Vajra Essence Ornament Tantra (Vajragarbha Alankara Tantra)* had not been previously translated, however after receiving them from Sugataśrī, I translated them into Tibetan and edited them.

Additional detail can be found in the holy biography of Sakya Paṇḍita written by Lhopa Kunkhyen Rinchen Pal.

2. How as a Result of Study Sakya Paṇḍita's Mind Reached the Stage of Liberation and Comprehension of the Five Major Sciences

This has two parts:

a. Attainment of liberation by understanding all knowable phenomena
b. Attainment of liberation by understanding each phenomenon exactly

2a. Attainment of Liberation by Understanding All Knowable Phenomena

In a multitude of previous lives, the great being Sakya Paṇḍita had relied upon many holy masters who were learned, accomplished, and well trained in all fields of knowledge. As a result, in this life, his mind was extremely sharp, and in this life he continued to train excellently, relying upon many great scholars. Tutelary deities personally guided his life and he attained unimpeded wisdom in all fields of knowledge. He completely learned all of the teachings listed above by hearing them once. The most difficult topics were fully understood by hearing them twice. For this reason, the Lord of Dharma himself stated:

> I am a linguist; I am a logician; no one can defeat evil challengers as well as me.
> I am expert in prosody; I am a poet, I am incomparable at explaining synomics.
> I know astrology and mathematics; I have realized all outer and inner sciences; I am in peerless in intellectual analysis.
> Who am I? I am the Sakyapa. Other scholars are like reflected images.

Regarding this statement, someone asked, "Sakya Paṇḍita, you state that you know everything that is well known among scholars. I wonder if you say this out of pride without real evidence that you have this knowledge? Or like a crazy person, are you saying this without careful reflection, without analyzing what you know and don't know? Or is this a genuinely honest statement based upon your knowledge of what you have thoroughly studied according to the system of the Noble Ones?"

His statement was not made without evidence. For example, for him to say "I am a linguist" is demonstrably true, because he was well trained through excellent study and was also able to teach and respond to others correctly according to Dharma.

His other statements are similar. Sakya Paṇḍita briefly explained his statement thus:

> Having trained in previous lives,
> relying upon many learned ones, and
> through detailed intellectual analysis,
> I am fearless with respect to all knowable things.

To explain this in detail, the fields of expert study known as the five major sciences are linguistics, logic, medicine, arts, and inner science.

Linguistics is a science based upon treatises that explain how to communicate through language. Among Sanskrit texts in this field, the crown jewel ornaments are *Kalāpa* and *Candra*. Sakya Paṇḍita was well trained in both of these, including their supplementary texts, so he had no difficulty understanding vocabulary and was an expert speaker, like the great scholars Candragomin, Vyāsa, Vasiṣṭha, Vālmīki, and Vāsuki.

Regarding Sakya Paṇḍita's skill in the science of logic, the principal among many treatises are the *Compendium of Valid Cognition* and the Seven Treatises on Valid Cognition by Dharmakīrti; Sakya Paṇḍita understood these well.

As a result of his correct understanding, his intellect was fully developed, like the body of a robust lion. He carried the many scriptures of the sugatas like a lion carries a dense mane. His ability to establish his own tradition and refute others' traditions was as sharp as a lion's claws and fangs, allowing him to utterly defeat inferior opponents. He even defeated opponents whose bodies of natural intelligence were strengthened through conceit as if they were as huge as elephants, with sharp tusks of foolish scriptures and logic who outshone the mass of ordinary scholars lacking intellectual analysis. Thus, Sakya Paṇḍita constantly and fearlessly proclaimed the view of selflessness and emptiness, like a roaring lion. In this ability he was equal to the great masters of India, such as Nāgārjuna, Dharmakīrti who was the originator of logic, and others.

Concerning Sakya Paṇḍita's skill in the science of arts, he was extremely learned in various branches of the arts such as drawing, proportion, the characteristics of the physical appearance of the buddhas in thangkas, various signs of auspiciousness, and the eight types of analytical analysis, including geomancy.

Some scholars consider astrology and mathematics to be included within the science of art. Concerning these, Sakya Paṇḍita was well trained in astrology as it is explained in the *Kālacakra Tantra*, which includes the five branches of arithmetic: numbers, addition, subtraction, multiplication, and division. He was also learned in the five branches of astrology: the weeks, days, and constellations, and their applications and their functions. He also knew the planets and their various individual movements: swift or slow, straight or crooked.

Based on this, Sakya Paṇḍita also understood the auspiciousness or inauspiciousness of dwellings and fortunes, the face of Rāhula, the fires at the end of an eon, eclipses of the sun and moon, and the appearance and disappearance of comets. He was a master in these and all other external astrological analyses, as well as the internal astrological phenomena such as nerves and veins and their airs; the internal sun, moon, planets, and constellations, and their times and applications; breath; moments; minutes; transferences; duration of hours; duration of sessions; duration of days and night; and occurrences of the eclipses of the sun and moon. Based on this, he comprehensively understood the arising and setting of primordial wisdom and how to accomplish perfect enlightenment as explained through internal astrology.

These days, some Tibetan masters are praised by their own disciples as peerless masters, but the only evidence proving this is that they know the proper proportions of statues and celestial mansions. Yet if they actually try to make something, they do not even know how to make a piece of cloth. Still they are proclaimed as learned in the five major sciences.

The great master Sakya Paṇḍita was not like that. He was extremely skilled and actually involved in making works of art. For example, Sakya Paṇḍita built the wooden shrine case for the statue of Mañjuśrī in the shrine of his great teacher, Drakpa Gyaltsen, which was located in Utsé Nyingma. (Lowo Khenchen states that the artistry of the backrest made by Sangtsa for that statue was even more detailed than this.)

Well-known foreign artists were later invited to Tibet, however, the detail of their workmanship could not be compared to even a hundredth of that of Sakya Paṇḍita.

Another work made by Sakya Paṇḍita's own hands was a very detailed drawing on fabric for a thangka made according to the instructions in the root tantra. This was presented to a Chinese leader and was drawn with great detail on white fabric.

Another of his personal works was a drawing of Mañjuśrī's special hand objects [a composite symbolic image of a lotus, sword, and two double-headed parrots representing Padmasambava, King Trisong Detsen, and translators Śāntarakṣita and Chogrong Lui Gyaltsen respectively] on the wall of Samyé Monastery. These days even famous and learned artists cannot come close to such detail.

Regarding Sakya Paṇḍita's skill in the science of medicine, as explained above, he was extremely well trained in a wide variety of medical theories. His skill in diagnosis was such that he could recognize the characteristics of various diseases through methods of analysis such as observation of the face, asking questions, and examination of the pulse. He was also skilled in prescribing appropriate medications for daily and occasional purposes. He was skilled in curing diseases through pacification, purification, and various procedures for both single and multiple ailments.

He understood the characteristics of diseases and the five methods of treatment, such as how each of the various diseases begin, develop, and completely ripen, and how each weaken, diminish, and completely disappear in the process of waxing and waning. He knew how to skillfully draw disease from the upper to the lower body as needed, or from the lower to the upper body, in order to skillfully extract it.

He also knew the methods of preventing diseases so that they would not occur in the first place; how to treat them once they had occurred; and, having treated them, how to prevent recurrence. Sakya Paṇḍita was thoroughly learned in these and many other medical treatments. He was skilled in the methods of recognizing characteristics of diseases that occur due to unbalanced elements and the methods of curing such diseases through pacification. In short, he was the equal of the skillful physician Jīvaka Kumārabhṛta.

Regarding the science of inner philosophy, Sakya Paṇḍita himself stated that inner science is summarized in the precious Tripiṭaka, the sacred teachings of the Sugata, which has two categories: Pāramitāyāna and Mantrayāna. The Pāramitāyāna has three categories: the Abhidharma, which primarily explains training in exalted wisdom; the Vinaya, which primarily explains training in exalted morality; and the Sūtra, which primarily explains training in exalted concentration. It can also be categorized as profound and vast, with profound teachings such as those of the Perfection of Wisdom (Prajñāpāramitā), vast teachings such as the *Gaṇḍavyūha*, and also the commentarial treatises on these. Sakya Paṇḍita was well trained in all of these.

Regarding the Mantrayāna, Sakya Paṇḍita was extremely well-trained in the kriyā, caryā, yoga, and anuyoga tantras, including their root and commentary tantras and commentarial treatises.

Concerning how to put these tantras into practice, there are two processes: maturation, which occurs through the process of initiation, and liberation, which occurs through meditation on the path. Sakya Paṇḍita comprehensively understood the method of liberation, which is characteristic of the path of meditation. He also understood the methods that cause the arising of meditative experience in those for whom it has not yet arisen, how to promote it in those for whom some experience has arisen, the borders of the path, how to dispel hindrances on the path, the signs of the heat of meditative absorption, and the process by which primordial wisdom gradually arises.

Sakya Paṇḍita also excellently understood the method of attaining the inner essence of the vajra verses in this very life through the essential points of the pith instructions of the Path Including the Result based on the *Vajra Verses*, which is the method that unmistakenly explains how to travel the paths and stages at both the worldly and beyond-worldly levels through the process of dependent arising. The result leads diligent practitioners to the excellent attainment of mahāmudrā without needing to abandon the body itself.

In addition, Sakya Paṇḍita excellently mastered most of the pith instructions that were well known among the great meditators of India who attained the stage of mahāsiddha, as well as those known to senior Tibetan practitioners, such as the teachings of the Kadam tradition, Method of Pacification, Dzokchen, Mahāmudrā, and even Chö. He received and mastered all of these teachings.

Sakya Paṇḍita also precisely understood how to engage in various paths, such as what are known as the gradual path and the sudden path. He knew the essential erring and unerring points well. Based on these paths, some absorptions can produce the experience of calm abiding; some can dispel various minor illnesses; some can protect from fear of human and nonhuman beings; some can produce beneficial thoughts; some can produce partial freedom from conceptual elaboration; some can elevate one to the formless realms; some make it possible to attain the stage of an arhat or pratekyabuddha; some make it possible to gradually establish the interconnections necessary for perfectly enlightened buddhahood after three countless eons; some make it possible to accomplish the eight worldly attainments; some make it possible to produce the primordial wisdom of the path of seeing through achieving the beyond-worldly attainments, based on which, through gradual promotion, the stage of a vajradhāra can be attained in a single life. Sakya Paṇḍita completely understood and accomplished all of these methods through the great kindness of his teacher, the Glorious Sakyapa Drakpa Gyaltsen, the Lord of Dharma, who was the embodiment of all the buddhas of the three times. Sakya Paṇḍita completely trained in every path without exception and understood them all without doubt.

Because of this Sakya Paṇḍita said, "I have realized the wisdom of all inner sciences." In these words, he summarized his own wisdom. He also stated, "I have realized all inner sciences." Sakya Paṇḍita also said, "I am peerless in intellectual analysis." He stated this because he had mastered unerring analysis and investigation, erudite terms and their meaning, the subtle meaning of what is confirmatory and contradictory, and also extremely subtle points that were previously both known and unknown among scholars. These points were so subtle that even some inferior scholars still could not understand them clearly after spending great effort for a long time. However, with very little effort, Sakya Paṇḍita comprehensively understood them without any difficulty.

As a result, when Sakya Paṇḍita engaged in dialogue or debate about any of the five major sciences that are well known among scholars, he could explain and respond correctly in each of the various fields. Realizing his own ability, he stated, "I am peerless in intellectual analysis."

Concerning the word "peerless," due to Sakya Paṇḍita's great wisdom and learning in various subjects, he attained the stage of great courage in composition, debate, and explanation. It is due to this that he boldly stated that he could understand any subject matter, at any time, as well as any person and their limitations. What would bring him to make such statements of assertion and refutation unless he actually knew these subjects, the time, and the capabilities of individuals?

Hence, Sakya Paṇḍita set the standard for who was with and without peer. Usually, worldly beings set the standard that forms the baseline of who is with and without peer. When asked, "Who makes this declaration that he knows the five major sciences?" he replied, "It is the Sakyapa." If he had been further asked, "Where does he live?" the answer would have been, "In the shrine of the glorious Sakya Monastery, as a fully ordained monk following Śākyamuni Buddha, whose name is known as Kunga Gyaltsen Palsangpo."

The reason why Sakya Paṇḍita said that other scholars are like reflected images is that some who seem to be scholars do not even correctly understand the meaning of the above description; they have not even heard the titles of these books, and not even a small portion of the meaning of their contents has arisen in their minds. Their minds know only a few narrow topics, like the recitations of talking parrots; still they declare that they are well trained. If someone were to ask them about or challenge them on the topics of Sanskrit, logic, synomics, poetry, prosody, or the classifications and summaries of words, and they were required to reply concerning these topics, they would have to remain as mute as a sheep. Yet out of pride and conceit, they declare themselves to be learned, believing that they can accomplish their goals by merely criticizing or saying unpleasant things about the genuinely learned. Such scholars are like reflected images because, like the image of a moon reflected on the water's surface, they appear in the shape of a moon but cannot accomplish the functions of a moon.

Sakya Paṇḍita did not suggest that well-trained scholars are like reflected images. How could he possibly say this? Genuine scholars are an object of veneration for both worldly and celestial beings and are the heart-sons of all the buddhas. Hence, his brief autobiography is an honest statement, for he knew that he was completely trained in all five of the major sciences that were well known among Indian scholars and that he had completely mastered all of the scriptures, treatises, and commentaries that existed in Tibet.

Sakya Paṇḍita naturally delighted in discussions concerning every aspect of knowable things. He had thoroughly analyzed his own mind and knew that he was well trained in these subjects. His statements were unbiased proof of his own intelligence. The depths of his knowledge could not be plumbed by unlearned ones immersed in contradictory traditions of knowledge, or by those who knew a few things about Sanskrit vocabulary, or who could ask questions, debate, and hold a dialogue on a few subjects, or who could ask a few questions about essential points of scriptures and pith instructions. To explain these good qualities through metaphor, Sakya Paṇḍita made the following statement:

> Traveling without impediment through the sky of knowledge,
> able to devour opponents, even the dazzling sun and moon,
> yet unable to be seen by anyone,
> Kunga Gyaltsen is like Rāhula in the sky.

Such an autobiographical statement is not a criticism of others made from pride; ancient scholars made such statements based on evidence. For example, although they had entirely overcome pride or conceit, great ancient scholars such as the glorious Dharmakīrti, Pang Lotsāwa Lodrö Tenpa, Prajñākaragupta, Śaṃkarānanda, Vādisiṃha, and many others made similar statements in their own biographies.

Statements such as these were made for the benefit of the great scholars who would appear in the future and for students with the sincere aspiration to become scholars so that that they would be able to fully understand from their biographies what these masters had studied. This helps the future students and scholars abandon the mental attitude of being contented with the knowledge of only a few aspects of knowable things. It also develops enthusiasm in fresh-minded intelligent youth, who will think, "How wonderful it would be if I could become a great scholar like that!" This is the reason that scholars make such bold statements.

For example, Dharmakīrti stated:

> Vālmīki stated that monkeys capture rabbits and put them in
> the ocean.
> Vyāsa proclaimed the untrue story of Arjuna.
> I explain the truth, weighing each word and its meanings.
> However, everyone criticizes, stretching their throats.
> I bow to the Possessor of Fame [Dharmakīrti].

Dharmakīrti also stated:

> If the sun of Dharmakīrti's
> words ever sets,
> genuine Dharma will sleep or die,
> and then artificial Dharma will arise.

Also, Pang Lotsāwa Lodrö Tenpa stated:

> Setting my knowledge on one side and
> setting all others' knowledge on the other,
> if such a scale were possible,
> the weight of my knowledge would be heavier.

Also, Prajñākaragupta stated:

> When the sun of Prajñākara's intellect rises,
> adorned by thousands of light rays of logical reasoning,
> like fireflies carrying a little light at night,
> heretics with inferior minds flee far away.

He also stated:

> When Prajñākara was born,
> if other schools' learned ones did not tremble,
> they were either insensible like a rock or
> actually fools, like cows.

The Brāhmin Ācārya Śaṃkarānanda stated:

> When Brāhmin paṇḍitas debated in Varanasi, because Śaṃkarānanda's words were so profound and deep, the other masters did not understand. Still they criticized his statements, saying, "Master, logical engagement has not yet arisen in your mind."
>
> Śaṃkarānanda responded:

When fishermen find a priceless precious jewel,
Hey! When an assembly of fools is handed precious jewels,
They are returned unheated, unbeaten, and unground.
Why not be happy they've been returned?
Śaṃkarānanda's situation is like this.

Vādisiṃha stated:

When others discuss logic, they stretch both hands
and quickly say whatever comes into their mind.
But if Vādisiṃha is the challenger
even Lord Śiva knows only the alphabet.

He wrote the above words on a long piece of bamboo in the shape of a pen and had them displayed.

Paṇḍita Ganaśri stated:

With the robust body of the Seven Treatises on Valid Cognition, the sharp fangs of the *Commentary on Valid Cognition*,
a heavy mane of exalted Dharma, and the very sharp claws of prosody:
who is this terror that eats the brains of heretical elephants?
It is Glorious Ganaśri, whose proclamations are a fearless lion's roar.

He also wrote this on a long piece of bamboo and posted it at the gate of King Kalinga's palace.

Thus, descriptions of these earlier scholars' own good qualities are found in the autobiographical accounts of their own lives. Such descriptions beautify them. On the other hand, proud and conceited descriptions of one's greatness of caste, wealth, and retinue, or of the greatness of one's force and power, are worldly concerns. Scholars scorn such things and would be ashamed to utter them; hence noble scholars do not proclaim such things. Readers should understand this distinction.

In summary, Sakya Paṇḍita stated:

In the beginning, I thoroughly learned every field of knowledge;
In the middle, I explained these meanings well to assemblies of scholars;
and later, I diligently meditated on the meaning of what my mind had become familiar with.
This is the intent of the practice of the buddhas of the three times.

2b. Attainment of Liberation by Understanding Each Phenomenon Exactly

The autobiography of the Lord of Dharma [Sakya Paṇḍita] stated:

> As for myself, when I was young, I requested the Great Jetsun [Drakpa Gyaltsen] to bestow the guru yoga blessing. He did not approve, saying, "You do not have the perception that I am a buddha. Your perception is that I am merely your uncle. Also, you are unable to perform hardship for your lama through offerings of your body and wealth."
>
> Terrifying signs of my death later occurred, accompanied by physical discomfort. At the same time, Jetsun Rinpoché Drakpa Gyaltsen also manifested discomfort for several days, during which time I continuously offered service day and night without break and without thought of sleep or food. This appears to have helped me to purify some sins.
>
> He then bestowed the guru yoga blessing upon me, which produced in me the perception that my guru was truly a buddha. I saw him as the real Mañjuśrī, the embodiment of all the buddhas, and genuine uncommon devotion to him arose in me. This liberated me from the signs of death, and I became physically comfortable again. Then I was able to understand the unmistaken essential points of scripture and logical reasoning, such as Mantrayāna, Paramitayāna, Abhidharma, and Vināya, as well as Sanskrit, logic, poetry, prosody, synonymics, and others. I also attained great fearless courage regarding the entire Tripiṭaka. Humans, celestial beings, and demons showed great

> kindness to me. Even conceited Indian kings came to request me to bestow Dharma teachings. Some genuine realization also arose in my mind.

Also, his homage states:

> When blessed with the profound path,
> you beheld your holy master as Mañjuśrī
> and realized all dharmas instantly;
> liberated mind, I bow my head to you.

Another source demonstrates that the great Lord Lama had been the spiritual master of great beings in many previous lives. Furthermore, Jetsun Drakpa Gyaltsen was Sakya Paṇḍita's teacher for many of his previous lives. It is said that one time when Dharma teachings were given in Sakya Monastery, a sound was heard in space, saying: "You have been a great paṇḍita, well trained in the *Commentary on Valid Cognition* for twenty-seven successive lives, and Jetsun Drakpa Gyaltsen was your spiritual master in each of those lives. No master other than him was able to tame you."

Another time, there was a similar occurrence that spoke of thirty-seven lives.

Also:

> One time when there was a Dharma teaching in Sakya, a sound was heard in the sky, saying, "Drakpa Gyaltsen was your spiritual master for an inconceivable number of previous lives." When I heard that sound, I was reminded of my previous lives.

I [Ngawang Kunga Sönam] have seen these passages. Also, Sakya Paṇḍita's autobiography states:

> The primordial wisdom body of all the buddhas,
> manifested in the pure body of an upāsika [Jetsun Drakpa Gyaltsen] has cut the web of my delusion.
> The words, "He has been your spiritual master for many lifetimes" were heard in space.
> I prostrate to you, Excellent Guide.

The Kadam master Namkha Bum asked him, "Please tell me, as heart advice without any concealment, what kind of positive qualities of scriptural realization have arisen in your mind? And has there been real evidence that there will be any benefit from your travel to Mongolia?"

Sakya Paṇḍita answered, "I have genuine, unmistaken devotion to Lord Buddha's doctrine, and I have some knowledge of the meaning of holy scriptures. There is not much realization that I can describe that has arisen in my mental continuum. The Mongol court summoned me, saying, 'You must come here to be an object of veneration. If you do not come here, I will send an army to Tibet.' On the basis of these words, I had to embark out of fear that if they were to send an army, it would cause destruction to Tibet. I am traveling there with the hope that it will be of benefit to sentient beings. Other than that, I have no real evidence that it will be of benefit. Generally, there is nothing that prevents me from giving away even my own body and life, if there is some benefit for sentient beings."

The homage quoted above states, "Liberated mind, I bow my head to you." Sakya Paṇḍita himself stated that the words "liberated mind" refer to his freedom from cognitive obscuration. "Realized all dharmas instantly" refers to comprehensive understanding of the suchness of all dharmas, which occurs only upon the first stage of the path of seeing.

Also, the willingness to give one's life for the purpose of Dharma is a sign of having attained the irreversible stage of dwelling on the path of seeing, because the *Ornament for Clear Realization* (*Abhisamayālaṃkāra*) states:

> Not observing even atoms of any phenomenon,
> certain concerning one's own stage,
> abiding on the three stages, and
> being willing to give one's life for the purpose of Dharma:
> thus upon sixteen moments,
> intelligent ones abide on the path of seeing.
> These are the marks of the irreversible stage.

A commentary on this [*Sphuṭārtha* by Ācārya Haribhadra] states:

> There are four aspects of the path: (1) Due to having realized an exalted stage of generosity and so forth, engagement and reengagement in miserliness, immorality, and so forth are each sep-

> arately rejected. (2) Because the three doors of liberation are the intrinsic nature of all phenomena, then not even a tiny atom of any knowable phenomenon is observed. (3) Due to attaining direct belief, one abides in exact certainty that the nature of one's own stage is the three omnisciences. (4) Due to exertion on a single point, one is willing to give one's own life for the purpose of Dharma and thus attain the state of omniscience.

These four aspects of the path summarize the sixteen moments of patience and understanding. Once these are genuinely attained, there is no clinging to either the subject or object and worldly phenomena are purified. In summary, such mental aspects are able to repel inclination toward any other resulting physical form; because of this, bodhisattvas are able to abide on the path of seeing. This very clearly explains the characteristics of the irreversible stage.

Further, it was foretold that in his third lifetime, Sakya Paṇḍita would become the highest of noble beings. In this life most disciples perceived in that way in their pure vision. Later, as a vidyādhara, he would abide in space and take birth as the son of King Nyimai Tophel.

This demonstrates that in reality Sakya Paṇḍita was a fully enlightened buddha, like Mañjuśrī. All of the events of his life that we perceived, including his positive qualities of realization and knowledge, should be understood as the manifestations of an emanation.

3. How He Acted for the Benefit of the Buddha's Doctrine and the Welfare of Sentient Beings by Reaching the Stage of a Fully Accomplished Great Paṇḍita

Sakya Paṇḍita's benefit to the doctrine and sentient beings has two aspects:

a. How he caused the development of the Buddha's doctrine through three types of scholarly activities
b. How he caused the flourishing of the Buddha's doctrine in the Land of Hor according to the prophecy of noble beings, such as the prophecy that begins, "In the northern regions of the earth. . . ."

3a. How Sakya Paṇḍita Caused the Development of the Buddha's Doctrine through the Three Types of Scholarly Activities

This has two parts:

1. How Sakya Paṇḍita caused the development of the Buddha's doctrine through the three types of scholarly activities of teaching, composition, and debate
2. How Sakya Paṇḍita performed the benefit of other sentient beings through myriad activities

3a1. How Sakya Paṇḍita Caused the Development of the Buddha's Doctrine through the Three Types of Scholarly Activities[11] of Teaching, Composition, and Debate

This has three parts:

a. How Sakya Paṇḍita caused the lotus garden of happiness and benefit to grow through the sunshine of his teachings
b. How he attracted the minds of scholars through compositions like a garland of jewels
c. How he crushed the rocky mountains of inferior views by the power of the thunderbolt of debate

3a1a. How Sakya Paṇḍita Caused the Lotus Garden of Happiness and Benefit to Grow through the Sunshine of His Teachings.

Over an inconceivable number of previous lives, the great being Sakya Paṇḍita made as many aspirations as the number of atoms in the oceans that he would become a teacher as exalted as he did become. As a result, he unmistakenly knew the meaning of each phenomena exactly and all phenomena entirely, as explained above. Sakya Paṇḍita also developed unbearable great compassion toward sentient beings in whom the eye of knowledge and wisdom is weakened by the cataract of ignorance, and whose footsteps have missed the path, searching for what is to be abandoned and what is to be adopted, and as a result have fallen from the cliff into the abyss of existence and experiencing unbearable agony. Seeing them as would a mother whose only child is drowning in a river, he taught the unmistaken suchness of all phenomena, which is the method of freeing them from suffering. As a teacher, he was like the sun arisen in the sky of knowledge, mounted on the vehicle of the wind, and he radiated the brilliant light of his elegant teachings in infinite directions, dispelling the darkness of the roots of ignorance and causing the lotus garden of happiness and benefit to fully develop throughout the ten directions.

Thus, his writings are a source of precious elegant words that provide philosophical teachings suited to the capacity of various disciples.

In particular, the root of the suffering of saṃsāra is strong clinging to the self, the antidote for which is primordial wisdom that realizes the absence of a self. This understanding must be preceded by the study of logical treatises, the chief among which are the Mādhyamaka treatises, which teach the view of freedom from all extremes and require studying commentaries by great masters in order to understand their meaning.

Although long ago the great master and translator Ngok Loden Sherab had established the tradition of the study of the *Commentary on Valid Cognition*, which is one of the three main treatises on logic, by the era of Sakya Paṇḍita this tradition had almost completely waned. With the intention to reestablish it and help this teaching flourish, as well as to establish the great path of the Kashmiri paṇḍita [Śākyaśribhadra], who kindly came to the Land of Snows and gave elaborate teachings, Sakya Paṇḍita made a commitment, as an offering of gratitude to his teacher, to always teach at least one session on one of the great treatises each day. Because of his strong commitment, this teaching tradition matured and continues to flourish to the present day.

On another topic, the great being Sakya Paṇḍita was frequently invited to visit various places by devoted people. At that time, some disciples directly requested teachings due to the root of their previous virtue; others did not request them, but gathered for the purpose of entertainment. To both, Sakya Paṇḍita gave either the elaborate or abbreviated forms of the bodhisattva vow in the Madhyamaka tradition with the intention of making it easy for them to preserve the commitments and with the thought that it would be of great benefit. For if within the minds of those practitioners genuine bodhicitta, which is the root of achieving unsurpassable enlightenment, were to develop, from that time onward, if it were not abandoned, then even if they committed the five irredeemable sins, their vow would not decline and their merit would increase equal to the boundaries of space.

If Sakya Paṇḍita remained in a particular place for a few additional days, he would give a complete teaching on the *Illumination of the Sage's Intent* in order that the bodhisattva vow would not decline but rather increase to greater heights. For this reason, at the end of that great text he stated, "Because I have taught this teaching in Central Tibet, Tsang, and Kham, all of my disciples have received its transmission. I have advised them to study it and explain its meaning to others." In this way, he bestowed this precious Dharma teaching and even gave advice on how to skillfully accomplish worldly activities for the benefit of other beings.

Sakya Paṇḍita's style of written expression, which is to say his tangible speech, was free of flaws such as repetition and possessed excellent qualities such as being extremely accurate in spelling, sounding pleasant when read, and being relevant in every case. Thus, all of his writing was greatly admired by others.

Therefore, Chögyal Phakpa stated:

> Learned ones,
> hearing such words proclaimed,
> become single-pointedly attracted to them
> without being interrupted by other distractions.
>
> What need to mention their ability to outshine other sounds,
> even not withstanding the examples of the
> pleasant songs of gandharva maidens
> and the beautiful melodious sounds of the nightingale.

As explained above, Sakya Paṇḍita's mental conduct was flawless. He possessed the good qualities he described as characterizing the learned:

> Teaching without discouragement, and
> solely with wisdom and compassion,
> with pure conduct of the three doors, and
> with devoted efforts to protect the doctrine.
> Possession of such conduct
> is known to benefit others through purity and wisdom.

This great master possessed these good qualities he described.

The *Ornament of the Mahāyāna Sūtras* (*Mahāyānasūtrālaṃkāra*) states:

> Intelligent ones, without discouragement and with
> compassion,
> with widely renowned reputation and with knowledge of correct ritual performance:
> such bodhisattvas are said to be excellent.
> Their explications possess the dignity of the sun among beings.

Also, from the same source:

> Those who are vast,
> having overcome doubt, and
> teach the two suchnesses without bias
> are known as magnificent bodhisattva teachers.

Sakya Paṇḍita possessed the positive qualities here described.

Sakya Paṇḍita established lineages of oral transmission of teachings on the great treatises: the *Commentary on Valid Cognition*, the *Treasury of Logic on Valid Cognition*, the *Treasury of Abhidharma*, and the three Hevajra tantras. Although not commonly classified as great treatises, among the still widely held teaching lineages that originated from him are the *Vajra Verses*, the *Illumination of the Sage's Intent*, and the *Jewel Treasury of Elegant Sayings*. All of these lineages of teachings continue to be widely held.

No doubt many of the oral explanation lineages originating from him have been broken, such those on texts other than the Seven Treatises on Valid Cognition, the *Compendium of Abhidharma*, the classical treatises of Maitreya Bodhisattva, the *Cakrasaṃvara Tantra*, the *Guhyasamāja Tantra*, and many commentaries on these.

In addition, among the oral explanation lineages that came from Sakya Paṇḍita and have continued to be taught without interruption through the centuries to the present and are still widely held are his teachings on the *prātimokṣa* vows, generating wishing and entering bodhicitta, initiations that are methods of maturation in the four classes of tantra, various blessings and empowerments, and reading transmissions.

3a1b. How Sakya Paṇḍita Attracted the Minds of Scholars through Compositions Like a Precious Garland of Jewels

Sakya Paṇḍita composed his flawless treatises in order to delight unbiased captain-like scholars and to clarify their minds with a precious garland of jewels, which arose from the churning of the ocean of wisdom and were impelled by the wind of his wish to explain; to dispel the darkness of ignorance of every sentient being with the Lord of Dharma's sun-like mandala; and to reveal the genuine mental liberation of the author. As it is said:

> A horse's worth is known in a race;
> an elephant's strength is known on the battlefield;
> the purity of gold and silver is known by smelting;
> a scholar is known by their composition of elegant sayings.

Sakya Paṇḍita's writings can be described in two different ways: the variety of treatises that this master composed and the quality of those treatises.

3a1b1. Concerning the Variety of Treatises

The *Jewel Treasury of Elegant Sayings* summarizes the subjects contained in treatises written by both Buddhist and non-Buddhist masters and demonstrates the path of the holy Dharma by explaining how noble worldly beings should behave.

Concerning linguistics, Sakya Paṇḍita wrote *Entry Door for Scholars*, *Generating Wisdom*, *Engaging in Wisdom,* and *Summary of Linguistics.*

Concerning logic, he wrote *Treasury of Logic on Valid Cognition* and its autocommentary, which distill the essence of the Seven Treatises on Valid Cognition.

Concerning art, Sakya Paṇḍita wrote *Treatise on Holy Images*, *Analysis of Geomancy*, and *Astrology of the Precious Doctrine.*

Concerning medicine, he wrote the *Summary of Eight Branches of Medical Treatment.*

Concerning inner science, Sakya Paṇḍita wrote *Articles of Petition to the Buddhas and Bodhisattvas of the Ten Directions*, which is a systematic illumination of the overall meaning of all Buddhist holy scriptures. He also wrote *Classification of Schools* and *Pāramitāyāna Teaching for Great Dharma Assemblies.*

The above works cover the subject of the common Pāramitāyāna.

Concerning the Mantrayāna, among Sakya Paṇḍita's many writings were his *Commentary on the Homage to Nairatmya by Drakpa Gyaltsen*; *Articles on the Five Interdependencies*, which is a pith instruction on Vajrayāna; *Explication of the Path*; *Guru Yoga of the Profound Path*; *Index of Commentaries on the Path Including the Result*; and many other works.

With regard to the five minor sciences, concerning prosody, Sakya Paṇḍita wrote *A Bouquet of Various Flowers of Prosody* and *Beseeching the Compassion of the Sugatas*, which demonstrates examples from the former text. Concerning poetry, Sakya Paṇḍita wrote *Poetry as an Ornament of Scholarly Speech*. Concerning synomics, he wrote *A Treasury of Words*. Concerning drama, he wrote *Engaging in Greatly Joyous Theatrical Performances* and *Treatise on Music*, which explains the music and songs for those performances.

During his era, this lord of Dharma was the single font of knowledge in the Land of Snows. He therefore wrote numerous letters responding to anyone who had questions concerning holy scripture, logical reasoning, pith instructions, or other topics. He answered various masters' questions, including those of Kadam masters such as Gelong Dorjé Sengé; great meditators such as Nyemo Gomchen; and various translators, including Shang Lotsāwa, Chak Lotsāwa, and Lowo Lotsāwa, to each of whom he wrote homage prayers.

Sakya Paṇḍita also wrote many other short works, such as praises of Buddha Śākyamuni and Mañjuśrī.

3a1b2. Concerning the Quality of Sakya Paṇḍita's Treatises

All of Sakya Paṇḍita's writing is said to have been composed spontaneously with very little effort. Vast meaning is demonstrated in his works by just a few words, and the meaning is clear and easy to understand even by those who are not learned.

Sakya Paṇḍita's words are like elegant ornaments that greatly delight the learned, with meaning so extremely profound that the depth of his analysis cannot be plumbed even by the combined knowledge of hundreds of others who are said to be scholars.

Concerning Sakya Paṇḍita's writing, Chögyal Phakpa wrote:

> The swiftness of his composition
> is even faster than the movement of light,
> arising effortlessly,
> as spontaneously as an ocean wave.
> The weight of its magnificent meaning is
> praised by all the intelligent.
> The subtlety of its analysis
> is like that of none before.
> He illuminates minds
> like sunlight illuminates snowy mountain peaks
> and generates complete joy
> like tasting the experience of absorption in samādhi.

Except for *Commentary on [Sönam Tsemo's] How to Easily Engage Beginners* and *Commentary on Homage to the Wheel of the Three Tantras*, the great master Sakya Paṇḍita did not write commentaries on books written by others. Neither did he write commentaries that analyze the meaning of tantric vocabulary. Sakya Paṇḍita did write sādhanas of Mañjuśrī, Vajravidāraṇa in the Virūpa tradition, wrathful Bhurkuṃkūṭa, and a few others, but otherwise, he did not write any grand mandala rituals, or ceremonies. He intended that the writings of the previous Sakya lamas, who were none other than Vajradhāra and who composed these in detail, would not decline.

The above generally explains Sakya Paṇḍita's oeuvre, however to list major texts in more detail by subject:

Linguistics: *Generating Wisdom*, *How to Enter Sanskrit*, *Summary of Linguistics*, *Summary of Vacana*, *Commentary on [Sönam Tsemo's] How to Easily Engage Beginners*, and *How to Compose Script*.

Logic: *Treasury of Logic on Valid Cognition* and an autocommentary on it.

Poetry: *Poetry as an Ornament of Scholarly Speech* and *Beseeching the Compassion of the Sugatas*.

Prosody: *A Bouquet of Various Flowers of Prosody*.

Synonymics: *A Treasury of Words*.

Drama: *Engaging in Greatly Joyous Theatrical Performances* and *Treatise on Music.*

Art: *Treatise on Holy Images* and *Analysis of Geomancy.*

Medical science: *Summary of Eight Branches of Medical Treatment.*

Inner science: Among the homages he wrote are an homage to the Buddha titled *What is to Be Attained*, *Homage to the Muni*, *Homage to the Greatly Compassionate Lord of the World* as well as another homage to Avalokiteśvara, *Homage to the Painting of the Special Hand Objects of Mañjuśrī*, *Homage to the Holy Site of Samyé Monastery*, and *Commentary on [Jetsun Drakpa Gyaltsen's] Homage to Mañjuśrī.*

Common vehicle: *Classification of Schools*, *Illumination of the Sage's Intent*, *Classification of the Three Vows*, and *The Great Resolve with Supplementary Scriptural Quotations.*

How to practice: *The Ten Dharma Activities*, *An Explanation of [Sachen Kunga Nyingpo's] Parting from the Four Attachments*, *Brief Framework of the Mahāyāna Path*, and *Explanation of Dedications.*

Useful general theory: *Entry Door for Scholars*, and *Elegant Theoretical Analysis*, and concerning worldly customs, *Jewel Treasury of Elegant Sayings.*

Miscellaneous: *Verses on How Harinanda Was Defeated*, *Explanation of the Word "Bagora" in Verse*, *Invitation to Various Intelligent People to Ask Questions*, and the root text *Eight "I Am's"* and an autocommentary on it.

Letters and responses: *Articles of Petition to the Buddhas and Bodhisattvas of the Ten Directions*, *Letter to Noble Masters*, *Letter to the Deities Who Delight in the Buddha's Doctrine*, *Letter to the Saṅgha Dwelling in Shingkun*, *Letter to the Ṣun*, *Letter to Lowo Lotsāwa*, *Advice to Shang Lotsāwa*, *Letter to the Geshé from Öjé*, *Letter to the Great Meditator from Nyemo*, *Response to Dogorwa*, and *Response to Chak Lotsāwa.*

Uncommon Mahāyāna vehicle: *Illumination of the Mañjuśrī Sādhana*; *Tārā Sādhana*; *Ritual of Offering to Grahamātṛikā, Mother of the Planets*; *Mother of the Planets Sādhana in a Lineage from Śāntarakṣita*; *Mandala Ritual Illuminating Indivisibility*; *Explanation of How to Meditate on Amitābha*; and *Wondrous Instructions on the Moment before Death.*

Anuttarayoga tantra: Two different homages to the lama [Jetsun Drakpa Gyaltsen]; *Homage to Lord of Mahasiddhas* [*Virupa*]; *Homage to the Lineage Lamas of Cakrasaṃvara*; *Great Guru Yoga*; *Outer, Inner, and Secret Mandalas*; *Index of Commentaries on the Path Including the Result*;

Giving Reading Transmissions for Practice; *The Five Interdependencies as the Complete Path*; *Explanation of the Hidden Path including its Root and Branches*; *Explanation of the Hidden Path*; *Ten Great Accomplishments*; *Eight Minor Accomplishments*; *Explanations of "Asta"*; *Articles Concerning the Wheel of Tsog*; *Commentary on [Drakpa Gyaltsen's] Homage to Nairātmyā*; *Qualities of the Six Types of Beings*; *Explanation of Merging into Primordial Wisdom*; *Simultaneously-Born Cakrasaṃvara Blessing*; *Explanation of Vajravidāraṇa in the Virūpa Tradition*; works on the Saṃpuṭa and Vajravidāraṇa tantras; and the treatise on the *Classification of the Three Vows*.

Sakya Paṇḍita wrote these and many other flawless texts to illuminate the Buddha's doctrine.

3a1c. How Sakya Paṇḍita Crushed the Rocky Mountains of Inferior Views by the Power of the Thunderbolt of Debate

The fame of this master's great learning spread to every region of the land like the rays of the sun upon the earth. In southern India roamed a Hindu logician known as Harinanda and a retinue of six other logicians who followed the sages Kapila, Vyāsa, and Kaṇāda, and who belonged to the Sāṃkhya, Vedānta, and Nyāya schools. They believed in and worshipped the gods Īśvara, Brahmā, Lakṣmī, King Vasava, and Agni. When they heard of Sakya Paṇḍita's fame, they declared, "We will travel to the Land of Snows, as we have heard that there is a monastic follower of Gautama who wears a woman's skirt. We want to convert him and reject his inferior views and conduct." With such proclamations, they arrived in Tibet.

In response, the great master Sakya Paṇḍita and his retinue also traveled toward the holy shrine of Ārya Wati in the region of Kyirong, where many people gather to barter merchandise. This is approximately sixty yojana[12] north of the Bodhi seat where the Buddha attained enlightenment. Our Lord Lama, like a lion able to subjugate inferior opponents, also declared his willingness to enter debate.

When the six logicians approached the Lord of Dharma, they uttered polite words of praise, but said, "It is not our tradition to prostrate to the shrine of the Sugata," and thus they sat upon their various seats. They proclaimed, "In our tradition, from the time of the Guru Brahmā until the present, none of our masters have relied upon Gautama's doctrine and we never take refuge in the Triple Gem. We are an extremely pure tradition of rishis." Thus the debate began.

The Lord of Dharma responded, "Are you oppressed by the sleep of great ignorance? Because Brahmā himself was extremely devoted to the Buddha Śākyamuni, for it is said:

> Extremely exalted, with four hands and faces looking in directions numbering half of half of sixteen,
> knower of consecrated recitations and authentic ritual, teacher of the *Rig Veda*:
> Great Brahmā was born from a flawless lotus yet fell asleep;
> our Guide who possesses ten powers is always awake, like early dawn.

Engaging in such dialogue, they discussed extremely subtle arguments on numerous subjects for a long time. Sakya Paṇḍita was able to refute the opponents' every challenge, word by word, rendering them speechless. Furthermore, he was able to influence them to give up their inferior views and to enter the flawless path. They took Buddhist vows, shaved their heavy loads of dreadlocks, and entered the path of renunciation, which contains the wealth of the precious jewels of the doctrine of Buddha Śākyamuni.

Furthermore, with the understanding that future challengers of the Buddhist doctrine might act in a similar way and with the intent to establish them on the path of liberation, Sakya Paṇḍita wrote the following poem:

> Hari and his retinue believed their god (Mahadev) to be
> the greatest god on this great earth, which is dressed in oceans and girdled with waters.
> The followers of the sages Kargā, Vyāsa, Vālmīki, Kaṇāda, Akśapāda, and Kapila.
> came with topknots, dressed in bark and leaves, bearing sticks and *kusha* grass,
> daubed in ashes, bearing loads of dreadlocks, well wrapped in *muza* grass, wearing deerskin upper robes,
> worshipping tridents with a symbolic design of three lines, and wearing Brahmin threads and sacred raiment made of silk.

Thus came the well-trained Vedics, skilled in reciting the *Veda*,
complete masters of linguistics and prosody,
holding the view that the self is existent,
proud of their performance of austerity.
The attitude of these heretics was like drunken elephants.
The crusher of their brains with a glorious lion's roar, possessed of a powerful intellect with sharp fangs of logic,
with robust limbs of grammatical treatises, dignified by the mane of the Sugāta's doctrine,
with eyes glaring, roaring in Sanskrit proclamations of proof and refutations through evidence:
Such a king of mountain lions
dwelt in Sakya in the Land of Snows.
Protector of other wise lions,
he conquered those inferior opponents
like a pack of foxes.
In the future, too, may the holy Dharma
defeat all those with mistaken views,
and may the Doctrine of the Sugātas,
the victory banner of infinite joy, be upheld.

Their dreadlocks can still be seen in Sakya in the temple of Utsé Nyingma. In the history of Tibetan Buddhism, only Sakya Paṇḍita was able to defeat heretical paṇḍitas through his knowledge of the Dharma.

3a2. How Sakya Paṇḍita Acted for the Benefit of other Sentient Beings through Myriad Activities

Although Sakya Paṇḍita's countless holy activities were amazing and beyond conception, just a few are recounted here.

When the great master Sakya Paṇḍita was eighteen years old, one amazing event occurred when he was asleep. He dreamed that he was in Sakya at Achi Bum temple and a bluish Indian paṇḍita appeared who was not thin in appearance; he realized it was Vasubandhu, a master second only to the Buddha. For a month, Sakya Paṇḍita received teachings on the *Abhidharmakośa* from him. When Sakya Paṇḍita awakened, he comprehensively and precisely understood all of the words of these teachings and their meanings. Later, when Sakya Paṇḍita studied the same text from the Kashmiri paṇḍita Śākyaśrībhadra, he said that there was no difference at all from what he had previously learned in his dream.

For this reason, in his biography of Sakya Paṇḍita, Jamyang Sherab Gyatso later referred to "the special tradition of explanation that originated from Ācarya Vasubandhu and Sakya Paṇḍita and has come down to me from them."

There is a story of another amazing dream. One night before the Kashmiri paṇḍita Śākyaśrībhadra came to Tibet, Sakya Paṇḍita dreamed that the master was singing a vajra song concerning the profound Dharma. Upon awakening, he clearly remembered the words and their meaning and did not forget them. Later, when Śākyaśrībhadra arrived in Tibet, Sakya Paṇḍita explained his dream and Śākyaśrībhadra responded, "That same night I also had the same dream."

Referring to this, Sakya Paṇḍita's homage states:

> You knew the *Abhidharma* without being taught
> and accomplished all good qualities as a youth.
> Sages extolled you in their assemblies.
> Wisdom-Endowed, I bow my head to you.

And:

> Because of your excellent study in every lifetime,
> holy teachers directly taught you
> all doors of Dharma, even in dreams.
> Immaculate One, I bow my head to you.

Another account describes how one night the Great Master dreamed that he was traveling on a mountain where there was a cave. Someone requested of him, "Please come here. You will be appointed holder of the throne of the great master Dignāga." Someone gave him a key to open the door of the cave. When he opened it, there were many layers of bookshelves filled with holy scriptures. After that, he effortlessly understood valid cognition.

On another occasion, when he was traveling in Kyirong, one night he dreamed that he was composing a praise for the Kyirong Jowo statue that began with the following words:

> Embodiment of the wisdom and compassion
> of the all the buddhas of the three times,
> your holy name is known as Greatly Compassionate One.
> prostrations to Avalokiteśvara.

When he awoke, he still remembered these first four lines, but could not remember the other lines.

In another story of an amazing dream, one night Sakya Paṇḍita dreamed that he was teaching the homage section of the *Commentary on Valid Cognition* in Sanskrit to a large assembly when the sun and moon arose from his right and left shoulders. The next day, he explained this to his teacher, Jetsun Drakpa Gyaltsen, who was very pleased and remarked, "Such an occurrence is extremely rare," so he made a tea offering to the assembly of five thousand monks.

On another occasion, the Great Master was invited by the leaders of Samyé Monastery to turn the wheel of Dharma there. Sakya Paṇḍita had completed explanation of most of the Lamdré teaching up to the beginning of the fifth chapter of the section on analysis of the tantra. Around that time, he received an invitation to preside over a ceremony at a gathering of the sangha in Sinpori. The night before he set out to perform the ceremony, many people came to request blessings, advice, and guidance on meditation, and due to all these activities, he had no time to sleep.

When it was nearly dawn, Sakya Paṇḍita took a short nap and in his dream, many lay people came and made prostrations and offerings. They asked, "Aren't all sentient beings extremely feeble, carried by the major rivers of birth, old age, illness, and death?" He replied, "Yes, that is the case." Again they asked, "Please, we request a prayer to be liberated from this." He replied, "You can pray thus:

> Despite understanding birth as birthless,
> I am still not freed from the cage of birth;
> in every birth, in whatever birth I take birth,
> protect me from birth in an inferior birth."

Again they asked, "Is it permissible to substitute the other three, old age, etc., for birth?" He responded, "Yes, it is." They thanked him, made prostrations, and disappeared. When he awoke, he said, "The protector king of this holy shrine appeared to be among those beings."

On another occasion, it is said that some pure-minded disciples perceived the great master as Mañjuśrī, and that he manifested himself thus and performed benefit for them. Bodong Tsöndrü Dorjé is said to have had such perception. Thus, Sakya Paṇḍita's homage states:

> The eyes of some pure-minded disciples
> beheld you as Mañjuśrī;
> for this, you were renowned even in the Land of the Noble.
> Spontaneously Arisen, I bow my head to you.

Another occasion is recounted in the autobiography of Jamyang Sherab Öser from Tsang Nagpugpa. He states that one night, in a dream, he flew to the east and reached the Five-Peaked Mountain, also known as Mount Wutai. There, in a very beautiful place on a pleasant grassy hill, was a mandala of Lord Mañjuśrī. Jamyang Sherab Öser performed many circumambulations and prostrations, but was unable to find the entrance door. Finally, he found a door on the eastern side and entered. Inside he beheld an extremely beautiful shrine, in the center of which was a huge throne made of precious jewels and upon it the great Dharma Lord Sakya Paṇḍita sat facing north. Thinking, "This is the real Mañjuśrī," he again did many prostrations, circumambulations, and supplications. He did not receive any verbal teaching, but was given a Dharma text wrapped in silks of many colors. Examining the text, he saw that it was *Litany of the Names of Mañjuśrī* written in golden ink. After that, for a long time, his mind was very clear during the day and he was able to engage in the meaning of emptiness, and many auspicious dreams occurred at night. He included this amazing story in his autobiography.

Another time, the Lord of Dharma was staying in Central Tibet, where he had been requested to turn the wheel of Dharma. To the south lived a geshé known as Yakdé Sönam Sangpo who was practicing in retreat. One evening, the geshé beheld the entire Hevajra mandala with the various deities. Not knowing the meaning of this dream, the next morning, as soon as he awoke, he set out to visit the Lord of Dharma, Sakya Paṇḍita.

When he arrived, the Lord of Dharma was performing the evening torma offering. The geshé immediately prostrated to him and offered his respects. The Lord of Dharma asked, "Did you come to visit me?" The geshé answered, "Yes." Sakya Paṇḍita asked, "Is there a specific reason?" The geshé replied, "Yes, I have a certain question to ask." Sakya Paṇḍita said, "Is it about last night? That was a miraculous performance by Gyalpo Pekar. Now that you have met me, things will not become extremely difficult, but you may still experience a serious illness." That year Yagde did experience a very serious illness and nearly died. But after he recovered, his practice increased. He became successful and very fortunate.

For this reason, Yagde used to say, "I have unshakable faith in the Lord of Dharma and believe him to be none other than a buddha." He told all of his disciples that the Lord of Dharma is the real Mañjuśrī himself and that he had great devotion toward Sakya Paṇḍita. This account is found in the biographies of the Lamdré lineage lamas written by Nyentö Dulwa Sengé.

In another story, after Umapa Sherab Bum received teachings on Lamdré, he meditated upon it and experienced a gathering of the elements. He went to the Lord of Dharma and explained what he had experienced and asked how to dispel it. The Lord of Dharma merely said, "If one has wisdom, there are no elements to gather." Umapa Sherab Bum carefully contemplated the meaning of these words and excellent meditative absorption arose within his mind. This is one of many amazing stories about how Sakya Paṇḍita benefitted sentient beings.

Another story is found in a biography. The Lamdré explains that signs of death associated with increase occur in only a few people. However, for those in whom they do occur, they signify that death is certain. After such signs occurred for Sharpa Sherab Jungné, he practiced only guru yoga with very strong supplications. He was completely freed from the signs of death and lived a very long life.

Another story explains that in any region where the noble Lord of Dharma dwelt, the community was free of epidemics caused by spirits, outer and inner conflicts, and crop disasters. Any difficulties that did occur were swiftly pacified through the blessings of this great master, and as a result, residents had loving and helpful thoughts toward each other. For this reason, as long as the Lord of Dharma dwelled in Tibet, the Mongol army did not attack, and inner conflicts did not arise.

Concerning Sakya Paṇḍita's holy activities of increase, inconceivable glory and success in both Dharma and worldly concerns arose in his life, and the lotus garden of explication and practice of the Buddha's doctrine fully blossomed. He produced countless disciples who became excellent scholars and mahāsiddhas.

Sakya Paṇḍita's lotus feet were venerated with great devotion by the most celebrated scholars of that time. For example, in those days, there was a well-known teacher known as Nyalshik Jampai Dorjé, whose disciples were also well reputed. Overwhelmed by Sakya Paṇḍita's fame, Nyalshik chose one of his own most intelligent disciples, known as Uyukpa Rikpai Sengé, and advised him to debate with Sakya Paṇḍita. Rigpai Sengé stayed for a few days in Sakya Paṇḍita's Dharma gathering but was unable to find anything that contradicted the Dharma. Unable to challenge anything, he developed unshakable faith in the Lord of Dharma and remained for a long time to receive teachings from him, eventually becoming one of Sakya Paṇḍita's chief disciples.

A brief account of the excellent disciples that Sakya Paṇḍita produced will be provided later. Details should be learned from more extensive biographies.

On another occasion, a nobleman known as Shākya Gön from the region of Samyé in Central Tibet invited Sakya Paṇḍita to Samyé to turn the wheel of Dharma. On the walls of the middle circumambulation path, Sakya Paṇḍita drew the designs of the special hand objects of Ārya Mañjuśrī and wrote verses of praise to the earlier bodhisattvas and Dharma rulers from the first period of the propagation of Dharma in Tibet. He also extensively turned the wheel of Dharma. For this specific occasion, Chögyal Phakpa wrote the following verses of homage:

> Glorious Sakyapa, who possessed the two eyes of Sanskrit and logic,
> with an intellect that gazed upon the mandala of all knowable things,
> vastly learned and well trained,
> you are a speaker of two languages.
>
> You clearly explained the jewel light of the holy Dharma
> so that the kingdom of omniscience would be attained

by all sentient beings equal to the boundary of space,
pleasing the Teacher of all living beings.

Glorious Sakyapa, for this world, you illuminated the doctrine
of the Teacher of living beings,
which is a jewel treasury of good qualities,
so that the pleasant aroma of its renown
pervaded every direction.

Holder of the Tripiṭaka, by whatever roots of virtue arose from
your explanation
of the profound and vast holy Dharma
in Samyé's great spontaneously accomplished temple,
may all living beings be liberated from the ocean of saṃsāra.

The rabbit-holding moon's cool light
illuminates both earth and sky at night,
outshining the misleading teachers who are like a multitude of
stars and
fully ripening the night-blooming jasmine flowers.

In regard to this, the great Dharma master Chögyal Phakpa wrote:

> These verses were composed to show how the Lord of Dharma, Sakya Paṇḍita, in the spontaneously accomplished temple of Samyé, sat upon the lion Dharma throne that had been the seat of the great master Kamalaśīla, the crown ornament of all scholars. There, by turning the profound and vast wheel of Dharma, he polished the precious jewel of the doctrine and benefitted a multitude of sentient beings. Seeing this, my mind rejoiced and was delighted, yet I felt some sadness in thinking of the genuine holy activities that earlier great masters had performed in this place, which had diminished due to the changing times and unruly actions of beings. With the aspiration that worldly beings' Dharma activities would be successful, Sakya Paṇḍita extended his right hand and drew images of Mañjuśrī's special hand objects and wrote verses of praise to illuminate the great masters' earlier

holy activities there. May the minds of any who see or recite them attain the primordial wisdom of those great masters.

3b. How Sakya Paṇḍita Caused the Flourishing of the Buddha's Doctrine in the Land of Hor

When the great master Sakya Paṇḍita was acting for the benefit of the Buddha's doctrine in the Land of Snows, there were cruel beings in the land known as Hor who were as deluded as animals concerning the virtues that should be adopted and the nonvirtues that should be abandoned. Their compassion was even less than that of the Lord of Death, their physical strength was greater than that of demons, their armies larger than the hosts of demigods, and their appearance was extremely fearsome. First, they conquered China, and eventually they controlled Minyak and all other northern lands. They compelled every man into military service and levied tribute and corvée, making no differentiation between the lay and ordained, causing even the word "Dharma" to disappear.

Seeing the situation worsening everywhere, including in his own country, the bodhisattva Sakya Paṇḍita developed unbearable compassion for them and made strong aspirations to tame their minds through the holy Dharma and lead them in the right direction. Seeing that the season for the ripening of these aspirations was nearing, Sakya Paṇḍita's own abbot, Śākyaśrībhadra, embarked for Singala.

Meanwhile, a king known as Lhanam Theu Karpo offered Śākyaśrībhadra an invitation to go to the Land of Hor. Śākyaśrībhadra prayed to Tārā, who responded with the advice, "If you go there, it will be of little benefit, but if one of your Tibetan disciples were to go, it would be of great benefit." The great paṇḍita repeated this prophecy to Sakya Paṇḍita.

Also, Jetsun Rinpoché Drakpa Gyaltsen prophesized shortly before he passed into parinirvāṇa, "In the latter part of your life, you will receive an invitation from the Mongols. If you go as they request, it will be of great benefit for the Buddha's doctrine and many sentient beings. Therefore, you must go at that time."

When the Lord of Dharma reached the age of sixty-one, in preparation, he performed a great turning of the wheel of Dharma. At the age of sixty-two, Godan Khan, who was the son of the universal emperor Genghis Khan's own son Potholoyon,[13] sent the following letter:

Decree of I, the emperor,
established by glorious foundation of great merit,
with the strength of the long-life spirit of the sky

A message to inform Sakya Paṇḍita Kunga Gyaltsen Palsangpo:

In order to repay the kindness of my father and mother, and the earth and sky, my investigations reveal that I require a spiritual teacher who will be able to teach me the unmistaken path of what is to be adopted and abandoned. You are the designee. You must come here without thinking of the hardship of the journey. If you were to say that you are too old, wouldn't it contradict your commitment and understanding of the Dharma? How many times did the Buddha previously give his own body for the purpose of others?

Whereas if through martial law I send a great military force, this will cause terrible destruction to many sentient beings. Aren't you afraid of this? For these reasons, thinking of the Buddha's doctrine and thinking of protecting many sentient beings from harm, you must come swiftly.

I will ensure you are respected by all the bhantes of the western province. As tokens of my invitation, I send five large measures of silver, one Dharma robe made of brocade with tassels of 6,200 pearls, a long monastic overcoat of brocade, one fine pair of shoes, two fine pair of *khatak*, two fine pair of *thonti khatak*, and twenty bolts of five-colored brocade. I send my emissary Dorsi Gon and nephew Wönjo Darma with these gifts.

Written on the new moon of the eighth lunar month of the Year of the Dragon.

Thus the letter of invitation from Mongolia arrived in Sakya.

Although the Lord of Dharma had reached an advanced age, he decided to embark, disregarding his own life and motivated by the reasons explained above.

At the age of sixty-three, Sakya Paṇḍita reached the northern area of Minyak. While he was there, he received a letter from Tönpa Lodrö Rabsal from Dokham requesting clarification on certain questions concerning the meaning of the scriptures. Sakya Paṇḍita's response was as follows:

> Questions, offerings, and *khatak*
> from Tönpa Lodrö Rabsal have arrived in my hand;
> by this, joy greatly increases.

> Concerning your first question, from the *Treasury of Logic on Valid Cognition*:
>
> > Whatever exists is impermanent, like a vase.
> > The impermanence of sound is naturally imputed.
>
> From the *Classification of the Three Vows*:
>
> > Ultimate reality does not exist,
> > because as Dharmakīrti clearly stated,
> > "Existence itself is pervaded by impermanence."
>
> You ask, "Should these statements be taken literally?" Glorious Dharmakīrti states:
>
> > Any ultimate that functions
> > exists ultimately here;
> > others exist relatively.
> > These explain the general and specific characteristics.
>
> Thus he characterized anything that has the ability to function as having ultimate existence. Anything that that does not have the ability to function is characterized as relative.
>
> Again, it is stated, "Impermanence is like result and existence." Thus, confirmation that the word impermanence is based on using the result as evidence. Existence is evidence of reality.
>
> > Thus, matter has no foundation.
> > Concerning the external foundation,

all proofs and refutations
are believed to depend on the meaning of sounds.

That, too, is taught as conventionally existent based on engagement in sounds.

Dharmakīrti stated, "Suchness is not nonexistent because of the meaning of sounds." Thus, he characterized the meaning of sounds as conventionally existent.

Dharmakīrti stated:

Regarding any object of observation,
What is observed is none other than existent.

Thus Dharmakīrti states that anything that is logically observable is characterized as existent. This means the following:

There are two types of existence here,
these are conventional and ultimate.
The ultimately existent functions;
the conventionally existent is the basis of proof and
refutation.

Your second question is, "Isn't ultimate reality an object of the intellect?" In response, the *Diamond Cutter Sūtra* (*Vajracchedikā Prajñāpāramitā Sūtra*) states:

The dharmakāya of all the buddhas
is the view of ultimate reality of these guides.
This ultimate reality is not an object of the intellect
because it is impossible to intellectualize.

Also, *Engaging in the Conduct of the Bodhisattva* states:

The ultimate is beyond the scope of the intellect;
the intellect is described as the relative.

As these quotations show, from the point of view of its nature, ultimate reality is beyond description in words, and is not an object that can be intellectualized. However, by the logical process of excluding the opposite, conventionally, it is said to be knowable.

The *Treatise on the Ultimate Continuum of the Mahāyāna* (*Ratnagotravibhāga Mahāyānottaratantra Śāstra*) states:

> If the Buddha had no elements,
> how could he feel pity for those who suffer?
> Also, there would be no interest in entering nirvāṇa
> or cherishing the aspiration to achieve it.

Also, *Distinguishing the Middle from the Extremes* (*Madhyānta-vibhāga*) states:

> Suchness, the extreme of perfection,
> signlessness, the ultimate, and
> the dharmadhātu are synonyms.
> They are not separate.
>
> The cessation of mistaken conceptual thought
> is the noble ones' object of experience
> and is the cause of their noble Dharma.
> These synonyms are in order.

The *Treasury of Abhidharma* states:

> From beginningless time, the ultimate
> is the place of all phenomena.
> Because the ultimate exists,
> all beings are able to achieve nirvāṇa.

This means as follows: The ultimate is free of the four extremes and all elaborations. At the relative level, existence and non-existence, and so forth, are shown to be contradictory due to the logical process of excluding the opposite. It is said, "If it has no existence, it is nonexistent."

The *Commentary on Valid Cognition* states:

Using conventional words created from sound,
there is nothing other than affirmation and rejection.

therefore nonexistence becomes inexpressible
because it does not exist.

The third question: Is the truth of cessation an inactive virtue?

In response, although the truth of cessation is inactive, it is not believed to have the real characteristic of a virtue.

The *Fundamental Verses on the Middle Way* (*Mūlamadhyamakakārikā*) by Nāgārjuna states:

If karma were inactive, it would imply
that meeting and disintegration are inactive.

The following faults would also be implied:
It would be impossible to abide in pure conduct,
And without doubt, all conventional things
Would contradict themselves,

It would be illogical to classify actions
as meritorious and nonmeritorious,
in the case of ripening results, it would imply that
ripening results would repeatedly occur again and again.

In this way, understand that the position that inactive virtues and nonvirtues possess real characteristics is rejected.

All of these well-asked questions,
which came from the intelligent Lodrö's intellect,
the one named Kunga has well discerned and realized,
just like the All-Knowing One.

This response [by Sakya Paṇḍita] to questions asked by the teacher from Eastern Tibet known as Lodrö Rabsal was recorded in a garden [in Dokham Mé] by [the scribe] Biji Rinchen Drak.

On another occasion, while Lord Sakya Paṇḍita, emanation of Mañjuśrī, was traveling toward the land of the Mongols, he was riding a horse along a path in the area of eastern Tibet. A good meditator known as Yogi Truma came to pay respects to the Lord of Dharma and offer outer and inner robes. The yogi asked the question, "Your treatise *Clarifying What Is and What Is Not Dharma* states:

> Fools meditate on mahāmudrā;
> most of them are said to fall to animal births,
> or if not, they take birth in the formless realms;
> alternatively, they fall into the cessation of the śrāvaka.
>
> Even if this meditation is done well,
> it cannot transcend the meditation of the Mādhyamika.
> Although the meditation of the Mādhyamika is good,
> it is still very difficult to accomplish."

The yogi asked, "What is the real meaning of this statement?" From the mouth of the Lord of Dharma came these words of advice:

> Calm abiding that shuts the mouth[14] of conceptual thought and
> insight wisdom with unimpeded[15] emptiness
> are major causes of falling into inferior birth;
> those who wish to become exalted, should abandon these.
>
> Calm abiding that does not illuminate the movement[16] of the mind and
> insight wisdom[17] that rejects perceptions of form
> are great causes for taking formless birth.
> Those who wish to be liberated[18] should abandon these.
>
> Calm abiding that lacks mindfulness and sensation[19] and
> insight wisdom[20] that rejects the six sensory organs
> are similar to the cessation of the śrāvaka.
> Those who desire supremacy, should abandon these.
>
> Calm abiding that is totally trained and blissful[21] and
> insight wisdom that thoroughly classifies all activity:[22]

these two are the great paths of the Pārimitāyāna.
Those who are the sons of buddhas should accomplish these.

Calm abiding that thoroughly pacifies the thought of characteristics[23] and
insight wisdom that is the integration of bliss and emptiness:[24]
these two are the excellent paths of Mantrayāna Mahāmudrā.
Those who wish liberation in this life, should accomplish these.

One who comprehensively understands the meaning of these five stanzas
will understand which mahāmudrā is right and which is wrong;
therefore, analyze these.

These five stanzas of instructions [by Sakya Paṇḍita] to Yogi Truma were recorded in a garden [in Dokham Met] in eastern Tibet by [the scribe] Biji. (These responses have never been seen before, however, they came into the hand of Vajradhara Kunga Wangchuk in Dokham, and as a result are reproduced here. The footnotes were written by Biji exactly according to the words of the Lord of Dharma.)

On another occasion when the Lord of Dharma was traveling in the city, someone offered a black cloth with many golden spots. Sakya Paṇḍita gave it to the physician Biji, saying:

Keep this well, for it indicates that our teachings will become as widespread as the stars in a clear sky. Some may say that the Sakyapa reject holy relics (*ringsel*). Concerning this, it is said:

Most relics are produced by spirits, but
it is possible that some are created by those oriented toward virtue.
Some are also produced by the four elements.
When they are from the three types of noble ones,[25]
holy relics arise from the power of good qualities,

like a precious jewel arises from an authentic source.
It is impossible to count them,
for such relics uninterruptedly increase beyond enumeration, and are impossible to count.

This is a fact. If any [relics] arise from me, they will be innumerable. Keep them, and use this cloth to cover them. But I jest. Don't relate this to others, as it will cause them to accumulate unwholesomeness.

The Dharma Lord and Protector of Living Beings Phakpa Rinpoché developed a connection with Setsen Khan [regnal name of Kublai Khan], the emperor of Mongolia. Under the emperor's dominion were people speaking many different languages who had little knowledge of the Triple Gem. However, this great master caused them to develop faith in the Triple Gem and to act according to what should be adopted and abandoned according to the law of cause and effect. People from the Land of Hor generated bodhicitta on the Mahāyāna path, received major empowerments, venerated the Triple Gem, were willing to benefit sentient beings, and abandoned some unwholesome actions, through which they entered the noble path.

Holders of monastic vows and Mantrayāna practitioners who possessed positive qualities of the Dharma in the lands of Tibet, Uyghur, and Minyak in eastern Tibet as well as Mentsé and other places were exempt from military draft, taxes, and corvée. In this way they were protected from harm. They also received necessities such as food, drink, and clothing, as well as gold, silver, fabric, and brocade, not just once but on many occasions. The Lord of Dharma was given noble titles such as *gushi* and others. In this way, the precious doctrine of the Buddha was venerated with devotion and material offerings for a long time.

The Land of Hor had an excessive population and plans for a secure future. Fearing revolt, each year males above nine years old were rounded up and, because it was difficult to kill them one by one, forced group by group into the ocean. Sakya Paṇḍita and Chögyal Phakpa generated tremendous compassion toward them; later, it became widely known that as an offering to receive initiation, this practice was discontinued. Thus, some of the happiness and joy of the people in the northern regions was due to the special kindness of the lords of Dharma, uncle and nephew [Sakya Paṇḍita and Chögyal Phakpa].

These days, even those with the title of *geshé* who have clear minds and the ability to analyze right and wrong, who are said to carry the heavy load of Dharma to benefit beings—it is needless to mention people with ordinary minds—pay no attention to such situations, due to their roughness and lack of compassion. In this way, unlike any of the geshes who have since appeared in the history of Tibet, these two, uncle and nephew, directly benefitted sentient beings.

Some criticize them, however, saying that the Sakya masters were distracted by the demonic sons of gods that had a strong connection with the emperor of Hor. Such criticism is unfounded. Although the fully ordained Sakyapa may have manifested some external appearances to appeal to the customs of the people of Hor, if he had not associated with them and their mentality, the Sakyapa would not have been able to bring them onto the path of Dharma. This is similar to the manner in which Buddha Śākyamuni performed holy deeds by engaging in worldly customs in order to engage worldly beings on the path. The consequences that would have occurred if the people of Hor had not been established in the path of Dharma have already been explained. Therefore, the goal of their activities was more important than any minor apparent contradictions.

In addition, this is a genuine holy biography of a great bodhisattva who demonstrated enormous courage. Sometimes, such activities are difficult for those with small minds to comprehend.

Even though it was toward the end of his holy life, Sakya Paṇḍita dwelled with these intentions in this situation. He stated:

> You, Lord, earnestly taught me
> exalted holy scripture;
> while I was diligently studying as hard as I could,
> you freed me from interruptions.
>
> Then just as you prophesized,
> according to the bonds of your holy words,
> it came about, accurate in every respect.
> I take refuge in you, who foretold the truth.

It is for these reasons that the Lord of Dharma traveled to the land of Hor. Externally, he may have appeared to travel reluctantly. Although such statements appear in a few biographies, in reality, he embarked to the Land of Hor with the realization such travel would bring about the profound causes and conditions for him to perform vast benefit for sentient beings.

Even Sakya Paṇḍita's response to a question by Dokorwa reveals this: "Due to some of my previous activities, the sun of the Dharma has arisen in the East. The hopes of the faithful in Utsang will be swiftly fulfilled by the wish-fulfilling jewel of study, contemplation, and meditation."

In the eighth lunar month of the Male Fire Horse Year (1247), in the Lord of Dharma's sixty-fifth year, he arrived at the palace in Lianzhou, China. At that time, the emperor Godan Khan was engaged in the coronation of Guyuk Khan[26] in Mongolia. After he returned, their first meeting occurred during first month of the Year of the Sheep (1248). The emperor was extremely pleased, and they had an extended discussion concerning both religious and secular matters.

Before that, some Tibetan monks had already come into the presence of the emperor. However, none of them had been able to influence the emperor toward Buddhist teachings. For instance, during gatherings for prayers and aspirations, the Mongolian priest Erkawun and the Mongolian oracles sat at the head of the assembly.

After the Lord of Dharma arrived and began to have numerous dialogues and discussions about the Dharma with the emperor, whenever the emperor had difficulty understanding some detail, some Uyghur masters assisted between the languages. In this way, the emperor received the excellent influence of the Dharma from Dharma Lord Sakya Paṇḍita.

As a result of their discussions, the emperor was extremely pleased and announced to his subjects, "From now onward, Erkawun and the oracles shall not sit above the Buddhist monks. The Lord of Dharma Lama Sakyapa [Sakya Paṇḍita] shall be honored at the head of everyone, and the chanting of prayers and aspirations shall be led by the Lord of Dharma." With the announcement of this decree, the crown of Buddhism was lifted high in the Land of Hor.

The emperor Godan had a skin disease. In order to cure it, the Lord of Dharma performed many rituals, including the Mañjuśrī torma water offering known as *Chabtor Jampalma*.

As a result of the rituals, on the eleventh day of the third month, as the

Lord of Dharma slept he had the following dream. A person with a crippled leg appeared whose body was completely covered by the rashes and sores of a skin disease. Sakya Paṇḍita asked, "Who are you?" The crippled one responded, "I have a leader who sent me to see you, saying, 'Lama Sakyapa is summoning me. See what he wants, for I can't go myself, so you must do so.'"

The Lord of Dharma responded, "The emperor Godan sent his messenger and invited me from afar. I came here to help him. He has an illness. What is the cause of his illness, and what will cure the disease?"

The crippled one explained, "My leader owned this area before anyone else did. In one of Emperor Godan's previous lives, he has born as the king of this area and accumulated merit toward Buddha Śākyamuni. After passing from that life, he was born the King of Minyak, and there built a house on the top of my leader's home. The King of Minyak invited Tibetan monks to perform rituals with musical instruments, chanting, and torma offerings to request use of the land. Yet they did not know how to properly perform the ritual to request the land, and as a result, my leader did not give permission. However, the King of Minyak began construction anyway, and their relationship with each other was unpleasant and waxed and waned. Eventually, due to the superior merit of the human race, my leader was unable to defeat the king, so he decided to move to this northern area and take up residence here. Again the emperor came to this area and burned the land above our homes, dug up the earth, and harmed us greatly; now we cannot find a place to stay. My leader was extremely angry at him. Gathering all the local spirits in this area, he said, 'This king expelled me twice. Now I shall take revenge. I request all of you spirits to join me in fighting this king.'

"The local spirits said, 'Because this king has accumulated merit toward Buddha Śākyamuni, we are unable to defeat him. Therefore, we recommend that you do not remain in this dry area. Take up residence where there are unowned springs, swamps, and wetlands.' My leader took their advice.

"Around that time, the king examined the records of previous kings and found that Buddhist monks had received too many stipends, and reduced this amount going forward. Also, wishing to determine whether a statue of Buddha Śākyamuni was solid gold or made of wood or stone, the king dug into the bottom of it with a chisel.

"The local spirits said, 'Due to these nonvirtuous actions, the king's merit will now decline, so we will be able to cause obstacles for him.' Although they went against the king, they were unable to defeat him because he was still very powerful and had tremendous merit. However, the spirits caused some of the king's ministers to break away, revolt against him, and finally assassinate him.

"Just before he died, the King made the aspiration, 'In my next life, may I be born as the son of a king in this area and be able to subdue all of you as my servants.' Through the power of this aspiration, Godan Khan was born as the grandson of Genghis Khan and came to this area. He disturbed all the swamps, wetlands, and springs in our territory with horseraces, and he spread the blood and carcasses of dead horses everywhere.

"Due to this contamination, my body was injured, and the creatures in the water, such as small fish and frogs, have also been greatly weakened and are nearly dead. Due to the warmth of my leader's body, they have not yet died, but their bodies are shriveling up. Seeing this situation some monks made aspirations and prayers, but none of those prayers helped our nāga leaders.

"But now, the Lord Sakyapa is giving medicine and food to us, which is greatly helping. I was previously unable to go anywhere, but now I am feeling a bit better and am able to travel a little. My leader is now close to death. If he dies, Godan Khan will also die. If my leader is cured, surely Godan will also be cured. A few small prayers will not be that effective. You must undertake a major effort to restore the health of both my leader and Godan Khan. If my leader is cured, Godan will also be cured. As a result, he will do well by you."

Just as the Lord of Dharma thought, "What would be of the most benefit in this matter?" the crippled one disappeared.

To benefit the emperor, the Lord of Dharma performed the ritual of Bodhisattva Siṃhanāda. The emperor was completely cured of his skin disease and became extremely devoted to Sakya Paṇḍita. He also took the bodhisattva vow, received many profound and vast Dharma teachings, and venerated Sakya Paṇḍita as an ornament upon his crown.

From this time forward, the Lord of Dharma gave Dharma teachings to people of many nationalities in many different languages, which caused those who did not have devotion to the Dharma to develop it, and thus enter the Mahāyāna path. In short, he established countless living beings in the state of maturation and liberation, and the Buddha's teachings spread and greatly flourished.

There is another story. When the Lord of Dharma visited Five-Peak Mountain, also known as Mount Wutai, in China, he encountered in the area a yogi known as Tokden Gyenpo. Sakya Paṇḍita gave him the major empowerment of Hevajra in the Ḍombi Heruka tradition, preceded by the blessing of Vajra Nairātmyā based on a mandala of *sindura* powder, and followed by profound instructions introducing the wisdom of mahāmudrā, with complete teachings on meditation beyond thought.

The following quotation from Sakya Paṇḍita's *Pith Instructions to Tokden Gyenpo* describes how he liberated that practitioner's mind.

> When the Lord of Dharma visited Five-Peak Mountain in China, also known as Mount Wutai, he encountered in the area a yogi known as Tokden Gyenpo. Sakya Paṇḍita gave him the major empowerment of Hevajra in the Ḍombi Heruka tradition, preceeded by the blessing of Vajra Nairātmyā based on a mandala of *sindura* powder, followed by profound instructions introducing the wisdom of mahāmudrā, with complete teachings on meditation beyond thought.
>
> While Dharma Lord Sakya Paṇḍita, an emanation of Mañjuśrī, dwelt on Five-Peak Mountain, the famous local meditator known as Tokden Gyenpo arrived, and offered prostrations, circumambulations, and praises to the Lord of Dharma.
>
> The Lord of Dharma said, "Circumambulations and prostrations are good, but in such a holy place, practicing the Dharma through meditation based on good instructions would be even better."
>
> Tokden Gyenpo contemplated for a while, then went to get a long white piece of cloth and offered it to the Lord of Dharma. He asked, "Do you believe that mahāmudrā meditation belongs to all vehicles? What is real mahāmudrā itself? Why do they call it mahāmudrā? How is it produced in the mind? How is progress on the path and stages interpreted in this system? Please give me pith instructions concerning mahāmudrā."
>
> The Lord of Dharma was pleased with his questions and bestowed the Hevajra empowerment in the tradition of Ḍombi

Heruka, followed by instructions on the accomplishment of simultaneously born mahāmudrā. He also gave complete pith instructions on meditation beyond thought according to the tradition of Toktsewa.

Sakya Paṇḍita explained:

> This is how our tradition leads practitioners in mahāmudrā. Don't expect to reach high attainment right away, but practice single pointedly. This will not deceive you. Keep the following brief responses to your questions in mind. Generally, the Pārimitāyāna tradition is said to be characterized by the four seals, which encapsulate the Buddhist view. The three lower tantric traditions are said to be sealed by the nonduality of profundity and clarity, but in these traditions, the word mahāmudrā is not conventionally used. Those traditions describe "excellent attainment," but do not describe the attainment of excellent mahāmudrā. Therefore, those meditations are not believed to have the genuine characteristics of mahāmudrā.
>
> Although those traditions explain profound emptiness, which is the goal to be realized, still they do not explain the profound path of the method, which is the realizer of that goal. Therefore it is not logically suitable that those could be genuine mahāmudrā. For example, although generosity, morality, and so forth are explained in the Śrāvaka tradition, because the special method of using wisdom as a support is not explained, it is unsuitable to term these methods "the perfection of generosity" and so on. But if the view itself is termed "mahāmudrā," like deeming a foolish person a "cow," I won't argue over a mere term.
>
> However, in reality, regarding the nature of mahāmudrā:
>
> > Mahāmudrā is unchangeable bliss.
> > The grasper and all that is grasped are completely
> > abandoned;
> > any form, conceptual thought, or expression
> > is like the city of gandhārvas, and
> > the nature of the performance of *pra*.[27]

The embodiment of method and wisdom yoga,
prostrations to the syllables *e* and *vam*.
Transcending the nature of atoms,
having the appearance of the performance of *pra*,
excellent in every aspect,
prostrations to that mahāmudrā.

As this states, what is known as abiding in natural suchness is emptiness, which is excellent in every respect. This is realized by the performance of *pra* and through personal experience that is beyond expression, even if one desires to express it. In this way, the inherent nature of that which is desired to be realized is primordial wisdom integrated with meditation. This is termed variously as "integration of appearance and emptiness," "integration of awareness and emptiness," "integration of bliss and emptiness," "integration of bliss and greatness," "simultaneously arising primordial wisdom," "naturally arisen primordial wisdom," "self-seeing primordial wisdom," and "primordial wisdom that realizes each individually," among many other synonyms.

The true method of realizing these is explained in the *Vajra Rosary: The Explanatory Tantra of Guhyasamāja*, which states: "Having excellently pleased the guru, completely receive authentic initiation and thoroughly analyze the meaning of suchness." Also, the *Analysis of Tantra* states, "Later, thoroughly analyze suchness." As these tantras state, one should receive authentic initiation as the method of maturation, then correctly meditate on the two processes, including their supplements, which is the method of liberation. Through this one will realize mahāmudrā.

As Nāgārjuna states:

The teachings of the buddhas
are completely based upon the two processes.
One is the process of creation,
the other is the process of completion.

As this explains, all methods of acquiring the unsurpassable wisdom of the Mantrayāna path are summarized within these two processes. This is the explanation's essential point.

Concerning the literal definition of *mahāmudrā*, some who are not trained in the Sanskrit language state that *mudrā* is translated into the Tibetan language as "chakgya." *Chak* means the primordial wisdom of emptiness, and *gya* means liberation from the net of saṃsāra. They say that this is explained in the *Guhyāgarba Tantra* and the *Mahāmudrā Droplet*, but such an explanation is erroneous.

The definition of *mahāmudrā* in Sanskrit is as follows. *Mahā* means great. *Mudrā* means seal, symbol, mark, or diacritical vowel mark, among many other meanings. Therefore, here the word *seal* is chosen. The actual meaning as stated by Mahāsiddha Avadhūti is:

> As it is accompanied by a seal, it is known as "sealed";
> this great seal of the three existences is a single taste.

The practice that seals all the phenomena of saṃsāra and nirvāṇa in the state of integration of bliss and emptiness is thus known as the view of mahāmudrā.

Regarding the process by which it arises, in a few fortunate beings, genuine primordial wisdom of mahāmudrā arises at the time of the descent of primordial wisdom during initiation; however, most practitioners must depend upon methods of meditation. Initially what arises is a mere semblance of mahāmudrā. Based upon this, later genuine mahāmudrā develops.

What is known as the "mere semblance" of mahumudra is of two types: a semblance in some aspects that possesses contamination and a bare semblance that possesses flaws. That which possesses contamination refers to an intellectual understanding, summarized as study and contemplation. Here and there occasional minor experiences of integration arise that are summarized as meditation, yet the waves of conceptual thought have not disappeared.

Regarding the bare semblance, there are several types: bare abiding, bare discriminating thought, bare appearance, bare emptiness aspect, and bare experience of body, speech, and mind. These refer to experiences of meditative absorption, such as for the body, an increase of bliss and heat, vibration, and trembling movement; for speech, expressing random words; for the mind, uncertain random experiences.

In addition, inferior mere semblance refers to fainting, cessation of the six sensory organs, and so forth.

Regarding the manner of traversing the path and stages, the path of accumulation according to the common vehicle begins with receiving empowerment, which is the method of ripening the sincere quest for enlightenment, and continues up to the completion of the arising of experience with flaws.

The second chapter of the root tantra states, "All-knowing primordial wisdom is thus." As this indicates, concerning the path of application, although genuine primordial wisdom of bliss and emptiness and the experience of nonconceptual thought continuously arise within the mental continuum, still there are subtle tendencies of conceptual thought, like the light of the sun at dawn. This is known as the arising of an example of primordial wisdom.

Litany of the Names of Mañjuśrī states:

> The transcendent nature of consciousness:
> bearing the manner of nondual primordial wisdom,
> spontaneously accomplishes nonconceptual thought.

What is known as the "path of seeing" begins at the time that the actual primordial wisdom of mahāmudrā arises. This is the genuine primordial wisdom of nonconceptual thought that directly realizes emptiness, excellent in every aspect.

Therefore, what is known as the "path of meditation" is continuous familiarization with that experience, which promotes it higher and higher, up to the attainment of the twelfth stage.

Then, what is known as the "path of no-more learning" is manifested in the attainment of ocean-like positive qualities, such as the four holy bodies and five primordial wisdoms, on the thirteenth stage.

To explain this, those who wish to manifest the stage of Vajradhāra in this life will no doubt become as accomplished as the Indian mahāsiddhas if they first practice the path of application according to the common tradition, then produce an example of genuine primordial wisdom of mahāmudrā according to the uncommon tradition, manifest actual primordial wisdom, and continuously practice the conduct and direct causes as explained in the tantras and the like.

Even if these activities cannot be accomplished, it is said that after producing an example of genuine primordial wisdom within the mind, accomplishment is still possible at the time of death or through instructions during the bardo.

Some talk of "mahāmudrā with a single chop," saying that counting the paths and stages is ignorant delusion. Rather, such talk is the real delusion. For example, *Litany of the Names of Mañjuśrī* refers to "Protector, Lord of the Tenth Stage."

Also, the *Abhidhāna* states:

> Extreme Joy and Stainless,
> likewise Producing Light and Radiant Light,
> Extremely Difficult to Train, Manifesting,
> Gone Far and Immovable,
> Excellent Intellect and Cloud of Dharma,
> Without Example, Great Primordial Wisdom, and
> Vajradhara, which is the thirteenth stage.

These and other elaborate explanations of the framework of the paths and stages were explicated by the great mahāsiddhas and are in the tantras.

The words in *Litany of the Names of Mañjuśrī*, "fully

enlightened buddhahood in a single moment," refer to the method of attaining perfect and complete enlightenment at the final end of all the paths and stages.

The *Wisdom of Passing Sūtra* states, "Mental realization is the Buddha. Do not search for any other mental involvement than the Buddha."

This statement is similar to one by Saraha:

> The nature of the mind alone is the seed of all,
> from which radiate both saṃsāra and nirvāṇa,
> and which produces the result of one's desires.
> Prostrations to that mind that is like a wish-fulfilling jewel.

This statement demonstrates that the all-base mental consciousness manifests both the relative and ultimate, travels through all the paths and stages, and manifests perfect enlightenment. Another source states:

> Outside of this precious mind,
> neither the Buddha nor sentient beings exist.
> Other than the actual state of consciousness,
> no external phenomena exist.

Another source states:

> The physical form of immaculate primordial wisdom
> and conceptual thoughts of saṃsāra:
> between these, there is not the slightest difference.

This explains the essential point that all perceptions of saṃsāara and nirvāṇa are a single taste within the mind.

Yogi Todgen, keep this in your heart and continue your practice. It will be of great benefit to you.

Yogi Tokden cherished this teaching, which is known as *Instrument to Open the Eyes Concerning Mahāmudrā: Instructions Given to Tokden Gyenpo*. It was given by the Lord of Dharma and copied down by Benji on Five-Peak Mountain and intensively practiced.

Another story tells of how when the Lord of Dharma was residing in Lanzhou Palace and giving Dharma teachings, at one point a number of pilgrims went to the holy place of Five-Peak Mountain on pilgrimage. One night, everyone dreamed that Mañjuśrī was not dwelling in the five peaks but giving Dharma teachings in Lanzhou Palace. Everyone had exactly the same dream. When they awoke and discussed their dreams with each other, they set out for Lanzhou Palace without a second thought. There they met the Lord of Dharma, who at that time was giving teachings on how to generate excellent enlightenment thought. This story is well known.

Another story tells of how the Lord of Dharma and Emperor Godan had numerous dialogues and conversations, in the course of which it was asserted that the *Sūtra of Golden Light* states that turtles do not have any hair. Following the discussion, the emperor disputed the statement, displaying to the Lord of Dharma a turtle skin as wide as the height of a human, upon which was long hair and a multicolored design like a rainbow.

The Lord of Dharma observed, "This could not be the regular skin of a common turtle. A sūtra states that some bodhisattvas take birth in a turtle-like form in order to benefit beings that dwell in the sea. No doubt this is the skin of such a being. As evidence, if the design is carefully examined and expertly interpreted, it will be seen that it is in the shape of a thousand buddhas surrounded by eight bodhisattvas." With these words, he pointed out each and every part of the design, and all in the gathering were amazed.

The emperor felt somewhat embarrassed and thought, "I must make some response to this." He summoned his ministers and asked them to invite magicians and have them create the appearance of a amazing temple with their occult powers. As he bade, they created such a temple, more enticing than any ever seen before.

The emperor himself came and said to the Lord of Dharma, "I invited you here as the object of veneration. You are skilled and learned and I have seen that you have a multitude of amazing positive qualities. This brings me great delight. Now, there is an amazing temple in an isolated place; come with me so that I may offer it to you." Having spoken thus, the great master with his disciples and the emperor and his retinue embarked for the temple.

As soon as the Lord of Dharma saw the temple, he knew that it had been created by magicians. There were many fearsome gatekeepers and door guardians, and he blessed them and bade them to heed him. There were also many holy statues and images, which he consecrated by strewing flowers. As a result, the magicians were unable to dissolve what they had created, and it became a real temple. It was named Emanation Temple and is said to still exist.

Thus Lord of Dharma Sakya Paṇḍita performed amazing holy activities and caused the Buddha's doctrine to flourish in the land of China.

The Lord of Dharma perceived that it would be of greater benefit to the Buddha's doctrine if he remained in China than if he returned to Tibet. He settled there and sent many material gifts to his students and the sangha in Tibet. As one of the Dharma gifts, he composed *Illumination of the Sage's Intent*, which explains how to engage step by step in the path of the bodhisattva. At the conclusion of the text he stated, "As I have given these teachings to all of my disciples who dwell in U, Tsang, and Kham, all of you have already received this reading transmission. Therefore, you should study this and explain it to others and practice according to this text." With this advice, he sent the following letter:

> *Om svasti siddhim*
> Prostrations to the Lama and the Protector Mañjugosha!
>
> A letter from the Palden Sakya Paṇḍita to all spiritual masters, their disciples, and people of U, Tsang, and Ngari.
>
> I came to this land of Hor with the intention to benefit the Buddha's doctrine and all sentient beings in general, and speakers of the Tibetan language in particular. When I arrived the great benefactor who invited me was extremely delighted and told me:
>
>> You came here with your relatives, bringing even very young relatives. I know that you came thinking of me. To you, I show my head; to others who come, I show my feet. You are the one I invited. Others come here from fear. Don't I know this?
>>
>> The two Phakpa brothers already know some Tibetan Dharma. Phakpa needs to learn still more Tibetan Dharma; his brother, Chana Dorjé, should study the language of Hor and the script of Hor.
>>
>> If I guide politics, which is the religion of humans, and you guide the Dharma, which is the religion of gods, don't

you think that the doctrine of Śākyamuni will spread
throughout the land to the oceans' shores?

This bodhisattva emperor is extremely devoted to the Buddha's doctrine, especially to the Triple Gem. He guides and protects his followers with good laws. He favors me in particular more greatly than others. In his own words, he told me, "Please teach the Dharma with a relaxed and happy mind. I will provide you with anything that you need. I know how to bring you success. Only the sky knows how to bring me success."

He also greatly favors the two Phakpa brothers. He has the noble intent to benefit every being under his dominion who lives according to the laws of the land. He told me, "Your Tibetan people should learn the laws of the land. I know how to bring success and happiness to their lives." Therefore, I request you all to pray for the longevity and success of the emperor and his lineage.

The reason I write this letter is that Mongolia possesses a military force that is limitless in size, and they have the intention to bring the entire world under their dominion. They treat the happiness and suffering of allies as equal to that of their own. However, toward those who do not follow their orders and confront them, they do not merely issue challenges, their policy is complete eradication.

Before they destroyed the Uyghurs, ambassadors and messengers were exchanged and accepted and the Uyghurs' gifts and citizens were accepted. Hor sent them officers and managers. Likewise, the same thing occurred in China, Minyak, and some parts of Mongolia, but because people did not follow orders, they were reduced to devastation and eventually forced to agree. Once they agreed, the emperor again sent emissaries, managers, generals, administrators, and leaders to these nations and treated the people well.

Some of our people are also impudent and hope to escape their armies by various methods, thinking, "We are so far away; they cannot come here." Some even imagine they can fight them.

Others demonstrate cunning, deception, and feigned compliance, which would cause great destruction to our nation.

Also, many Tibetan people have individually come to Mongolia to meet with government officials. However, since not many people have the experience to deal with the officials, and since most were rude and unskilled, only a few were appointed to high government positions whereas most were assigned to lower levels.

Additionally, there are signs that the government officials here are not pleased with the Tibetan people, because they are seen as offering little benefit in either skill or wealth. For the past few years, no armies have entered Tibet, because I came with various people in my retinue to meet with the officials. I explained to them the good things that the individual people have done, and the officials have treated me well. They have also treated the Tibetan people in Ngari and U-Tsang who cooperated with them well. The benefit of this cooperation has been that the armies of Hor have been absent from Tibet during the past few years. Most people in Western Tibet may not be aware of this.

The Tibetan people who previously came to Hor made two mistakes: they came with little wealth, and they mistrusted those with whom they needed to make connections. This resulted in armed conflict that devastated many areas. I believe that you may have heard of and know about these things.

When the Tibetans faced military action, many believed that they lived in a secure place, were a brave people, had a large army, and were well armed and skilled in the use of their weapons. Hoping that they would win, they miscalculated, lost the battles, and were destroyed.

Many believe that people in the land of Hor pay few taxes and have a light military draft, while, in comparison, the subjugated nations must pay heavy taxes and endure a heavy burden of forced military service and corvée labor. The reality is the opposite.

In the case of Tibet, if we carefully follow their orders, the Mongol officials will allow us to appoint our own local leaders and manage our land and people by ourselves. Therefore, I advise you to assemble the Sakyapa officials who hold the ranks of golden seal (*gser yig*) and silver seal (*dngul yig*) and ask them to identify the most qualified candidates to be appointed as local leaders. You should write introductory letters for those whom you chose, and send these letters by trusted messenger. Write the letters in triplicate. Send one to me, keep another copy in the office of the Sakyapa, and keep another copy in the office of the local leader. The letters should clearly differentiate between those who follow the advice of the Sakyapa from those who do not. If this differentiation is not made, the negative consequences that befall those who do not follow orders will also fall upon those who do follow them.

Also, it is important for the Sakyapa golden seal officials to carefully explain and discuss the situation with local leaders. They must perform their duties well in order to benefit sentient beings and must not abuse their authority over the local leaders. The local leaders must not act unilaterally, not consulting the Sakyapa golden seal officials. No laws should be made without consultation with the higher authorities, because if an incident arises, it will be difficult to explain. In short, I ask that all of you work harmoniously.

Furthermore, if you follow the rules of the land of Mongolia, the future will be good. Treat the golden seal officials with fine favors, such as welcoming parties, farewells, and acts of service. You should do this because the new golden seal officials will ask the people, "Did you evade the previous golden seal official? Did you oppose him? Did you treat the previous golden seal official well? Did you send his messengers appropriately to spread his words to the public? Are those who treated the golden seal official well now in a stable situation?" These will be the first questions that they ask. If the golden seal officials are not pleased with your answers, they have the ability to harm those who oppose them. If they are pleased, they have the ability to benefit those who please them. As I have seen myself, if you do not follow the words of the golden seal officials, it will be very difficult to accomplish your aims.

If people wish to come to Mongolia, it is best that those who come be skilled and prosperous. Local leaders who wish to succeed should associate with the Sakyapa, offer them resources, and be forthcoming about the types and quantities of resources that they have. I, myself, will oversee this. By acting thus, when these local leaders return home, things will go well for them and for others.

Generally, since last year, I have sent a person to give advice such as this about how to act properly. However, most of you seem to not be the type to follow such advice. What do you expect will happen? Are you waiting to surrender after they bring destruction, and only then to come and listen to their advice? It seems that you don't understand what you hear.

In any case, please do not say, "The Sakyapa went to Mongolia but did not help us at all." My purpose in coming here was to benefit all speakers of the Tibetan language. My wholehearted thought is to cherish beings other than myself.

Those of you who follow my advice will benefit, but most of you do not see this. You who hear this may even find it hard to believe and may still dream of victory over the Mongols. Although you are now living comfortably, you may suddenly find yourself oppressed as if by evil forces, and I fear that all the youth of Ü and Tsang will be sent off to Mongolia.

Whatever happens to me personally—whether I succeed or fail—I have no regrets. It is possible that the future may bring success due to the kindness and blessings of my lamas and the Triple Gem. I urge all of you to pray to the Triple Gem, too.

The emperor shows special favor to us above all others. As a result, many people of different nationalities—including leaders and spiritual masters from the lands of China, Uygur, Minyak, Mongolia, and some other parts of Tibet—are amazed that this has occurred. They come forward to receive Dharma teachings with great devotion. Hence, you do not have to worry about what the people of Mongolia will do to those of us who have come here. I wish to tell you that you can relax your minds concerning our situation, for all show favor to us.

To those who wish to come here bringing material wealth,

> I should tell you which materials are particularly valued here. Gold is of the highest value, then silver, elephant tusks, and large pearls. Also highly valued are vermillion; madder; *ruta* root; medicinal animal bile (*gi wang*); skins of tigers, leopards, snow leopards, and otters; high-quality Tibetan shoes; and fine woolen fabric from Central Tibet. There are other materials that may be highly valued in other places that are not particularly valuable here. But, in particular, if you have gold here, you can fulfill any wish.
>
> Keep these things in mind. May the doctrine of Lord Buddha spread and flourish in every direction. Mangalam!

This letter was written by Sakya Paṇḍita and sent to disciples, benefactors, and others in Ü and Tsang. This letter brought joy and increased the delight of all who read it.

Thus, until the age of seventy, this great lama—the second omniscient teacher to appear in this degenerate age—performed great service to the Buddha's teachings, and established countless sentient beings in the stage of maturation and liberation. I herein describe [according to the master Biji] the manner of the withdrawal of the manifestation of great master's form body at the conclusion of his holy life.

> In the ninth month of the year (1251), when the master manifested his intent to depart for the benefit of beings elsewhere, it is said that eighteen great signs occurred.
>
> On the eighth day of the ninth lunar month, a great trembling of the earth occurred. I, the physician Biji asked what this portended. The Dharma master responded, "When great sons of victors intended to depart for the benefit of others, such signs occurred. It seems that we are also following their footsteps."
>
> At midnight on the twenty-ninth day of the month, the Lord of Dharma told me that the buddha King Proclaimer of Inexhaustible Melodious Sounds directly manifested in saṃbhogakāya form, with one face and two hands. He told me, "Light incense," and so I lit incense. As the night ended and dawn broke, the Lord

of Dharma again said, "Eleven-Faced Avalokiteśvara has directly come and blessed me. Light incense."

On the sixth day of the tenth month of Mindruk, the sounds of myriad celestial instruments were heard. I was in [the Lord of Dharma's] presence and said, "There are many people in the shrine room. It seems that they are performing the ritual of Uṣṇīṣa Vijaya." The Lord of Dharma said, "Go to the shrine room and see whether or not they are performing the ritual." When I went to the shrine room, I realized that the people there had also heard the sounds of the instruments, and they said, "What could these sounds be? Ask the Lord of Dharma." When I asked him, he responded, "I received a welcome reception from celestial beings. Now I need to depart for my own and others' benefit." The same day, there was a shower of many snowflakes in the shape of flowers, which were visible in the air, but did not accumulate on the earth.

On the thirteenth day of the month, while we sat in the remaining sunlight, a beautifully shaped long white cloud appeared. The Lord of Dharma smiled and, pointing his finger at the sky, said, "Did you see that?" I responded, "I can't see anything, but I feel very joyful." He said, "It seems that you have fewer sins, but that you still have some stain-like sins, so you should perform practices for eliminating them. I beheld Lord Buddha Śākyamuni seated upon a lion throne with a retinue of śrāvakas." He asked me to light incense, so I lit incense.

On the morning of the fourteenth day, while we were sitting in the sun, a similar cloud appeared. The Lord of Dharma told me, "I have clearly seen the mandala of Śrī Hevajra. Light incense."

On the morning of the fifteenth day, while we were sitting outside, a similar cloud again appeared. He told me, "I have seen Mañjuśrī thrice." He asked me to light incense, so I lit incense three times.

Finally, the Lord of Dharma gazed at me and smiled. I asked him, "What is happening?" He told me, "Mañjuśrī and Maitreya bodhisattva are having a dialogue." He even told me what they were saying, but I have forgotten the words.

Later, when we were circumambulating, the attendant Chokgyin Pal was carrying a small throne in the shape of a table in one hand and holding a cushion on top of it. We proceeded along, and I held the Lord of Dharma's left hand. When we reached the shrine room, the Lord of Dharma sat upon the small throne. He advised Chokgyin Pal, "Go make tea for us." He then said to me, "You go and light some incense." When I lit the incense and brought it to him, he said, "Ayuh Tārā!" It seems that he had perceived Tārā.

At midnight on the seventeenth day, I was standing in the presence of the Lord of Dharma, who was also standing. He asked me, "Don't you see anything?" I heard the sounds of singing and musical instruments. There were many others with us, including Lopön Joden, who also heard the sounds of the instruments but did not perceive anything unusual about the sounds. The Lord of Dharma gazed upon me and said, "I saw thirteen different mandalas—the mandala of Cakrasaṃvara, and also many male and female virās, all dancing and singing songs." He then quoted a number of the words of the songs, but I could not catch them. Lopön Joden seems to have remembered some of the verses, but I do not write them here because the Lord of Dharma said, "Do not tell others as it will cause them to accumulate negativity."

Then, a geshé known as Dorang was taken seriously ill in Jugur Memar. The Lord of Dharma sent my disciple Rinchen Gyaltsen there to see him. When he returned, Rinchen Gyaltsen explained that Dorang was extremely ill. Because he had no assistant, his bed was filled with excrement and urine. The Lord of Dharma said, "Seeing this, why don't all the buddhas and bodhisattvas act with compassion?"

That night, early in the morning, Mahāsiddha Virūpa, Kṛṣṇapa, and the Lord of Dharma's own lama, Jetsun Drakpa Gyaltsen, appeared together and told him, "Do not feel disappointed about this. This contaminated body has four great torrents of birth, aging, illness, and death." Virūpa smiled, and Kṛṣṇapa joined him, saying, "That is correct." Mahāsiddha Virūpa used his ring finger to take nectar from a skull in his hand. He told the Lord of Dharma, "Extend your tongue, and touch this droplet." At the moment that he did, every form of conceptual and nonconceptual thought was transcended, and a nonconceptual experience of bliss and clarity arose in his mind. There is no more exalted experience than this, even in the minds of the buddhas.

Then his own lama, Jetsun Drakpa Gyaltsen, told him:

> When it is your time to depart this place for the benefit of other beings, you will become a vidyādhara who dwells in space toward the east, beyond many worlds of existence. You will please a multitude of tathāgatas, completely purify the environment as a buddha realm, and bring about the maturation of many yet-unmatured beings. By then, you will have traveled most of the paths and stages. In your third birth, you will be born on this earth, the son of King Nyimai Thopel, to the southeast of India in a land known as Mumuni. While a youth, you will perform many Dharma activities, such as teaching and composition. You will possess clairvoyance and, thus, be able to see the entire world of existence, helping you to lead hundreds of thousands of devoted disciples to liberation. At that time, you will also be part of my retinue, for we have a Dharma connection and I have given initiation to you.

The Lord of Dharma told me what the length of that life would be, but I do not remember.

> Then, after departing that life, you will become a fully enlightened buddha known as Glorious Stainless One, and act for the benefit of other sentient beings.

Then Jetsun Drakpa Gyaltsen asked Mahāsiddha Virūpa, "Isn't that true?" The Mahāsiddha responded, "That is correct." Kṛṣṇapa likewise concurred. Then the Lord of Dharma asked me to arrange a *tsok* offering, so I set it up.

Due to the power of practicing the profound path, the Lord

of Dharma's secret organ receded so that it could not be seen. An *uṣṇīṣa* clearly emerged on the top of his head. Between his two eyebrows, a long hair curled in the shape of a conch shell. These and many other signs of perfection clearly appeared on his holy body.

On the seventh day of the eleventh month, the sound of celestial musical instruments clearly resounded. Everyone who gathered at the Emanation Temple clearly heard this. I asked the Lord of Dharma, "What does this signify?" He responded, "All of you should diligently perform prayers. According to the sūtras, a single moment of service to the guru from whom you have received empowerment generates more merit than offering even your own body—including head, limbs, and other parts!"

Because I had offered everything to my guru, I had nothing left to offer. However, I had previously received a new red *chamtsé* as a token of appreciation from a practitioner whose leg I had cured. Because the Lord of Dharma was using it, I decided that I wanted to offer it to him. When this thought entered my head, the Lord of Dharma smiled at me and said:

> You do not have to give this to me. I have already used it, so it has already been offered to me. When I reach excellent enlightenment, I will perceive all of you disciples, and the services you have offered as clearly as if I were looking at an *arura* fruit in my palm. Whatever connections we have—Dharma conversation, touching my hand, seeing me, remembering me, receiving initiation, receiving the bodhisattva vow, and so forth—will not be meaningless; they will ensure that you will be free of the suffering of lower rebirths. Because you have performed much service to me, you should rejoice in this.

One night, I attempted to support the Lord of Dharma the entire night, from dusk until dawn, sometimes from his back and sometimes from the side of his body. He told me, "Ask Dulwa Gyaltsen to come here." When he arrived, the Lord of Dharma said, "Bring the *chamtsé* (heavy monastic robe) that was offered by Lady Sorokta." When it was brought, he told me, "Use this. You and I have many connections from previous lives, too. In this life, at first you were my tea server. Then, I sent you to Jobum Gukshri in Minyak Garu. Later, despite the invasion by the armies of Hor, you didn't die, but came here, and now you serve me. In the next life, it is inevitable that you will take birth in my presence."

Early in the morning on the fourteenth day of the eleventh month,[28] the Lord of Dharma peacefully departed. Many sounds of celestial instruments were heard, victory banners were seen, a variety of offering melodies were heard, and the earth trembled.

On the twenty-fifth day of the month, the cremation was performed. All of the smoke appeared in the form of rainbows, and everyone who gathered at the ceremony heard many sounds of musical instruments. All of the holy relics which remained were in the shape of round *ringsel*, with the largest ones bearing images of deities. In such ways, inconceivable signs naturally occurred, which continue to act for the benefit of beings.

The *Liberation Homage* (*Rnam thar bstod pa*) written by Yarlungpa Drakpa Gyaltsen describes these wonderous signs as follows:

In the middle of your exalted crown, Hevajra's image and
a stainless image of Mañjuśrī clearly appeared;
on your forehead, Cakrasaṃvara;
on the back of your head, the Blessed Buddha;
on your shoulder, Kasarpaṇi;
on your marrow bone, Avalokiteśvara;
on your spine, the four secret mothers;
on your kneecaps, Tārā and Acala;
on the nāga tree of the right arm bone, Maitreya with the wheel-turning mudra.
These ten emanation appearances arose on your holy physical base.

As a symbol of the lion's roar of emptiness, the pleasant melody of Brahma,

a raised letter *A* clearly appeared, symbolizing birthlessness;
a victory stupa above each ear;
and a samaya vajra marked with a *hūṃ* in the center,
symbolizing the dharmakāya, the natural purification of the
holy mind.

With respect to the monastic seats (*gdan sa*) of this great master, they can be divided in three categories: major, moderate, and minor. The major ones are glorious Sakya Monastery and Emanation Temple in the north.[29] He also built four monasteries in Langzhou, including Shar Trulpai Dé, Lhowang Dé, Nup Pemoi Dé, and Jang Gyatso Dé. The moderate seats are Samyé Monastery, Nyangtö Monastery in Nyang Valley, and Shang Sekshing Monastery.[30] The minor seats are many and are spread throughout the regions of Kham, Tsang, and Ü. He oversaw all of these, teaching the Dharma in general and, in particular, the special system of Buddhist logic.

Before embarking for the Land of Hor, Sakya Paṇḍita appointed Dharma teachers and leaders as his representatives to lead these places. In Sakya, he appointed Uyukpa Rikpai Sengé as master of logic and science. He appointed Master Dodé Pal from Shang as teacher of Mantrayāna to the assembly. He appointed Geshé Shākya Sangpo as overall leader of the assembly. After making all of these appointments, he embarked on his journey.

It is said that in those times, there were around eighty sons, grandsons, and nephews in the main Sakya family. After the Lord of Dharma entered parinirvāṇa, the schools which strictly followed the system of the Lord of Dharma's explication of *pramāṇa* and other topics, were Pal Sakya Thupten Lhachen [the main Sakya temple], Jang Ngamring, Nalendra, Serdokchen, Kyitsal, Thupten Namgyal, Thupten Yangchen, and Ü Tsethang.

These and many other places greatly flourished. Likewise, the number of large and small temples that followed his personal tradition of Mantrayāna also greatly increased.

From these and other points of view, the Lord of Dharma came to be beyond compare to other masters. Especially during this time in which religion was in a difficult state, his holy activities helped to greatly increase it. As he himself stated, "One must understand that the method of upholding the Buddha's doctrine is to act to according to scriptures accepted by the learned, whereas explaining only the visual forms of buddhas and bodhisattvas is simply a method of generating amazement in the childlike." Indeed, by ensuring the continuation of all of his exalted and holy activities, he provided an example of how to reach liberation.

Thus, the Lord of Dharma who knew the five sciences,
great Sakya Paṇḍita, who is the second Buddha,
having seen a part of your holy biography,
I have attained unshakable faith, even in my youth.

The Paṇḍita who was well trained in countless previous lives
became an omniscient teacher who knows all knowable things.
Now fully enlightened in the name of Glorious Immaculate
One,
I take refuge in you who has accomplished the two purposes.
You embarked for the land of Hor
with the sole intent of benefitting beings in the Land of Snows.

Through your power, the doctrine of the glorious Sakyapa
spread throughout Jambudvīpa.
The manner of your unfathomable kindness
was clearly known by earlier beings.

Alas! These days, in this dark age,
people have not seen such a system
so well-sourced, and free of error.
How astonishing that they accept as exalted newly-arisen
doctrines.

Alas! Foolish ones lack the experience of the holy Dharma;
following their conceit is the custom of worldly beings.
Therefore, to facilitate my spreading of the Buddha's doctrine,
Lord of Dharma, may you gaze upon me from the realm of the
kingdom of Dharma.

This supplication to the Lord of Dharma was written down just as it spontaneously arose.

Postscript Concerning Sakya Paṇḍita's Younger Brother, Sangtsa Sönam Gyaltsen

This great lama's younger brother was known as Sangtsa Sönam Gyaltsen. He was born at Kyawo Khadang in the Male Wood Dragon Year (1184), when his mother was twenty-three and his father was thirty-five.

Sönam Gyaltsen was also well trained in all the Dharmas of his father and ancestors. His main practices were Hevajra and Vajrakīlaya. Mahākāla and Mahākālī were subdued as his retinue. Among the activities that he accomplished were the building of the Utsé Nyingma shrine, and a wall around the entire temple. He planned to build a fence to enclose Mön Creek, Bal Creek, and the Sakya Gray Earth Mountain as a backrest. However, his elders advised him that this was too ambitious, so, instead, he built a fence that began about the length of one arrow shot from the large field known as Shingmo Ché.

Sönam Gyaltsen also established an annual fair at Sithang where a multitude of people gathered to trade. He planned to hold these fairs in other places, such as Dromtö, Dromé, Takthok, Mangkhar Drilchen, Tsang Barphuk, Shab Tömé, and Tanak. He also helped to create native villages in Jangchung, Khabso, Komdré, Garphuk, and other places. He also helped to establish horse and cattle ranches in Rasa and other places.

Sönam Gyaltsen relied on many masters who upheld the Buddha's doctrine, and he offered the necessities for the practice of Dharma. He also built many shrines for images of the Buddha's holy body, the scriptures, and stupas. He also endowed continuous offerings at those places and endowed annual offerings on the anniversary days of past lamas. He performed these and many other activities.

He also had clairvoyance concerning where he would be reborn in the future. When he entered parinirvāṇa, he stated, "I will take birth as a Dharma practitioner who practices the profound path as a hidden yogi in the south near a grassy mountain and give initiation to some disciples." There exists an ear-whispered teaching that this was an indication that one of his future births would be that of Nasa Drakphukpa.

The great lama Sönam Gyaltsen lived until the age of fifty-six. On the twenty-second day of the twelfth month in the year of the Female Earth Pig (1239), he had many pure perceptions and perceived the guru and tutelary deities to be inseparable. He said, "This Lord of Dharma is none other than the Buddha. You should develop strong devotion toward him without any doubts. Stating thus, he passed away in the area north of Palri Mountain. Before he had passed away, he had mentioned this mountain, declaring, "My body should be cremated on it. There is an auspicious connection that my son and my lineage will have dominion over the entire country." His followers did exactly as he instructed.

Some say that Sangtsa Sönam Gyaltsen's mother was from Tarerong. Their family was of noble lineage, and her father was known as José from Sang. Her younger son was named Sangtsa Sönam Gyaltsen and was the brother of Sakya Paṇḍita. Some say that Sönam Gyaltsen and Sakya Paṇḍita did not have the same mother because Dharma Lord Sakya Paṇḍita was not called "Sangtsa." Although some believe this to be the case, Jetsun Drakpa Gyaltsen's genealogical articles written to the King of Garing did not mention that Sönam Gyaltsen and Sakya Paṇḍita had different mothers, so this is evidence that they shared the same mother.

Acknowledgments

TRANSLATION OF THESE BIOGRAPHIES was supported by a 2008 grant from the Khyentse Foundation, with additional contributions by the Hiroshi Sonami Fund, Kristy Chakravatri, and Jia-Jing Lee. Early drafts of the translations were edited by Dewayne Dean and Tenzin Kalsang, and numerous questions were clarified by Venerable Khenpo Khenrab Woser and Venerable Jamyang Chophel. The manuscript was put into final form and prepared for publication by Wisdom Publications editorial and production manager Laura Cunningham, editor Brianna Quick, and production editor Ben Gleason. Patty McKenna served as marketing manager.

Sincerest gratitude to all of these people and organizations who have made this book possible. By the merit of these efforts, may the blessings and teachings of Sakya Paṇḍita spread throughout the world.

Sakya Paṇḍita's Writings Included in This Work

As categorized by Jamgön Ameshab

Note: Where works have abbreviated titles in common use and complete longer titles, both appear below in transliterated Tibetan and Tibetan script.

Linguistics

Commentary on [Sönam Tsemo's] How to Easily Engage Beginners
Byis pa bde blag tu 'jug pa'i 'grel pa/ བྱིས་པ་བདེ་བླག་ཏུ་འཇུག་པའི་འགྲེལ་པ།

Engaging in Wisdom
Shes rab la 'jug pa/ ཤེས་རབ་ལ་འཇུག་པ།

Generating Wisdom
Shes rab 'phro pa/ ཤེས་རབ་འཕྲོ་པ།

How to Compose Script
Yi ge'i sbyor ba/ ཡི་གེའི་སྦྱོར་བ།

How to Enter Sanskrit
Sgra la 'jug pa/ སྒྲ་ལ་འཇུག་པ།

Summary of Linguistics
Sgra nyer bar bsdus pa/ སྒྲ་ཉེར་བར་བསྡུས་པ།

Summary of Vacana
Smra sgo'i gnas kyi bsdus pa/ སྨྲ་སྒོའི་གནས་ཀྱི་བསྡུས་པ།

Logic

Treasury of Logic on Valid Cognition
Tshad ma rigs gter/ ཚད་མ་རིགས་པའི་གཏེར།
Rigs gter/ རིགས་གཏེར།

Treasury of Logic on Valid Cognition with Autocommentary
Tshad ma rigs pa'i gter gyis rang 'grel/ ཚད་མ་རིགས་པའི་གཏེར་གྱི་རང་འགྲེལ།
Rigs gter rang 'grel/ རིགས་གཏེར་རང་འགྲེལ།

Medical Science

Summary of the Eight Branches of Medical Treatment
Sman dpyad kyi bstan bcos yan lag brgyad pa'i bsdus don/ སྨན་དཔྱད་ཀྱི་བསྟན་བཅོས་ཡན་ལག་བརྒྱད་པའི་བསྡུས་དོན།
Yan lag brgyad pa'i bsdus don/ ཡན་ལག་བརྒྱད་པའི་བསྡུས་དོན།

Inner Science

Articles on the Petition to the Buddhas and Bodhisattvas of the Ten Directions
Phyogs bcu'i sangs rgyas dang byang chub sems dpal rnams la zhu ba'i 'phrin yig/ ཕྱོགས་བཅུའི་སངས་རྒྱས་དང་བྱང་ཆུབ་སེམས་དཔལ་རྣམས་ལ་ཞུ་བའི་འཕྲིན་ཡིག

Classification of Schools
Grub mtha' rnam 'byed/ གྲུབ་མཐའ་རྣམ་འབྱེད།

Commentary on [Jetsun Drakpa Gyaltsen's] Homage to Mañjuśrī
'Jam dbyangs kyi bstod pa'i rnam bshad/ འཇམ་དབྱངས་ཀྱི་བསྟོད་པའི་རྣམ་བཤད།

Homage to Avalokiteśvara
Spyan ras gzigs kyi bstod pa/ སྤྱན་རས་གཟིགས་ཀྱི་བསྟོད་པ།

Homage to the Compassionate Lord of the World
'Jig rten dbang phyags thugs rje chen po la bstod pa/ འཇིག་རྟེན་དབང་ཕྱུགས་ཐུགས་རྗེ་ཆེན་པོ་ལ་བསྟོད་པ།
Spyan ras gzigs kyi bstod pa/ སྤྱན་རས་གཟིགས་ཀྱི་བསྟོད་པ།

Homage to the Holy Site of Samyé Monastery
Bsam yas lhun gyis grub pa'i gnas chen la bstod pa/ བསམ་ཡས་ལྷུན་གྱིས་གྲུབ་པའི་གནས་ཆེན་ལ་བསྟོད་པ།

Homage to the Muni
Thub pa'i bstod pa/ ཐུབ་པའི་བསྟོད་པ།

Homage to the Painting of the Special Objects of Mañjuśrī
'Jam dbyangs kyi phyag mtshan ri mo la bstod pa/ འཇམ་དབྱངས་ཀྱི་ཕྱག་མཚན་རི་མོ་ལ་བསྟོད་པ།

Homage to the Sugatas [in Lhasa]
Bde bar gshegs pa'i bstod pa/ བདེ་བར་གཤེགས་པའི་བསྟོད་པ།
Lha sa'i bde bar gshegs pa rnams la bstod pa/ ལྷ་སའི་བདེ་བར་གཤེགས་པ་རྣམས་ལ་བསྟོད་པ།

Homage to What Is to Be Attained
Sangs rgyas kyi bstod pa thob bya'i ma/ སངས་རྒྱས་ཀྱི་བསྟོད་པ་ཐོབ་བྱའི་མ།

Instrument to Open the Eyes Concerning Mahāmudrā: Instructions Given to Tokden Gyenpo
Rtogs ldan rgyan po la gdams la phyag rgya chen po'i mig thur/ རྟོགས་ལྡན་རྒྱན་པོ་ལ་གདམས་ལ་ཕྱག་རྒྱ་ཆེན་པོའི་མིག་ཐུར།

Parāmitāyāna Teaching for Great Dharma Assemblies
Pha rol phyin pa'i gzhung lugs spyi'i tshogs chos chen mo/ ཕ་རོལ་ཕྱིན་པའི་གཞུང་ལུགས་སྤྱིའི་ཚོགས་ཆོས་ཆེན་མོ།

Art

Analysis of Geomancy
Sa brtag pa/ ས་བརྟག་པ།

Treatise on Holy Images
Sku gzugs kyi bstan bcos/ སྐུ་གཟུགས་ཀྱི་བསྟན་བཅོས།

Astrology

Astrology of the Precious Doctrine
Bstan pa rin po che'i rtsis/ བསྟན་པ་རིན་པོ་ཆེའི་རྩིས།

Poetry

Poetry as an Ornament of Scholarly Speech
Snyan ngag mkhas pa'i kha rgyan/ སྙན་ངག་མཁས་པའི་ཁ་རྒྱན།

Synonymics

A Treasury of Words
Tshig gi gter ཚིག་གི་གཏེར།

Prosody

Beseeching the Compassion of the Sugatas
Bde bar gshegs pa'i thugs rje la bskul ba/ བདེ་བར་གཤེགས་པའི་ཐུགས་རྗེ་ལ་བསྐུལ་བ།

Bouquet of Various Flowers of Prosody
Sdeb sbyor sna tshogs me tog gi chun po/ སྡེབ་སྦྱོར་སྣ་ཚོགས་མེ་ཏོག་གི་ཆུན་པོ།
Sdeb sbyor me tog gi chun po སྡེབ་སྦྱོར་མེ་ཏོག་གི་ཆུན་པོ།

Drama

Engaging in Greatly Joyous Theatrical Performance
Zlos gar rab dga'i 'jug pa/ ཟློས་གར་རབ་དགའི་འཇུག་པ།

Treatise on Music
Rol mo'i bstan bcos/ རོལ་མོའི་བསྟན་བཅོས།

Useful General Theory

Entry Door for Scholars
Mkhas pa 'jug pa'i sgo མཁས་པ་འཇུག་པའི་སྒོ།

Mkhas pa 'jug མཁས་འཇུག

Excellent Analysis of Theory
Gzhung lugs legs bshad/ གཞུང་ལུགས་ལེགས་བཤད།

Jewel Treasury of Elegant Sayings
Legs par bshad pa rin po che'i gter/ ལེགས་པར་བཤད་པ་རིན་པོ་ཆེའི་གཏེར།
Sa skya legs bshad/ ས་སྐྱ་ལེགས་བཤད།

Common Vehicle

Brief Framework of the Mahāyāna Path
Theg pa chen po'i lam gyi rnam gzhag mdor bsdus/ ཐེག་པ་ཆེན་པོའི་ལམ་གྱི་རྣམ་གཞག་མདོར་བསྡུས།

Classification of Schools
Grub mtha'i rnam 'byed/ གྲུབ་མཐའི་རྣམ་འབྱེད།

Classification of the Three Vows (also known as "Clarifying What Is and What Is Not Dharma")
Sdom pa gsum gyi rab tu dbye ba/ སྡོམ་པ་གསུམ་གྱི་རབ་ཏུ་དབྱེ་བ།
Sdom gsum rab dbye/ སྡོམ་གསུམ་རབ་དབྱེ།
Chos dang chos ma yin pa rnam par 'byed pa/ ཆོས་དང་ཆོས་མ་ཡིན་པ་རྣམ་པར་འབྱེད་པ།

Explanation of Dedications
Bsngo ba yon bshad dang bcas pa rnams mjing/ བསྔོ་བ་ཡོན་བཤད་དང་བཅས་པ་རྣམས་མཇིང་།

An Explanation of Parting from the Four Attachments
Zhen pa bzhi bral gyi gdams pa/ ཞེན་པ་བཞི་བྲལ་གྱི་གདམས་པ།

Illumination of the Sage's Intent
Thub pa'i dgongs pa rab tu gsal pa/ ཐུབ་པའི་དགོངས་པ་རབ་ཏུ་གསལ་པ།
Thub pa dgongs gsal/ ཐུབ་པ་དགོངས་གསལ།

The Great Resolve with Supplementary Scriptural Quotations

Sems bskyed chen mo lung sbyor dang bcas pa/ སེམས་བསྐྱེད་ཆེན་མོ་ལུང་སྦྱོར་དང་བཅས་པ།

How to Practice
Chos nyams su blang pa'i rim pa/ ཆོས་ཉམས་སུ་བླང་པའི་རིམ་པ།

The Tenfold Dharma Activities
Chos spyod bcu pa/ ཆོས་སྤྱོད་བཅུ་པ།

Uncommon Mahāyāna Vehicle

How to Meditate on Amitābha
Snang ba mtha' yas bsgom don/ སྣང་བ་མཐའ་ཡས་བསྒོམ་དོན།

Illumination of the Mañjuśrī Sādhana
'Jam dpal gyi sgrub thabs kyi gsal byed/ འཇམ་དཔལ་གྱི་སྒྲུབ་ཐབས་ཀྱི་གསལ་བྱེད།

Mandala Ritual Illuminating Indivisibility
Zung 'jug gsal ba'i dkyil 'khor gyi cho ga/ ཟུང་འཇུག་གསལ་བའི་དཀྱིལ་འཁོར་གྱི་ཆོ་ག

Ritual of Offering to Grahamātṛikā, Mother of the Planets
Gza' yum gyi mchod pa'i cho ga/ གཟའ་ཡུམ་གྱི་མཆོད་པའི་ཆོ་ག

Wonderous Instructions on the Moment Before Death
'Chi kha ma'i gdams ngag ngo mtshar can/ འཆི་ཁ་མའི་གདམས་ངག་ངོ་མཚར་ཅན།

Mantrayāna

Articles on the Five Interdependencies
Rten 'brel lnga'i yi ge/ རྟེན་འབྲེལ་ལྔའི་ཡི་གེ

Commentary on [Drakpa Gyaltsen's] Homage to Nairātmyā
Bdag med ma'i bstod pa'i 'grel ba/ བདག་མེད་མའི་བསྟོད་པའི་འགྲེལ་བ།
Rje btsun pas mdzad pa'i bdag med ma'i bstod pa'i 'grel ba/ རྗེ་བཙུན་པས་མཛད་པའི་བདག་མེད་མའི་བསྟོད་པའི་འགྲེལ་བ།

Explication of the Path
Lam sbas bshad/ ལམ་སྦས་བཤད།

Guru Yoga of the Profound Path
Lam zab mo bla ma'i rnal 'byor/ ལམ་ཟབ་མོ་བླ་མའི་རྣལ་འབྱོར།

Index of Commentaries on the Path Including the Result
Lam 'bras bu dang bcas pa'i khrid kyi dkar chag/ ལམ་འབྲས་བུ་དང་བཅས་པའི་ཁྲིད་ཀྱི་དཀར་ཆག
Khrid kyi dkar chag/ ཁྲིད་ཀྱི་དཀར་ཆག

Anuttarayogatantra

Articles Concerning the Wheel of Tsok
Tshogs kyi 'khor lo'i yi ge/ ཚོགས་ཀྱི་འཁོར་ལོའི་ཡི་གེ

Commentary on Homage to the Wheel of the Three Tantras
Bstod pa rgyud gsum 'khor lo'i 'grel ba/ བསྟོད་པ་རྒྱུད་གསུམ་འཁོར་ལོའི་འགྲེལ་བ།

Eight Minor Accomplishments
Phra mo brgyad kyi man ngag/ ཕྲ་མོ་བརྒྱད་ཀྱི་མན་ངག

Explanations of "Asta"
ASh+Ta'i bzhi bshad/ ཨཥྚའི་བཞི་བཤད།

Explanation of the Hidden Path
Lam sbas bshad/ ལམ་སྦས་བཤད།

Explanation of the Hidden Path Including Its Root and Branches
Lam sbas bshad rtsa ba yan lag dang bcas pa/ ལམ་སྦས་བཤད་རྩ་བ་ཡན་ལག་དང་བཅས་པ།

Explanation of Merging into Primordial Wisdom
Ye shes bsre ba'i bshad pa/ ཡེ་ཤེས་བསྲེ་བའི་བཤད་པ།

Explanation of the Vajravidāraṇa Sādhana in the Virūpa Tradition
Rnam 'joms bir lugs kyi bshad pa/ རྣམ་འཇོམས་བིར་ལུགས་ཀྱི་བཤད་པ།

The Five Interdependencies as the Complete Path
Rten 'brel lngas lam yongs su rdzogs pa/ རྟེན་འབྲེལ་ལྔས་ལམ་ཡོངས་སུ་རྫོགས་པ།

Giving Reading Transmissions for Practice
Sgrub pa lung sbyin/ སྒྲུབ་པ་ལུང་སྦྱིན།

Great Guru Yoga
Bla ma'i rnal 'byor chen mo/ བླ་མའི་རྣལ་འབྱོར་ཆེན་མོ།

Homage to the Lineage Lamas of Cakrasaṃvara
Bde mchog brgyud pa'i bstod pa/ བདེ་མཆོག་བརྒྱུད་པའི་བསྟོད་པ།

Homage to the Lord of Mahāsiddhas Virūpa
Rnal 'byor dbang phyug gi bstod pa/ རྣལ་འབྱོར་དབང་ཕྱུག་གི་བསྟོད་པ།
Birlu pa la bstod pa/ བིརླུ་པ་ལ་བསྟོད་པ།

Outer, Inner, and Secret Mandalas
Phyi nang gsang gsum gyi maN+Dala/ ཕྱི་ནང་གསང་གསུམ་གྱི་མཎྜལ།

Qualities of the Six Types of Beings
Rigs drug gi mtshan don/ རིགས་དྲུག་གི་མཚན་དོན།

Simultaneously Born Cakrasaṃvara Blessing
Dge mchog lhan skyes kyi byin rlabs/ དགེ་མཆོག་ལྷན་སྐྱེས་ཀྱི་བྱིན་རླབས།

Ten Great Accomplishments
Grub chen bcu/ གྲུབ་ཆེན་བཅུ།

Two Homages to Jetsun Rinpoche Drakpa Gyaltsen
Rje btsun rin po che grags pa rgyal mtshan gyi bstod pa gnyis/ རྗེ་བཙུན་རིན་པོ་ཆེ་གྲགས་པ་རྒྱལ་མཚན་གྱི་བསྟོད་པ་གཉིས།

A work on the *Saṃputa Tantra* (untitled)
Sam+bu Ta/ སམྦུ་ཊ།

A work on the *Vajravidāraṇa Tantra* (untitled)
Rdo rje rnam 'jom kyi rgyud/ རྡོ་རྗེ་རྣམ་འཇོམ་ཀྱི་རྒྱུད།

Sādhanas

Mother of the Planets Sādhana in a Lineage from Śāntarakṣita
Zhi ba 'tsho las brgyud pa'i gza' yum gyi sgrub thabs/ ཞི་བ་འཚོ་ལས་བརྒྱུད་པའི་གཟའ་ཡུམ་གྱི་སྒྲུབ་ཐབས།

Sādhana of Bhurkumkūta
Khro bo sme brtsigs kyi sgrub thabs/ ཁྲོ་བོ་སྨེ་བརྩེགས་ཀྱི་སྒྲུབ་ཐབས།

Sādhana of Mañjuśrī
'Jam pa'i dbyangs kyi sgrub thabs/ འཇམ་པའི་དབྱངས་ཀྱི་སྒྲུབ་ཐབས།

Sādhana of Vajravidāraṇa in the Virūpa Tradition
Rnam 'joms bir lugs kyi sgrub thabs/ རྣམ་འཇོམས་བིར་ལུགས་ཀྱི་སྒྲུབ་ཐབས།

Tārā Sādhana
Sgrol ma'i sgrub thabs/ སྒྲོལ་མའི་སྒྲུབ་ཐབས།

Letters and Responses

Advice to Shang Lotsāwa
Zhang lo tsA ba la gdams pa/ ཞང་ལོ་ཙཱ་བ་ལ་གདམས་པ།

Letter to Lowo Lotsāwa
Glo bo lo tsA ba la springs yig/ གློ་བོ་ལོ་ཙཱ་བ་ལ་སྤྲིངས་ཡིག

Letter to Noble Masters
Skyes bu dam pa rnams la sprin ba'i yi ge/ སྐྱེས་བུ་དམ་པ་རྣམས་ལ་སྤྲིན་བའི་ཡི་གེ་

Letter to the Deities Who Delight in the Buddha's Doctrine
Bstan pa la dga' ba'i lha rnams la springs yig/ བསྟན་པ་ལ་དགའ་བའི་ལྷ་རྣམས་ལ་སྤྲིངས་ཡིག

Letter to the Geshé from Öjé
'Od 'je ba'i dge bshes la springs yig/ འོད་འཇེ་བའི་དགེ་བཤེས་ལ་སྤྲིངས་ཡིག

Letter to the Great Meditator from Nyemo

Snye mo sgom chen la springs yig/ སྙེ་མོ་སྒོམ་ཆེན་ལ་སྤྲིངས་ཡིག

Letter to the Sangha Dwelling in Shingkun
Shing kun na bzhugs pa'i dge 'dun rnams la springs yig/ ཤིང་ཀུན་ན་བཞུགས་པའི་དགེ་འདུན་རྣམས་ལ་སྤྲིངས་ཡིག

Letter to the Sun
Nyi ma la springs yig/ ཉི་མ་ལ་སྤྲིངས་ཡིག

Response to Chak Lotsāwa
Chag lo tsA ba'i zhus lan/ ཆག་ལོ་ཙཱ་བའི་ཞུས་ལན།

Response to Dogorwa
Do gor ba'i zhus lan/ དོ་གོར་བའི་ཞུས་ལན།

Miscellaneous

Eight "I Ams" root text and autocommentary
Nga brgyad ma'i rtsa 'grel/ ང་བརྒྱད་མའི་རྩ་འགྲེལ།

Explanation of the Word "Bagora" in Verse
Ba go ra zhes bya ba'i sgra las drangs pa'i tshigs bcad/ བ་གོ་ར་ཞེས་པའི་སྒྲ་ལས་དྲངས་པའི་ཚིགས་བཅད།

Invitation to Various Intelligent People to Ask Questions
Blo gsal ba'i skyes bu rnams la ji ltar dri ba'i tshigs bcad/ བློ་གསལ་བའི་སྐྱེས་བུ་རྣམས་ལ་ཇི་ལྟར་དྲི་བའི་ཚིགས་བཅད།

Verses on How Harinanda Was Defeated
'Phrog byed dga' bo pham par byas pa'i tshigs bcad/ འཕྲོག་བྱེད་དགའ་བོ་ཕམ་པར་བྱས་པའི་ཚིགས་བཅད།

Table of English, Sanskrit, and Tibetan Proper Nouns

Note: For a list of Sakya Paṇḍita's writings, see page 145. This table is organized alphabetically by English terms first and if there is no English term, next by Sanskrit or phonetic Tibetan.

English	Sanskrit	Phonetic Tibetan[1]	Transliterated Tibetan	Tibetan (Uchen)
	Abhidhāna	*Abhidhāna*	*A b+hi d+ha na*	ཨ་བྷི་དྷ་ན།
	Acala	Mikyowa Karpo	Mi g.yo ba Dkar po	མི་གཡོ་བ་དཀར་པོ།
	Ācara	Atsara	A tsa ra	ཨ་ཙ་ར།
	Ācārya Haribhadra	Lopön Sengé Sangpo	Slob dpon seng ge bzang po	སློབ་དཔོན་སེང་གེ་བཟང་པོ།
		Aché Mangchungma	A ce Mang chung ma	ཨ་ཅེ་མང་ཆུང་མ།
		Achi Bum	A phy'i 'bum	ཨ་ཕྱིའི་འབུམ།
Achi stupa		Achi chörten	A phyi'i mchod rten	ཨ་ཕྱིའི་མཆོད་རྟེན།
	Agni	Jinsa	Byin za	བྱིན་ཟ།
		Ajo Phaktön	A jo Phag ston	ཨ་ཇོ་ཕག་སྟོན།
	Akśapāda	Kangmik	Rkang mig	རྐང་མིག
amalaki fruit		kyurula	skyu ru la	སྐྱུ་རུ་ལ།
Analysis of Commentary		*Drelwa Takpa*	*'Grel ba brtag pa*	འགྲེལ་བ་བརྟག་པ།
Analysis of Tantra		*Taknyi*	*Brtag gnyis*	བརྟག་གཉིས་
	anuyogatantra	naljor lamé gyü	·rnal 'byor bla med rgyud	རྣལ་འབྱོར་ བླ་མེད་རྒྱུད།
	Arali	Arali	A ra li	ཨ་ར་ལི།

1. As per the Wisdom Publications style sheet.

English	Sanskrit	Phonetic Tibetan	Transliterated Tibetan	Tibetan (Uchen)
Articles of Petition to the Buddhas and Bodhisattvas of the Ten Directions		*Chokchui Sangyé kyi Trinyik*	*Phyogs bcu'i sangs rgyas dang byang chub sems dpal rnams la zhub'i 'phrin yig*	ཕྱོགས་བཅུའི་སངས་རྒྱས་དང་བྱང་ཆུབ་སེམས་དཔལ་རྣམས་ལ་ཞུབའི་འཕྲིན་ཡིག
Ārya tradition		Phakpai kor	'Phags pa'i skor	འཕགས་པའི་སྐོར།
	Ārya Wati	Phakpa Wati	'Phags pa Wa ti	འཕགས་པ་ཝ་ཏི།
Ascertaining the Simultaneity of the Object	*Sahāvalambanirṇayasiddhi*	*Lhenchik Mikpar Ngepa*	*Lhan cig dmigs par nges pa*	ལྷན་ཅིག་དམིགས་པར་ངེས་པ།
Ascertainment of Valid Cognition	*Pramāṇaviniścaya*	*Tsema Nampar Ngepa*	*Tshad ma rnam par nges pa*	ཚད་མ་རྣམ་པར་ངེས་པ།
Auspicious Power Tantra Requested by Susiddhi	*Subahuparipṛccha Susiddhi Tantra*	*Pungwa Sangpoi Lekdrup kyi Gyü*	*Dpung ba bzang po'i legs grub kyi rgyud*	དཔུང་བ་བཟང་པོའི་ལེགས་གྲུབ་ཀྱི་རྒྱུད།
	Avadhūti	Avadhūti	A wa d+hU tI	ཨ་ཝ་དྷཱུ་ཏཱི།
	Avalokiteśvara	Chenrezik	Spyan ras gzigs	སྤྱན་རས་གཟིགས།
	Avataṃsaka Sūtra	*Sangyé Phalpo Chedo*	*Sangs rgyas phal po che mdo*	སངས་རྒྱས་ཕལ་པོ་ཆེ་མདོ།
Bal Creek		Baldrok	'Bal grog	འབལ་གྲོག
		Bari Lotsāwa Rinchen Drak	Ba ri Lo tsA ba Rin chen grags	བ་རི་ལོ་ཙཱ་བ་རིན་ཆེན་གྲགས།
		Bartön Dorjé Gyaltsen	Bar ston Rdo rje rgyal mtshan	བར་སྟོན་རྡོ་རྗེ་རྒྱལ་མཚན།
	Bhalendra	Bhalendra	Bha len+dra	བྷ་ལེནྡྲ།

English	Sanskrit	Phonetic Tibetan	Transliterated Tibetan	Tibetan (Uchen)
		Bhante	Ban de	བན་དེ།
	Bhatu	Bhatu	Bha Tu	བྷ་ཊུ།
	Bhikṣukārikā	*Gelongi Kārikā*	*Dge slong gi kA ri kA*	དགེ་སློང་གི་ཀཱ་རི་ཀཱ།
	Bhitam	*Bhitama*	*B+hi ta ma*	བྷི་ཏ་མ།
	Bhota Rāhula	Bhota Rāhula	b+ho ta rA hu la	བྷོ་ཏ་རཱ་ཧུ་ལ།
		Biji Rinchen Drak	Bi ji Rin chen grags	བི་ཇི་རིན་ཆེན་གྲགས།
	Bodhgaya	Dorjé Den	Rdo rje gdan	རྡོ་རྗེ་གདན།
Bodhisattva Tak		Jangchup Sempa Tak	Byang chub sems dpas Stag	བྱང་ཆུབ་སེམས་དཔས་སྟག
		Bodong	Bo dong	བོ་དོང་།
		Bodong Tsöndrü Dorjé	Bo dong brtson 'grus rdo rje	བོ་དོང་བརྩོན་འགྲུས་རྡོ་རྗེ།
Bouquet of Various Flowers of Prosody		*Debjor Natshok Metoki Chunpo*	*Sdeb sbyor sna tshogs me tog gi chun po*	སྡེབ་སྦྱོར་སྣ་ཚོགས་མེ་ཏོག་གི་ཆུན་པོ།
Bright Lamp		*Drönma Salwa*	*Sgron ma gsal ba*	སྒྲོན་མ་གསལ་བ།
	Buddha Vimalāśrī	Sangyé Drima Mepai Pal	Sangs rgyas Dri ma med pa'i dpal	སངས་རྒྱས་དྲི་མ་མེད་པའི་དཔལ།
	Cakrasaṃvara	Khorlo Dechok	'Khor lo Bde mchog	འཁོར་ལོ་བདེ་མཆོག
	Cakrasaṃvara Root Tantra	*Dechok Tsagyü*	*Bde mchog rtsa rgyud*	བདེ་མཆོག་རྩ་རྒྱུད།
	Candapa	*Tsandapa*	*Tsa NDa pa*	ཙ་ཎྜ་པ།

English	Sanskrit	Phonetic Tibetan	Transliterated Tibetan	Tibetan (Uchen)
	Candra	*Tsandrapa*	*Tsa n+dra pa*	ཙནྡྲ།
	Candragomin		Can+dra go mi	ཙནྡྲ་གོ་མི།
	caryātantra	chögyü	spyod rgyud	སྤྱོད་རྒྱུད།
		Chagen	Cha gan	ཆ་གན།
		Chak Lotsāwa	Chag Lo tsA ba	ཆག་ལོ་ཙཱ་བ།
		Chak Lotsāwa Chöjé Pal	Chos rje dpal Chag Lo tsA ba	ཆོས་རྗེ་དཔལ་ཆག་ལོ་ཙཱ་བ།
		Chambu	Lcam bu	ལྕམ་བུ།
		Cham Lhakhang	Lcam Lha khang	ལྕམ་ལྷ་ཁང་།
		chamtsé	phyam tshe	ཕྱམ་ཚེ།
	Chandoratnākara[2]	*Debjor Rinchen Jungné*	*Sdeb sbyor rin chen 'byung gnas*	སྡེབ་སྦྱོར་རིན་ཆེན་འབྱུང་གནས།
		Changtön Tsöndrü Drak	Cang ston brtson 'grus grags	ཅང་སྟོན་བརྩོན་འགྲུས་གྲགས།
		Chapa	Phya pa[3]	ཕྱ་པ།

2. Treatise on Sanskrit prosody by the Indian author Ratnākaraśānti. Derge Tengyur (D 4303) sgra mdo, se 351b1–360b7.

3. Chapa Chökyi Sengé (Phya pa chos kyi seng ge, 1109–69).

English	Sanskrit	Phonetic Tibetan	Transliterated Tibetan	Tibetan (Uchen)
		Charup Sengé Palsangpo	Phya rub Seng ge dpal bzang po	ཕྱ་རུབ་སེང་གེ་དཔལ་བཟང་པོ།
		Chim Namkha Drak	Mchims Nam mkha' grags	མཆིམས་ནམ་མཁའ་གྲགས།
		Chiring	Spyi rings	སྤྱི་རིངས།
		Chiwo Lhepa Jangchup Ö	Spyi bo Lhas pa Byang chub 'od	སྤྱི་བོ་ལྷས་པ་བྱང་ཆུབ་འོད།
		Chö	Gcod	གཅོད།
Chögön from Rilung Phukpa		Rilung Phuk Rongpa Chögön	Ri lung Phug pa Chos mgon	རི་ལུང་ཕུག་པ་ཆོས་མགོན།
		Chökyi Gönpo	Chos kyi mgon po	ཆོས་ཀྱི་མགོན་པོ།
		Chokjin Pal	Mchog sbyin dpal	མཆོག་སྦྱིན་དཔལ།
		Chumik Ringmo	Chu mig ring mo	ཆུ་མིག་རིང་མོ།
		Chungpa	Gcung pa	གཅུང་པ།
Classification of the Three Vows		*Domsum Rabtu Jewa*	*Sdom gsum rab tu dbye ba*	སྡོམ་གསུམ་རབ་ཏུ་དབྱེ་བ།
Collection of the Bodhisattva's Previous Lives		*Jangchup Sempai Kyewai Rab*	*Byang chub sems dpa'i skyes ba'i rabs*	བྱང་ཆུབ་སེམས་དཔའི་སྐྱེས་པའི་རབས།
Collection of Madhyamaka Reasoning	*Madhyamaka Yuktikāya*	*Uma Riktsok*	*Dbu ma rigs tshogs*	དབུ་མ་རིགས་ཚོགས།

English	Sanskrit	Phonetic Tibetan	Transliterated Tibetan	Tibetan (Uchen)
Commentary on Valid Cognition	*Pramāṇavārttika*	*Tsema Namdrel*	*Tshad ma rnam 'grel*	ཚད་མ་རྣམ་འགྲེལ།
Compendium of Abhidharma	*Abhidharmasamuccaya*	*Ngönpa Kuntü*	*Mngon pa kun btus*	མངོན་པ་ཀུན་བཏུས།
Compendium of Valid Cognition	*Pramāṇasamuccaya*	*Tsema Kunlé Tüpa*	*Tshad ma kun las btus pa*	ཚད་མ་ཀུན་ལས་བཏུས་པ།
Complete Nobility		*Kunsang*	*Kun bzang*	ཀུན་བཟང་།
Comprehensive Conduct		*Kuntu Jöpa*	*Kun tu spyod pa*	ཀུན་ཏུ་སྤྱོད་པ།
Condensation of Vajrayāna		*Dorjé Thekdü*	*Rdo rje theg bsdus*	རྡོ་རྗེ་ཐེག་བསྡུས།
Condensed Ulitmate Tantra of All the Tathāgatas	*Sarvatathāgatasaṃgraha Tantra*	*Deshin Shekpa Thamché kyi Dekhona Nyi Düpai Gyü*	*De bzhin gshegs pa thams cad kyi de kho na nyid bsdus pa'i rgyud*	དེ་བཞིན་གཤེགས་པ་ཐམས་ཅད་ཀྱི་དེ་ཁོ་ན་ཉིད་བསྡུས་པའི་རྒྱུད།
Crimson Rishi		*Drangsong Marser*	*Drang srong dmar ser*	དྲང་སྲོང་དམར་སེར།
		Daka Yeshé	*'Da' ka ye shes*	འདའ་ཀ་ཡེ་ཤེས།
		Dampa Kunga Drak	Dam pa Kun dga' grags	དམ་པ་ཀུན་དགའ་གྲགས།
	Dānaśilā	Dānaśīla	dA na shA+i la	དཱ་ན་ཤཱི་ལ།
	Daṇḍin	Lopön Jukpachen	Slob dpon Dbyug pa can	སློབ་དཔོན་དབྱུག་པ་ཅན།
		Dawa Gyaltsen	Zla ba rgyal mtshan	ཟླ་བ་རྒྱལ་མཚན།

English	Sanskrit	Phonetic Tibetan	Transliterated Tibetan	Tibetan (Uchen)
		Denpa Joden	Ldan pa Jo gdan	ལྡན་པ་ཇོ་གདན།
Description of the Lama		*Ngönjö Lama*	*Mngon brjod bla ma*	མངོན་བརྗོད་བླ་མ།
		Deshek Khampa Dorgyal	Bde gshegs Khams pa Rdor rgyal	བདེ་གཤེགས་ཁམས་པ་རྡོར་རྒྱལ།
		Detön Könchok Drak	Sde ston dkon mchog grags	སྡེ་སྟོན་དཀོན་མཆོག་གྲགས།
	Deva Mati	Deba Mati	De lba ma ti	དེ་ལྦ་མ་ཏི།
		Dewachen	Bde ba chen	བདེ་བ་ཆེན།
	dhāraṇī	sung	gzungs	གཟུངས།
	Dharmakīrti	Chökyi Drakpa	Chos kyi grags pa	ཆོས་ཀྱི་གྲགས་པ།
	Dharmapāla	Dharmapāla Rakṣita	D+harmA pA la rak+Shita	དྷརྨཔཱལ།
	Dharmottara	Chöchok	Chos mchog	ཆོས་མཆོག
Diamond Cutter Sūtra	*Vajracchedikā Prajñāpāramitā Sūtra*	*Dorjé Tsöpa*	*Rdo rje btsod pa*	རྡོ་རྗེ་བཙོད་པ།
	Dignāga	Chökyi Langpo	Phyogs kyi glang po	ཕྱོགས་ཀྱི་གླང་པོ།
Distinguishing the Middle from the Extremes	*Madhyāntavibhāga*	*Ütha Namjé*	*Dbus mtha' rnam 'byed*	དབུས་མཐའ་རྣམ་འབྱེད།
Dodé Pal from Shang		Shangtsun Dodé Pal	Zhang btsun Mdo sde dpal	ཞང་བཙུན་མདོ་སྡེ་དཔལ།
		Dokham	Do khams	མདོ་ཁམས།
		Dokorwa	Do skor ba	དོ་སྐོར་བ།

English	Sanskrit	Phonetic Tibetan	Transliterated Tibetan	Tibetan (Uchen)
		Doktö	Mdogs stod	མདོགས་སྟོད།
		Doktön Chugupa	Ldog ston Gcu gu pa	ལྡོག་སྟོན་གཙུ་གུ་པ།
	Ḍombi Heruka	Dombi Heruka	Dom bi He ru ka	ཌོམ་བི་ཧེ་རུ་ཀ
Dong clans		Dong rüchen	Ldong rus chen	ལྡོང་རུས་ཆེན།
		Dongtön	Ldong ston	ལྡོང་སྟོན།
		Dönmori	Don mo ri	དོན་མོ་རི།
		Dorang	Rdo rang	རྡོ་རང་།
		Dorjé Nyingpo	Rdo rje snying po	རྡོ་རྗེ་སྙིང་པོ།
		Dorjé Öser	Rdo rje ’od zer	རྡོ་རྗེ་འོད་ཟེར།
		Dorjé Rinpoché	Rdo rje Rin po che	རྡོ་རྗེ་རིན་པོ་ཆེ།
		Dorsi Gon	Rdor sri dgon	རྡོར་སྲི་དགོན།
		Dorta	Dor ta	དོར་ཏ།
		Drakpa Gyaltsen	Grags pa rgyal mtshan	གྲགས་པ་རྒྱལ་མཚན།
Draksang from Thangpé		Thangpewa Draksang	Thang dpe bag rags bzang	ཐང་དཔེ་བ་གྲགས་བཟང་།
		Drangkhang Nyingpa	Brang khang Rnying pa	བྲང་ཁང་རྙིང་པ།
		Drangti Darma Nyingpo	Brang ti Dar ma snying po	བྲང་ཏི་དར་མ་སྙིང་པོ།
		Dratön Yeshé Sengé	Bra ston Ye shes seng ge	བྲ་སྟོན་ཡེ་ཤེས་སེང་གེ
Drawo Valley		Drawo	Bra bo	བྲ་བོ།

English	Sanskrit	Phonetic Tibetan	Transliterated Tibetan	Tibetan (Uchen)
		Drilchen	Dril chen	དྲིལ་ཆེན།
Dro Valley		Dro	’Bro	འབྲོ།
		Drogön Chakna	’Gro mgon Phyag na	འགྲོ་མགོན་ཕྱག་ན།
		Drogön Chögyal Phakpa	’Gro mgon Chos rgyal ’phags pa	འགྲོ་མགོན་ཆོས་རྒྱལ་འཕགས་པ།
		Drokmi Lotsāwa	’Brog mi Lo tsA ba	འབྲོག་མི་ལོ་ཙཱ་བ།
		Dromé	Grom smad	གྲོམ་སྨད།
		Drompa Yutsé	Grom pa G.yu rtse	གྲོམ་པ་གཡུ་རྩེ།
		Dromtö	Grom stod	གྲོམ་སྟོད།
Droplet of Reasoning	*Nyāyabindu*	*Tsema Rikthik*	*Tshad ma rigs thigs*	ཚད་མ་རིགས་ཐིགས།
Drops of Logic	*Hetubindu*	*Tenshikyi Thikpa Drelwa*	*Gtan tshigs kyi thigs pa ’grel ba*	གཏན་ཚིགས་ཀྱི་ཐིགས་པ་འགྲེལ་བ།
		Drosang	’Bro gsang	འབྲོ་གསང་།
Drup and Tsok		Drup Tsok	Grub Tshogs	གྲུབ་ ཚོགས།
		Drup Nyingpo Dorjé Palsangpo	Grub Snying po Rdo rje dpal bzang po	གྲུབ་སྙིང་པོ་རྡོ་རྗེ་དཔལ་བཟང་པོ།
		Drupthop Yönten Palsangpo	Grub thob Yon tan dpal bzang po	གྲུབ་ཐོབ་ཡོན་ཏན་དཔལ་བཟང་པོ།

English	Sanskrit	Phonetic Tibetan	Transliterated Tibetan	Tibetan (Uchen)
		Dulwa Gyaltsen	'Dul ba Rgyal mtshan	འདུལ་བ་རྒྱལ་མཚན།
Dzayasena from Nepal		Balpo Dzayasena	Bal po dza ya se na	བལ་པོ་ཛ་ཡ་སེ་ན།
		Dzokchen	Rdzogs chen	རྫོགས་ཆེན།
earth-blessing ritual		sa choka	sa cho ga	ས་ཆོ་ག
Eight Branches of Medicine		Menyen Lakgyepa	*Sman yan lag brgyad pa*	སྨན་ཡན་ལག་བརྒྱད་པ།
Eighteen Thousand		*Namdrelgyi Gyantö Draktso Gyepa*	*Rnam 'drel gyi rgyan stod brag btso brgyad pa*	རྣམ་འདྲེལ་གྱི་རྒྱན་སྟོད་བྲག་བཙོ་བརྒྱད་པ།
Emanation Temple		Trulpai Lhakhang	Sprul pa'i Lha khang	སྤྲུལ་པའི་ལྷ་ཁང་།
Engaging in Greatly Joyous Theatrical Performances		*Logar Rabgai Jukpa*	*Zlos gar rab dga'i 'jug pa*	ཟློས་གར་རབ་དགའི་འཇུག་པ།
Engaging in the Conduct of the Bodhisattva	*Bodhisattvacaryāvatāra*	*Jangchup Sempai Chöpala Jukpa*	*Byang chub sems dpa'i spyod pa la 'jug pa*	བྱང་ཆུབ་སེམས་དཔའི་སྤྱོད་པ་ལ་འཇུག་པ།
Engaging Youth		*Jepa Jukpa*	*Byes pa 'jug pa*	བྱེས་པ་འཇུག་པ།
Entry Door for Scholars		*Khepala Jukpai Go*	*Mkhas pa la 'jug pa'i sgo*	མཁས་པ་ལ་འཇུག་པའི་སྒོ།
		Erkawun	Erka 'un	ཨེརྐ་འུན།
Essence of Attainment		*Drupnying*	*Grub snying*	གྲུབ་སྙིང་།

English	Sanskrit	Phonetic Tibetan	Transliterated Tibetan	Tibetan (Uchen)
Excellent Glorious Diamond Pinnacle Tantra	*Vajraśekhara*	*Dorjé Tsemo Pal Chok*	*Rdo rje tse mod pal mchog*	རྡོ་རྗེ་རྩེ་མོ་དཔལ་མཆོག
Five Droplets		*Thiklé Nga*	*Thig le lnga*	ཐིག་ལེ་ལྔ།
Five-Peak Mountain (Mount Wutai)		Ribo Tsenga	Ri bo Rtse lnga	རི་བོ་རྩེ་ལྔ།
Five Treatises of Maitreya		Jamchö Dé Nga	Byams chos sde lnga	བྱམས་ཆོས་སྡེ་ལྔ།
four Sijili brothers		Sijili punshi	Si ji li Spun bzhi	སི་ཇི་ལི་སྤུན་བཞི།
Fundamental Verses on the Middle Way	*Mūlamadhyamakakārikā*	*Tsawa Sherab*	*Rtsa ba shes rab*	རྩ་བ་ཤེས་རབ།
	Gaṇḍavyūha	*Dongpo Köpa*	*Sdong po bkod pa*	སྡོང་པོ་བཀོད་པ།
		Ganden	Dga' ldan	དགའ་ལྡན།
		Gandenpa Chökyi Gyaltsen	Dga' ldan pa Chos kyi rgyal mtshan	དགའ་ལྡན་པ་ཆོས་ཀྱི་རྒྱལ་མཚན།
		Gangla Cha	Gang la Cha	གང་ལ་ཅ།
Garland of Melodies	*Sarasvatikaṇṭhābharaṇa*	*Yangchen Gulgyen*	*Dbyangs can mgul rgyan*	དབྱངས་ཅན་མགུལ་རྒྱན།
		Garphuk	Gar phug	གར་ཕུག
		Garpu	Gar pu	གར་པུ།
		Gatön Dorjé Drak	Rga ston Rdo rje grags	རྒ་སྟོན་རྡོ་རྗེ་གྲགས།

English	Sanskrit	Phonetic Tibetan	Transliterated Tibetan	Tibetan (Uchen)
		Gelong Dorjé Sengé	Dge slong rdo rje seng ge	དགེ་སློང་རྡོ་རྗེ་སེང་གེ
Genghis Khan		Jingir Gan	Jing gir Gan	ཇིང་གིར་གན།
		geshé	dge bshes	དགེ་བཤེས།
		Gethong	Dge mthong	དགེ་མཐོང་།
Godan Khan (son of Ogedei Khan)		Godan Khan	Go dan Khan	གོ་དན་ཁན།
going to heroism (samādhi)	śūraṁgama	palwar drowa	dpal bar 'gro ba	དཔལ་བར་འགྲོ་བ།
Golden-Colored Realm		Khamser Dokchen	Khams gser mdog can	ཁམས་གསེར་མདོག་ཅན།
		Gomchen Tagen	Sgom chen Rta rgan	སྒོམ་ཆེན་རྟ་རྒན།
		Gompa Kyibar	Sgom pa kyi 'bar	སྒོམ་པ་ཀྱི་འབར།
		Gompa Ödrak	Sgom pa 'Od grags	སྒོམ་པ་འོད་གྲགས།
		Gö Khukpa	'Gos Khug pa	འགོས་ཁུག་པ།
	Guhyāgarba Tantra	*Sangwai Nyingpo*	*Gsang ba'i snying po*	གསང་བའི་སྙིང་པོ།
	Guhyasamāja	*Sangwai Düpa*	*Gsang ba'i 'dus pa*	གསང་བ་འདུས་པ།
Gunbu Gumuk Forest		Gunbu Gunmuk Nak	Gun bu rgun mug nags	རྒུན་བུ་རྒུན་མུག་ནགས།
		Gungthang	Gung thang	གུང་ཐང་།
		Gungthang Nalatsé Nesar	Gung thang Na la rtse gnas gsar	གུང་ཐང་ན་ལ་རྩེ་གནས་གསར།

English	Sanskrit	Phonetic Tibetan	Transliterated Tibetan	Tibetan (Uchen)
		Gushi	Gu shI	གུ་ཤྲཱི།
		Guyuk Khan	Gu yug khan	གུ་ཡུག་ཁན།
Great Secret		*Sangwa Chenpo*	*Gsang ba chen po*	གསང་བ་ཆེན་པོ།
		Gyagom Tsultrim Drak	Rgya sgom Tshul khrims grags	རྒྱ་སྒོམ་ཚུལ་ཁྲིམས་གྲགས།
		Gyalpo Nyimai Tophel	Rgyal po Nyi ma'i stobs 'phel	རྒྱལ་པོ་ཉི་མའི་སྟོབས་འཕེལ།
		Gyalpo Pekar	Rgyal po dpe dkar	རྒྱལ་པོ་དཔེ་དཀར།
		Gyalwa Yangönpa	Rgyal ba Yang dgon pa	རྒྱལ་བ་ཡང་དགོན་པ།
		Gyalwapa	Rgyal ba dpal	རྒྱལ་བ་དཔལ།
Handfuls of Flowers from the Ornamental Tree of Paradise		*Gyen Jönshing Nyimpai Metok*	*Rgyan ljon shing snyim pa'i me tog*	རྒྱན་ལྗོན་ཤིང་སྙིམ་པའི་མེ་ཏོག
	Harinanda	*Trokjé Gapo*	*'Phrog byed dga' bo*	འཕྲོག་བྱེད་དགའ་བོ།
	Hevajra Mūlatantra Rāja	*Taknyi*	*Brtag gnyis*	བརྟག་གཉིས།
Hevajra Root Tantra		*Kyé Dorjé Tsawai Gyü*	*Kye rdo rje'i rtsa ba'i rgyud*	ཀྱེ་རྡོ་རྗེའི་རྩ་བའི་རྒྱུད།
How to Enter the Door of Dharma		*Chöla Jukpai Go*	*Chos la 'jug pa'i sgo*	ཆོས་ལ་འཇུག་པའི་སྒོ།
Illumination of the Sage's Intent		*Thupai Gongpa Rabtu Salwa*	*Thub pa'i dgongs pa rab tu gsal ba*	ཐུབ་པའི་དགོངས་པ་རབ་ཏུ་གསལ་བ།

English	Sanskrit	Phonetic Tibetan	Transliterated Tibetan	Tibetan (Uchen)
Illumination of the Twenty Thousand Stanzas		Nyitri Nangwa	*Nyi khri snang ba*	ཉི་ཁྲི་སྣང་བ།
Immortal Treasury of Synonymy	*Amarakośa*	*Ngönjö Chimé Dzö*	*Mngon brjod 'chi med mdzod*	མངོན་བརྗོད་འཆི་མེད་མཛོད།
	Īśvara	Wangchukma	Dbang phyug ma	དབང་ཕྱུག་མ།
		Jakshong	'Jag shongs	འཇག་ཤོངས།
		Jang	Ljang	ལྗང་།
		Jangchung	Byang gcung	བྱང་གཅུང་།
		Jangchup Ö	Byang chub 'Od	བྱང་ཆུབ་འོད།
		Jang Ngamring	Byang Ngam ring	བྱང་ངམ་རིང་།
		Jangsem Ngagyal	Byang sems nga rgyal	བྱང་སེམས་ང་རྒྱལ།
Mañjuśrī torma water offering		chabtor jampalma	chab gtor 'jam dpal ma	ཆབ་གཏོར་འཇམ་དཔལ་མ།
		Jamyang Nyithokpa	'Jam dbyangs Nyi thog pa	འཇམ་དབྱངས་ཉི་ཐོག་པ།
		Jamyang Sherab Gyatso	'Jam dbyangs Shes rab rgya mtsho	འཇམ་དབྱངས་ཤེས་རབ་རྒྱ་མཚོ།
Jamyang Sherab Öser from Tsangnak Phukpa		Tsangnak Phukpa Jamyang Sherab Öser	Tsang nags phug pa 'Jam dbyangs shes rab 'od zer	གཙང་ནགས་ཕུག་པ་འཇམ་དབྱངས་ཤེས་རབ་འོད་ཟེར།

English	Sanskrit	Phonetic Tibetan	Transliterated Tibetan	Tibetan (Uchen)
		Jang Gyatso Dé (Chinese: Beihaizang Si)	Byang Rgya mtsho sde	བྱང་རྒྱ་མཚོ་སྡེ།
		Jarchöpa	Dbyar chos pa	དབྱར་ཆོས་པ།
Jātaka tales	*Jātaka*	*Kyerab*	*Skyes rabs*	སྐྱེས་རབས།
	Jayadeva	Gyalpoi Lha	Rgyal bo'i lha	རྒྱལ་པོའི་ལྷ།
		Jetso	Rje mtsho	རྗེ་མཚོ།
		Jetsun Drakpa Gyaltsen	Rje btsun Grags pa rgyal mtshan	རྗེ་བཙུན་གྲགས་པ་རྒྱལ་མཚན།
		Jetsun Puhrang Lochung	Rje btsun Pu hrangs lo chung	རྗེ་བཙུན་པུ་ཧྲངས་ལོ་ཆུང་།
		Jetsun Sönam Tsemo	Rje btsun Bsod nams rtse mo	རྗེ་བཙུན་བསོད་ནམས་རྩེ་མོ།
Jewel Garland		*Rinchen Trengwa*	*Rin chen phreng ba*	རིན་ཆེན་ཕྲེང་བ།
	Jīvaka Kumārabhṛta	Tsojé Shönu	'Tsho byed Gzhon nu	འཚོ་བྱེད་གཞོན་ནུ།
		Jiwolhé	Spyi bo lhas	སྤྱི་བོ་ལྷས།
Jñānapada tradition		Yeshé Shab	Ye shes zhabs	ཡེ་ཤེས་ཞབས།
		Jobum Gukshrī	Jo 'bum Gug shrI	ཇོ་འབུམ་གུག་ཤྲཱི།
		Jocham Phurmo	Jo lcam phur mo	ཇོ་ལྕམ་ཕུར་མོ།
		Joden	Jo gdan	ཇོ་གདན།

English	Sanskrit	Phonetic Tibetan	Transliterated Tibetan	Tibetan (Uchen)
		Joden Jangchup Palzangpo	Jo gdan Byang chub dpal bzang po	ཇོ་གདན་བྱང་ཆུབ་དཔལ་བཟང་པོ།
		Joden Jangthang	Jo gdan Byang thang	ཇོ་གདན་བྱང་ཐང་།
		Jomo Mangchungma	Jo mo Mang chung ma	ཇོ་མོ་མང་ཆུང་མ།
		Jomo Shangmo	Jo mo Zhang mo	ཇོ་མོ་ཞང་མོ།
		Jongtön Sherab Palsangpo	Ldong ston Shes rab dpal bzang po	ལྡོང་སྟོན་ཤེས་རབ་དཔལ་བཟང་པོ།
		José Chakyi Dorjé	Jo sras lcags kyi rdo rje	ཇོ་སྲས་ལྕགས་ཀྱི་རྡོ་རྗེ།
José from Chiwolhé		Chiwo Lhepa José	Spyi bo lhas pa jo sras	སྤྱི་བོ་ལྷས་པ་ཇོ་སྲས།
José from Sang		Sangkyi José	Zangs kyi Jo sras	ཟངས་ཀྱི་ཇོ་སྲས།
	Jñāna Vajra	Jñāna Vajra	Dz+nyA na bdzra	ཛྙཱན་བཛྲ།
		Jugur Memar	Ju gur Me mar	ཇུ་གུར་མེ་མར།
		Kadam	Bka' dams	བཀའ་དམས།
	Kālacakra Tantra	*Dükyi Khorloi Gyü*	*Dus kyi 'khor lo'i rgyud*	དུས་ཀྱི་འཁོར་ལོའི་རྒྱུད།
	Kalāpa	*Kalāpa*	*Ka lA pa*	ཀ་ལཱ་པ།
	Kālidāsa	Nakmo Khol	Nag mo khol	ནག་མོ་ཁོལ།
	Kaṇāda	Sheksen	Gzegs zan	གཟེགས་ཟན།
	Kapila	Serkya	Ser skya	སེར་སྐྱ།

English	Sanskrit	Phonetic Tibetan	Transliterated Tibetan	Tibetan (Uchen)
	Kargā	Karga	Skar dga'	སྐར་དགའ།
		Karmo Nyida	Dkar mo Nyi zla	དཀར་མོ་ཉི་ཟླ།
		Kar Shākya Drak	Dkar shAkya grags	དཀར་ཤཱཀྱ་གྲགས།
	Kasarpaṇi	Kasarpaṇi	Ka sar pa Ni	ཀ་སར་པ་ཎི།
	Kauśāmbī	Kaushambhi	Ka'u shaM b+hi	ཀའུ་ཤཾ་བྷི།
		Khampa Aseng	Khams pa A seng	ཁམས་པ་ཨ་སེང་།
		Khampa Galo	Khams pa Rga lo	ཁམས་པ་རྒ་ལོ།
		Khangtön Öser Gyaltsen	Khang ston 'Od zer rgyal mtshan	ཁང་སྟོན་འོད་ཟེར་རྒྱལ་མཚན།
		Khabso	Khab so	ཁབ་སོ།
		Khabso Takthok	Khab so Stag thog	ཁབ་སོ་སྟག་ཐོག
		khatak (ceremonial scarf)	kha btags	ཁ་བཏགས།
		Khaupa Öden Palsangpo	Kha 'ub pa 'Od ldan dpal bzang po	ཁ་འུབ་པ་འོད་ལྡན་དཔལ་བཟང་པོ།
		Khenpo Chöjé	Mkhan po Chos rje	མཁན་པོ་ཆོས་རྗེ།
		Khenpo Drakpa Sengé	Mkhan po Grags pa seng ge	མཁན་པོ་གྲགས་པ་སེང་གེ
		Khenpo Sengé Silnön	Mkhan po Seng ge zil non	མཁན་པོ་སེང་གེ་ཟིལ་ནོན།

English	Sanskrit	Phonetic Tibetan	Transliterated Tibetan	Tibetan (Uchen)
		Khön	’Khon	འཁོན།
		Khön Barkyé	’Khon Bar skyes	འཁོན་བར་སྐྱེས།
		Khön Dorjé Rinchen	’Khon Rdo rje rin chen	འཁོན་རྡོ་རྗེ་རིན་ཆེན།
		Khön Gekyab	’Khon Dge skyabs	འཁོན་དགེ་སྐྱབས།
		Khön Gyichuwa	’Khon Sgyi chu ba	འཁོན་སྒྱི་ཆུ་བ།
		Khön Könchok Gyalpo	’Khon Dkon mchog rgyal po	འཁོན་དཀོན་མཆོག་རྒྱལ་པོ།
		Khön Pawoché	’Khon Dpa’ bo che	འཁོན་དཔའ་བོ་ཆེ།
		Khön Sherab Yönten	’Khon Shes rab yon tan	འཁོན་ཤེས་རབ་ཡོན་ཏན།
		Khön Tsuktor Sherab	’Khon Gtsug tor shes rab	འཁོན་གཙུག་ཏོར་ཤེས་རབ།
		Khön Tsultrim Gyalpo	’Khon Tshul khrims rgyal po	འཁོན་ཚུལ་ཁྲིམས་རྒྱལ་པོ།
		Khönrok Sherab Tsultrim	’Khon Rog Shes rab tshul khrims	འཁོན་རོག་ཤེས་རབ་ཚུལ་ཁྲིམས།
		Khöntön Balpo	’Khon ston Bal po	འཁོན་སྟོན་བལ་པོ།
		Khöntön Shākya Lodrö	’Khon ston ShAkya blo gros	འཁོན་སྟོན་ཤཱཀྱ་བློ་གྲོས།
		Khyin Lotsāwa	’Khyin Lo tsA ba	འཁྱིན་ལོ་ཙཱ་བ།
		Khyung Rinchen Drak	Khyung Rin chen grags	ཁྱུང་རིན་ཆེན་གྲགས།
King Kalinga		Kalingai Gyalpo	Ka ling ga’i rgyal po	ཀ་ལིང་གའི་རྒྱལ་པོ།
King of Garing		Garing Gyalpo	Ga ring rgyal po	ག་རིང་རྒྱལ་པོ།

English	Sanskrit	Phonetic Tibetan	Transliterated Tibetan	Tibetan (Uchen)
King Vasava		Norlhai Bu	Nor lha'i bu	ནོར་ལྷའི་བུ།
		Komdré	Kom 'dre	ཀོམ་འདྲེ།
		Könpa Lhajé Gungtak	Dkon pa Lha rje gung stag	དཀོན་པ་ལྷ་རྗེ་གུང་སྟག
	Kṛṣṇapa	Nakpopa	Nag po pa	ནག་པོ་པ།
	kriyātantra	jagyü	bya rgyud	བྱ་རྒྱུད།
	Kumudi	*Kumuti*	*Ku mu ti*	ཀུ་མུ་ཏི།
		Kunga Bar	Kun dga' 'Bar	ཀུན་དགའ་འབར།
		Kunga Gyaltsen	Kun dga' rgyal mtshan	ཀུན་དགའ་རྒྱལ་མཚན།
Kunga Mönlam from Nyithok		Nyithokpa Kunga Mönlam	Nyi thog pa Kun dga' smon lam	ཉི་ཐོག་པ་ཀུན་དགའ་སྨོན་ལམ།
		Kunga Nyingpo	Kun dga' snying po	ཀུན་དགའ་སྙིང་པོ།
		Kunga Sengé	Kun dga' seng ge	ཀུན་དགའ་སེང་གེ
Kunmön from Sulung		Sulung Kunmön	Sru lung Kun smon	སྲུ་ལུང་ཀུན་སྨོན།
Kunsö from Ganden		Gandenpa Kunsö	Dga' ldan pa Kun bsod	དགའ་ལྡན་པ་ཀུན་བསོད།
	Kurukullā	Rikjema	Rig byed ma	རིག་བྱེད་མ།
kusha grass		kusha	ku sha	ཀུ་ཤ།
		Kyangdurwa	Rkyang 'Dur ba	རྐྱང་འདུར་བ།
		Kyareng Trakmé	Skya reng Khrag med	སྐྱ་རེང་ཁྲག་མེད།

English	Sanskrit	Phonetic Tibetan	Transliterated Tibetan	Tibetan (Uchen)
		Kyaring Trakmé	Skya ring Khrag med	སྐྱ་རིང་ཁྲག་མེད།
		Kyawo Khadang	Skya bo Kha gdangs	སྐྱ་བོ་ཁ་གདངས།
Kyawo Khadang in Yeru		Yeru Kyawo Khadang	G.yas ru Skya bo Kha gdangs	གཡས་རུ་སྐྱ་བོ་ཁ་གདངས།
		Kyirong	Skyid grong	སྐྱིད་གྲོང་།
		Kyitsal	Skyid tshal	སྐྱིད་ཚལ།
		Kyopa Pal Rinpoché	Skyob pa Dpal Rin po che	སྐྱོབ་པ་དཔལ་རིན་པོ་ཆེ།
		Kyormolung	Skyor mo lung	སྐྱོར་མོ་ལུང་།
		Kyotön Drimé Palsangpo	Skyo ston Dri med dpal bzang po	སྐྱོ་སྟོན་དྲི་མེད་དཔལ་བཟང་པོ།
		Kyura Akyab	Skyu ra A skyabs	སྐྱུ་ར་ཨ་སྐྱབས།
		Kyura Akyab	Skyur ra A skyabs	སྐྱུར་ར་ཨ་སྐྱབས།
		Lachen	Bla chen	བླ་ཆེན།
	Lakṣmī	Nyinmo Longpa	Nyin mo long pa	ཉིན་མོ་ལོང་པ།
		Lama Dampa Sönam Gyaltsen	Bla ma Dam pa Bsod nams rgyal mtshan	བླ་མ་དམ་པ་བསོད་ནམས་རྒྱལ་མཚན།
		Lama Martön Chökyi Gyalpo	Bla ma Dmar ston Chos kyi rgyal po	བླ་མ་དམར་སྟོན་ཆོས་ཀྱི་རྒྱལ་པོ།
		Lama Öser Shākya	Bla ma 'Od zer shA kya	བླ་མ་འོད་ཟེར་ཤཱ་ཀྱ།

English	Sanskrit	Phonetic Tibetan	Transliterated Tibetan	Tibetan (Uchen)
		Lama Sé	Bla ma Se	བླ་མ་སེ།
Path Including the Result		Lamdré	Lam 'bras	ལམ་འབྲས།
Land of Hor (epithet for Mongol lands)		Horgyi Yul	Hor gyi yul	ཧོར་གྱི་ཡུལ།
		Langriwa	Glang ri ba	གླང་རི་བ།
Lanydza script		Lanydza	la nya+dza	ལ་ཉྫ།
Lanzhou		Lingchu	Ling chu	ལིང་ཆུ།
		Latö	La stod	ལ་སྟོད།
		Lhanam Theu Karpo	Lha gnam the'u dkar po	ལྷ་གནམ་ཐེའུ་དཀར་པོ།
		Lhathok Yönten Sung	Lha thog Yon tan bzung	ལྷ་ཐོག་ཡོན་ཏན་བཟུང་།
		Lhawang Lo	Lha dbang Blo	ལྷ་དབང་བློ།
		Lho and Mar	Lho Dmar	ལྷོ་དམར།
		Lhowang Dé (Chinese: Jinta Si)	Lho dbang sde	ལྷོ་དབང་སྡེ།
		Lhopa Kunkhyen Rinchen Palsangpo	Lho pa Kun mkhyen Rin chen dpal bzang po	ལྷོ་པ་ཀུན་མཁྱེན་རིན་ཆེན་དཔལ་བཟང་པོ།
		Lhopa Thamché Khyenpa	Lho pa Thams cad mkhyen pa	ལྷོ་པ་ཐམས་ཅད་མཁྱེན་པ།

English	Sanskrit	Phonetic Tibetan	Transliterated Tibetan	Tibetan (Uchen)
Litany of the Names of Mañjuśrī	*Mañjuśrīnāmasaṃgīti*	*Jampal Tsenjö*	*'Jam dpal mtshan brjod*	འཇམ་དཔལ་མཚན་བརྗོད།
		Lodrö Gyaltsen Palsangpo (a.k.a. Chögyal Phakpa)	Blo gros Rgyal mtshan dpal bzang po	བློ་གྲོས་རྒྱལ་མཚན་དཔལ་བཟང་པོ།
		Lo Lotsāwa	Glo Lo tsA ba	གློ་ལོ་ཙཱ་བ།
		Lopön Lhatsun	Slob dpon Lha btsun	སློབ་དཔོན་ལྷ་བཙུན།
		Lopön Dralé Namgyal	Slob dpon Dgra las rnam rgyal	སློབ་དཔོན་དགྲ་ལས་རྣམ་རྒྱལ།
		Lopön Rinchen Pal	Slob dpon Rin chen dpal	སློབ་དཔོན་རིན་ཆེན་དཔལ།
		Lopön Yeshé Jungné	Slob dpon Ye shes 'byung gnas	བ་དཔོན་ཡེ་ཤེས་འབྱུང་གནས།
		Lotön Dorjé Wangchuk	Lo ston Rdo rje dbang phyug	ལོ་སྟོན་རྡོ་རྗེ་དབང་ཕྱུག
		Lotsāwa Palchok Dangpoi Dorjé	Lo tsA ba Dpal mchog dang po'i rdo rje	ལོ་ཙཱ་བ་དཔལ་མཆོག་དང་པོའི་རྡོ་རྗེ།
		Lotsāwa Sherab Rinchen	Lo tsA ba Shes rab rin chen	ལོ་ཙཱ་བ་ཤེས་རབ་རིན་ཆེན།
Lotus-Born Hevajra Sādhana		Drupthap Tsokyé	Sgrub thabs mtsho skyes	སྒྲུབ་ཐབས་མཚོ་སྐྱེས།

English	Sanskrit	Phonetic Tibetan	Transliterated Tibetan	Tibetan (Uchen)
Lotus with a Garland of Pearls		*Mutik Trengwa Pema Chen*	*Mu tig phreng ba pad+ma can*	མུ་ཏིག་ཕྲེང་བ་པདྨ་ཅན།
		Lowo Khenchen	Glo bo mkhan chen	གློ་བོ་མཁན་ཆེན།
		Lucham Drama	Klu cham Bra ma	ཀླུ་ཆམ་བྲ་མ།
		Luipa	Lu'i pa	ལུའི་པ།
		lung	rlung	རླུང་།
		Lui Wangpo Sungwa	Klu'i Dbang po srung ba	ཀླུའི་དབང་པོ་སྲུང་བ།
		Machik Dorjé Den	Ma gcig Rdo rje ldan	མ་གཅིག་རྡོ་རྗེ་ལྡན།
		Machik Jondro	Ma gcig Jo 'bro	མ་གཅིག་ཇོ་འབྲོ།
		Machik Kunkyi	Ma gcig Kun skyid	མ་གཅིག་ཀུན་སྐྱིད།
		Machik Nyitri Cham	Ma chen Nyi khri lcam	མ་གཅིག་ཉི་ཁྲི་ལྕམ།
		Machik Ödrön	Ma gcig 'Od sgron	མ་གཅིག་འོད་སྒྲོན།
		Machik Shangmo	Ma gcig Zhang mo	མ་གཅིག་ཞང་མོ།
	Madhyamaka	Uma	Dbu ma	དབུ་མ།
	Magadha	Magadha	Ma ga d+ha	མ་ག་དྷ།
	Mahākalā	Nakpo Chenpo	Nag po chen po	ནག་པོ་ཆེན་པོ།
	Mahākālī	Chamdral	Lcam bral	ལྕམ་བྲལ།
	Mahāmudrā	Chakgya Chenpo	Phyag rgya chen po	ཕྱག་རྒྱ་ཆེན་པོ།

English	Sanskrit	Phonetic Tibetan	Transliterated Tibetan	Tibetan (Uchen)
Mahāmudrā Droplet		*Chakgya Chenpoi Thiklé*	*Phyag rgya chen po'i thig le*	ཕྱག་རྒྱ་ཆེན་པོའི་ཐིག་ལེ།
	Mahāvairocana Abhisaṃbodhi	*Namnang Ngönpar Jangchupa*	*Rnam snang mngon par byang chub pa*	རྣམ་སྣང་མངོན་པར་བྱང་ཆུབ་པ།
	Maitreya	Jampa	Byams pa	བྱམས་པ།
		Mal Lotsāwa	Mal Lo tsA ba	མལ་ལོ་ཙཱ་བ།
		Malpo	Smal po	སྨལ་པོ།
		Mangjo Jangyen	Mang jo byang rgyan	མང་ཇོ་བྱང་རྒྱན།
	Mañjuśrī	Jampalyang	'Jam dpal dbyangs	འཇམ་དཔལ་དབྱངས།
		Mangkhar Drilchen	Mang mkhar dril chen	མང་མཁར་དྲིལ་ཆེན།
	Mārīcī	Öser Chenma	'Od zer can ma	འོད་ཟེར་ཅན་མ།
		Masang	Ma sangs	མ་སངས།
Master Ngok		Geshé Ngok	Dge bshes Rngok	དགེ་བཤེས་རྔོག
		Medikpa	Me dig pa	མེ་དིག་པ།
		Mé Lhangtser	Me Lhang tsher	མེ་ལྷང་ཚེར།
		Mentsé	Sman rtse	སྨན་རྩེ།
Method of Pacification		Shijé	Zhi byed	ཞི་བྱེད།
		Minyak	Mi nyag	མི་ཉག
		Minyak Prajnā Dzala	Mi nyag Pradz+nyA dzwa la	མི་ཉག་པྲཛྙཱ་ཛྭ་ལ།

English	Sanskrit	Phonetic Tibetan	Transliterated Tibetan	Tibetan (Uchen)
		Mindruk	Smin drug	སྨིན་དྲུག
		Mithup Dawa	Mi thub zla ba	མི་ཐུབ་ཟླ་བ།
		Nyitri Yum	Nyi khri yum	ཉི་ཁྲི་ཡུམ།
	Mokṣākaragupta	Tharpa Jungné	Thar pa 'byung gnas	ཐར་པ་འབྱུང་གནས།
		Moktön	Rmog ston	རྨོག་སྟོན།
Mon family		Mönsa	Mon bza'	མོན་བཟའ།
Mon Creek		Möndrok	Mon grog	མོན་གྲོག
month of Tra		Tra dawa	Khra zla ba	ཁྲ་ཟླ་བ།
Mount Wutai		Gyanak Riwo Tseda	Rgya nag ri bo rtse lda	རྒྱ་ནག་རི་བོ་རྩེ་ལྡ།
		Mu	Dmu	དམུ།
Mu Dembu		Musa Dem	Dmu bza' ldem	དམུ་བཟའ་ལྡེམ།
		Mumuni	Mu mu ni	མུ་མུ་ནི།
		Mutsu Jangchup Drak	Mu tshu byang chub Grags	མུ་ཚུ་བྱང་ཆུབ་གྲགས།
muza grass		muza	mu dza	མུ་ཛ།
Nāgarī script		Naga rada	Na gar a da	ན་ག་ར་ད།
	Nāgārjuna	Ludrup	Klu sgrub	ཀླུ་སྒྲུབ།
		Nakgom Sönam Gyaltsen	Nags sgom Bsod nams rgyal mtshan	ནགས་སྒོམ་བསོད་ནམས་རྒྱལ་མཚན།

English	Sanskrit	Phonetic Tibetan	Transliterated Tibetan	Tibetan (Uchen)
	Nalendra	Nalendra	Na len dra	ནམ་མཁའ་འུ་པ།
		Nam Khaupa	Nam mkha' 'u pa	ནམ་མཁའ་འུ་པ།
		Namkha Bum	Nam mkha 'bum	ནམ་མཁའ་འབུམ།
		Namkha Drimé	Nam mkha' dri med	ནམ་མཁའ་དྲི་མེད།
		Namlha Yuring	Gnam lha g.yu ring	གནམ་ལྷ་གཡུ་རིང་།
		nang jewa	nang rje ba	ནང་རྗེ་བ།
	Nāropā	Naropa	Na ro pa	ན་རོ་པ།
		Nasa Drakphukpa	Na bza' Brag phug pa	ན་བཟའ་བྲག་ཕུག་པ།
		Natsok Salwa	*Sna tshogs gsal ba*	སྣ་ཚོགས་གསལ་བ།
		Netso Baltön	Ne tsho Sbal ston	ནེ་ཚོ་སྦལ་སྟོན།
		Ngari Drakseng	Mnga' ris Grags seng	མངའ་རིས་གྲགས་སེང་།
		Ngawang Kunga Sönam	Ngag dbang Kun dga' bsod nams	ངག་དབང་ཀུན་དགའ་བསོད་ནམས།
		Ngok Loden Sherab	Rngog blo ldan shes rab	རྔོག་བློ་ལྡན་ཤེས་རབ།
		Ngurmik	Ngur smrig	ངུར་སྨྲིག
Nonconceptualization		*Tokpamepa*	*Rtog pa med pa*	རྟོག་པ་མེད་པ།
		Nupa Rikzin Drak	Nub pa rig 'dzin grags	ནུབ་པ་རིག་འཛིན་གྲགས།

English	Sanskrit	Phonetic Tibetan	Transliterated Tibetan	Tibetan (Uchen)
		Nup Pemoi Dé (Chinese: Xilianhu Si)	Nub Pad mo'i sde	ནུབ་པད་མོའི་སྡེ།
		Nyalshik Jampai Dorjé	Snyal zhig 'jam pa'i rdo rje	སྙལ་ཞིག་འཇམ་པའི་རྡོ་རྗེ།
		Nyak Wangyal	Gnyag Dbang rgyal	གཉག་དབང་རྒྱལ།
		Nyangmé Gyengong	Nyang smad rgyan gong	ཉང་སྨད་རྒྱན་གོང་།
		Nyangtö	Nyang stod	ཉང་སྟོད།
		Nyangtö Kyangdul	Nyang stod rkyang 'dul	ཉང་སྟོད་རྐྱང་འདུལ།
Nyangtö Monastery in Nyang		Nyangtö Kangthur	Nyang stod Rkang thur	ཉང་སྟོད་རྐང་ཐུར།
	Nyāya	Rikpa Chenpa	Rig pa can pa	རིག་པ་ཅན་པ།
		Nyemo Gomchen	Snye mo sgom chen	སྙེ་མོ་སྒོམ་ཆེན།
		Nyen Darma Sengé	Gnyan Dar ma seng ge	གཉན་དར་མ་སེང་གེ
		Nyen Tsathar Gyi Yachang	Gnyan rtsa thar gyi ya changs	གཉན་རྩ་ཐར་གྱི་ཡ་ཆངས།
		Nyentö Dulwa Sengé	Gnyan stod 'dul ba seng ge	གཉན་སྟོད་འདུལ་བ་སེང་གེ
		Nyen Tsuktor Gyalpo	Gnyen Gtsug tor rgyal po	གཉེན་གཙུག་ཏོར་རྒྱལ་པོ།
		Nyen Ösung	Gnyan 'Od srung	གཉན་འོད་སྲུང་།
Nyitri Cham from Mangkhar		Mangkhar Nyitri Cham	Mang mkhar Nyi khri lcam	མང་མཁར་ཉི་ཁྲི་ལྕམ།

English	Sanskrit	Phonetic Tibetan	Transliterated Tibetan	Tibetan (Uchen)
		Nyung Chung	Nyung chung	ཉུང་ཆུང་།
Ocean of Ḍākinīs		*Khandro Gyatso*	*Mkha' 'gro rgya mtsho*	མཁའ་འགྲོ་རྒྱ་མཚོ།
	Oḍḍiyāna	Orgyen	O rgyan	ཨོ་རྒྱན།
Origin of Heruka		*Heruka Ngönjung*	*He ru ka mngon byung*	ཧེ་རུ་ཀ་མངོན་བྱུང་།
Origin of the Protector		*Gönpo Ngönpar Jungwa*	*Mgon po mngon par 'byung ba*	མགོན་པོ་མངོན་པར་འབྱུང་བ།
Origin of Vajravārāhī		*Dorjé Phakmo Ngönpar Jungwa*	*Rdo rje phag mo mngon par 'byung ba*	རྡོ་རྗེ་ཕག་མོ་མངོན་པར་འབྱུང་བ།
Ornament for Clear Realization	*Abhisamayālaṃkāra*	*Ngöntok Gyen*	*Mngon rtogs rgyan*	མངོན་རྟོགས་རྒྱན།
Ornament of Rhetoric	*Kāvyādarśa*	*Gyengyi Tenchö*	*Rgyan gyi bstan bcos*	རྒྱན་གྱི་བསྟན་བཅོས།
Ornament of Saṃpuṭa		*Gurgyen Shupai Mishi*	*Gur rgyan zhus pa'i mi bzhi*	གུར་རྒྱན་ཞུས་པའི་མི་བཞི།
Ornament of the Mahāyāna Sūtras	*Mahāyānasūtrālaṃkāra*	*Thekpa Chenpoi Dodé Gyen*	*Theg pa chen po'i mdo sde rgyan*	ཐེག་པ་ཆེན་པོའི་མདོ་སྡེ་རྒྱན།
Öser Sherab from Bumpa		Bumpa Öser Sherab	'Bum pa 'Od zer shes rab	འབུམ་པ་འོད་ཟེར་ཤེས་རབ།
Öser Sherab from Taktön		Taktön Öser Sherab	Stag ston 'Od ser shes rab	སྟག་སྟོན་འོད་སེར་ཤེས་རབ།
	Padmaśrī	Padmashrī	Pad+ma shrI	པདྨ་ཤྲཱི།

English	Sanskrit	Phonetic Tibetan	Transliterated Tibetan	Tibetan (Uchen)
		Palchen Öpo	Dpal chen 'Od po	དཔལ་ཆེན་འོད་པོ།
		Palri	Dpal ri	དཔལ་རི།
		Pal Sakya Thupten Lhachen	Dpal Sa skya Thub bstan lha chen	དཔལ་ས་སྐྱ་ཐུབ་བསྟན་ལྷ་ཆེན།
		Palsangpo	Dpal bzang po	དཔལ་བཟང་པོ།
	Paṇḍita Ganaśri	Paltuk	Dpal stug	དཔལ་སྟུག
Pang Lotsāwa Lodrö Tenpa		Pang Lotsāwa Lodrö Tenpa	Dpang Lo tsA ba Blo gros brtan pa	དཔང་ལོ་ཙཱ་བ་བློ་གྲོས་བརྟན་པ།
Parting from the Four Attachments		*Shenpa Shidrel*	*Zhen pa bzhi bral*	ཞེན་པ་བཞི་བྲལ།
Perfection of Wisdom	*Prajñāpāramitā*	*Sherabkyi Pharoltu Chinpa*	*Shes rab kyi pha rol tu phyin pa*	ཤེས་རབ་ཀྱི་ཕ་རོལ་ཏུ་ཕྱིན་པ།
Perfection of Wisdom in Eight Thousand Verses	*Aṣṭasāhasrikā Prajñāpāramitā*	*Pharoltu Chinpa Gyé Tongpa*	*Pha rol tu phyen pa brgyad stong pa*	ཕ་རོལ་ཏུ་ཕྱིན་པ་བརྒྱད་སྟོང་པ།
performance of pra		praphab	pra phab	པྲ་ཕབ།
Phamthing brothers		Phamthingpa kuché	Pham mthing pa sku mched	ཕམ་མཐིང་པ་སྐུ་མཆེད།
physician Darma Sengé		Darma Sengé	Lha rje Dar ma seng ge	ལྷ་རྗེ་དར་མ་སེང་གེ
		Pönpo Ri	Dpon po Ri	དཔོན་པོ་རི།
		Potala	Po ta la	པོ་ཏ་ལ།

English	Sanskrit	Phonetic Tibetan	Transliterated Tibetan	Tibetan (Uchen)
		Potholoyon	Po tho lo yon	པོ་ཐོ་ལོ་ཡོན།
Practical Instructions on Performing Activities		*Drupthap Letsok*	*Sgrub thabs las tshogs*	སྒྲུབ་ཐབས་ལས་ཚོགས།
	Prajñākaragupta	Sherab Jungné Bepa	Shes rab 'byung gnas sbas pa	ཤེས་རབ་འབྱུང་གནས་སྦས་པ།
	Prātimokṣa	*Sosor Tharpa*	*So sor thar pa*	སོ་སོར་ཐར་པ།
	Prātiya	*Pratiya*	*Bra ti ya*	བྲ་ཏི་ཡ།
Proof of Other Minds	*Saṃtānāntarasiddhi*	*Gyüshen Drupa*	*Rgyud gzhan Grub pa*	རྒྱུད་གཞན་གྲུབ་པ།
Protectors' Enlightenment Tantra		*Gönpo Ngönpar Jungwai Gyü*	*Mgon po mngon par 'byung ba'i rgyud*	མགོན་པོ་མངོན་པར་འབྱུང་བའི་རྒྱུད།
Proving the Validity of the Brahmin		*Bramsei Tsema Drupai Rabtu Jepa*	*Bram ze'i tshad ma grub pa'i rab tu byed pa*	བྲམ་ཟེའི་ཚད་མ་གྲུབ་པའི་རབ་ཏུ་བྱེད་པ།
		Puhrang Lotsāwa	Pu hrangs Lo tsA ba	པུ་ཧྲངས་ལོ་ཙཱ་བ།
phurba		phurba	phur ba	ཕུར་བ།
	Rakta Yamāri	Shinjé Shemar	Gshin rje gshed dmar	གཤིན་རྗེ་གཤེད་དམར།
		Rasa	Ra sa	ར་ས།
	Ratnakūṭa	*Könchok Tsekpa*	*Dkon mchog brtsegs pa*	དཀོན་མཆོག་བརྩེགས་པ།
Reasoning of Debate	*Vādanyāya*	*Tsöpai Rikpa*	*Brtsod pa'i rigs pa*	བརྩོད་པའི་རིགས་པ།

English	Sanskrit	Phonetic Tibetan	Transliterated Tibetan	Tibetan (Uchen)
		Rikden Sherab Rinchen	Rigs ldan shes rab rin chen	རིགས་ལྡན་ཤེས་རབ་རིན་ཆེན།
Rinchen Dorjé from Ngonba		Ngönpa Rinchen Dorjé	Mngon pa Rin chen rdo rje	མངོན་པ་རིན་ཆེན་རྡོ་རྗེ།
		Rinchen Gyaltsen	Rin chen rgyal mtshan	རིན་ཆེན་རྒྱལ་མཚན།
		Rinchen Jungné	*Rin chen 'byung gnas*	རིན་ཆེན་འབྱུང་གནས།
		Rinchen Kyopa Palsangpo	Rin chen Skyob pa dpal bzang po	རིན་ཆེན་སྐྱོབ་པ་དཔལ་བཟང་པོ།
	Rishi	Drangsong	Drang srong	དྲང་སྲོང་།
		Rutsam	Ru mtshams	རུ་མཚམས།
		Salwa Wangchuk Drak	Gsal ba dbang phyugs grags	གསལ་བ་དབང་ཕྱུགས་གྲགས།
		Sakthang Ding	Sag thang Ding	སག་ཐང་དིང་།
		Sakya Paṇḍita	Sa skya PaNDita	ས་སྐྱ་པཎྜིཏ།
	Śākyaśribhadra	Khaché Paṇchen	Kha che PaN chen	ཁ་ཆེ་པཎ་ཆེན།
Samantabhadra's Aspiration to Noble Conduct		*Sangchö Mönlam*	*Bzang spyod smon lam*	བཟང་སྤྱོད་སྨོན་ལམ།
	Śaṃkarānanda	Śaṃkarānanda	shaM ka ra nan+da	ཤཾ་ཀ་ར་ནནྡ།
	Saṃpuṭa Tantra	*Saṃpuṭa*	*SaM pu Ta*	སཾ་པུ་ཊ།

English	Sanskrit	Phonetic Tibetan	Transliterated Tibetan	Tibetan (Uchen)
	Saṃghaśrī	Saṃghaśrī	SaM ga shri	སཾ་ག་ཤྲི།
	Sāṃkhya	Drangchenpa	Grangs can pa	གྲངས་ཅན་པ།
		Samyé	Bsam yas	བསམ་ཡས།
		Sangphu	Gsang phu	གསང་ཕུ།
		Sangdong	Zangs sdong	ཟངས་སྡོང་།
		Sangpo Pal	Bsang po dpal	བཟང་པོ་དཔལ།
		Sangtsa Sönam Gyaltsen	Zangs tsha Bsod nams rgyal mtshan	ཟངས་ཚ་བསོད་ནམས་རྒྱལ་མཚན།
Sangyé Bum from Central Tibet		Üpa Sangyé Bum	Dbus pa Sangs rgyas 'bum	དབུས་པ་སངས་རྒྱས་འབུམ།
	Śāntideva	Shiwa Lha	Zhi ba lha	ཞི་བ་ལྷ།
	Saraha	Saraha	Sa ra ha	ས་ར་ཧ།
	Sarvadurgatipariśodana	*Ngensong Jongwa*	*Ngan song sbyong ba*	ངན་སོང་སྦྱོང་བ།
		Satön Ripa	Sa ston Ri pa	ས་སྟོན་རི་པ།
Secret General Tantra Ritual of All the Maṇḍalas	*Sarvamaṇḍala Sāmānyavidhīnāṃ Guhyatantra*[4]	*Kyilkhor Thamché Kyichi Choga Sangwai Gyü*	*Dkyil 'khor thams cad kyi spyi'i cho ga gsang ba'i rgyud*	དཀྱིལ་འཁོར་ཐམས་ཅད་ཀྱི་སྤྱིའི་ཆོ་ག་གསང་བའི་རྒྱུད།

4. Dege Kangyur, Toh 806.

English	Sanskrit	Phonetic Tibetan	Transliterated Tibetan	Tibetan (Uchen)
Secret Jewel Droplet		*Sangwa Norbui Thiklé*	*Gsang ba nor bu'i thig le*	གསང་བ་ནོར་བུའི་ཐིག་ལེ།
Secret of Everything Equal to the Limit of Space		*Khanyam Thamché Sangwa*	*Mkha' mnyam thams cad gsang ba*	མཁའ་མཉམ་ཐམས་ཅད་གསང་བ།
Secret Ornament		*Sangwa Gyen*	*Gsang ba rgyan*	གསང་བ་རྒྱན།
Segön Wish-Fulfilling Mahākāla		Segön	Bse mgon yid bzhin nor bu	བསེ་མགོན་ཡིད་བཞིན་ནོར་བུ།
		Serdokchen	Gser mdog can	གསེར་མདོག་ཅན།
		Serö Nampar Tsenpoi Gyalpo	Gser 'od Rnam par Rtsen po'i rgyal po	གསེར་འོད་རྣམ་པར་རྩེན་པོའི་རྒྱལ་པོ།
		Setsen Khan	Se chen	སེ་ཆེན།
Seven Treatises on Valid Cognition		Tsema Dedun	Tshad ma sde bdun	ཚད་མ་སྡེ་བདུན།
		Shab	shab	ཤབ།
		Shab Gongar	Shab sgo lngar	ཤབ་སྒོ་ལྔར།
		Shab Tömé	Shab stod smad	ཤབ་སྟོད་སྨད།
		Shākya Gön	ShAkya mgon	ཤཱཀྱ་མགོན།
Shākya Jangchup from Doklo		Dokloba Shākya Jangchup	Mdog glo ba ShAkya byang chub	མདོག་གློ་བ་ཤཱཀྱ་བྱང་ཆུབ།

English	Sanskrit	Phonetic Tibetan	Transliterated Tibetan	Tibetan (Uchen)
		Shākya Sangpo	ShAkya bzang po	ཤཱཀྱ་བཟང་པོ།
		Shang	zhang	ཞང་།
		Shang Dodé Palsangpo	Zhang Ddo sde dpal bzang po	ཞང་མདོ་སྡེ་དཔལ་བཟང་པོ།
		Shang Gönpawa	Zhang Dgon pa ba	ཞང་དགོན་པ་བ།
		Shang Gyalwa Palsangpo	Zhang Rgyal ba dpal bzang po	ཞང་རྒྱལ་བ་དཔལ་བཟང་པོ།
		Shang Lotsāwa	Zhang Lo tsA ba	ཞང་ལོ་ཙཱ་བ།
		Shang Könchok Pal	Zhang Dkon mchog dpal	ཞང་དཀོན་མཆོག་དཔལ།
		Shang Sekshing	Shangs sreg Shing	ཤངས་སྲེག་ཤིང་།
		Shangshung	Zhang zhung	ཞང་ཞུང་།
		Shang Sumthokpa	Zhang gsum thog pa	ཞང་གསུམ་ཐོག་པ།
		Shang Tsultrim Drak	Zhang tshul khrims grags	ཞང་ཚུལ་ཁྲིམས་གྲགས།
		Sharpa Jamyang Rinchen Gyaltsen	Shar pa 'Jam dbyangs Rin chen rgyal mtshan	ཤར་པ་འཇམ་དབྱངས་རིན་ཆེན་རྒྱལ་མཚན།
		Sharpa Sherab Jungné	Shar pa Shes rab 'byung nas	ཤར་པ་ཤེས་རབ་འབྱུང་ནས།
		Sharpa Yeshé Gyaltsen	Shar pa Ye shes rgyal mtshan	ཤར་པ་ཡེ་ཤེས་རྒྱལ་མཚན།
		Shar Trulpai Dé (Chinese: Baita Si)	Shar Sprul pa'i sde	ཤར་སྤྲུལ་པའི་སྡེ།
		Shengom Dorjé Sengé	Gshen sgom Rdo rje seng ge	གཤེན་སྒོམ་རྡོ་རྗེ་སེང་གེ

English	Sanskrit	Phonetic Tibetan	Transliterated Tibetan	Tibetan (Uchen)
		Sherab Pal	Shes rab dpal	ཤེས་རབ་དཔལ།
		Sherab Rinchen	Shes rab rin chen	ཤེས་རབ་རིན་ཆེན།
		Sherab Sangwa	Shes rab gsang ba	ཤེས་རབ་གསང་བ།
		Shigatsé	Gzhis ka rtse	གཞིས་ཀ་རྩེ།
		Shing Thangchen Thangchung	Zhing Thang chen Thang chung	ཞིང་ཐང་ཆེན་ཐང་ཆུང་།
		Shönu Jungwa	*Gzhon nu 'byung ba*	གཞོན་ནུ་འབྱུང་བ།
		Shu	Zhu	ཞུ།
		Shuhrul	Zhu hrul	ཞུ་ཧྲུལ།
		Shujé Ngodrup	Zhus byes Dngos grub	ཞུས་བྱེས་དངོས་གྲུབ།
	Siṃhanāda	Sengé Drai Choka	Seng ge Sgra'i cho ga	སེང་གེ་སྒྲའི་ཚོ་ག
	Sindūra	Sindura	sin+d+h+u ra	སིན་དྷུ་ར།
	Singala	Singala	Sing+ga la	སིངྒ་ལ།
		Sinpori	Srin po Ri	སྲིན་པོ་རི།
		Sinshing	Zin shing	ཟིན་ཤིང་།
		Sithang	Zi thang	ཟི་ཐང་།
six-limbed sādhana		Yenlak Drukpa	Yan lag drug pa	ཡན་ལག་དྲུག་པ།
		Sönam Gyaltsen	Bsod nams rgyal mtshan	བསོད་ནམས་རྒྱལ་མཚན།

English	Sanskrit	Phonetic Tibetan	Transliterated Tibetan	Tibetan (Uchen)
		Sönam Thayé	Bsod nams mtha' yas	བསོད་ནམས་མཐའ་ཡས།
		Sönam Tsemo	Bsod nams rtse mo	བསོད་ནམས་རྩེ་མོ།
		Sölchawa Dulwa Gyaltsen	Gsol bya ba 'Dul ba rgyal mtshan	གསོལ་བྱ་བ་འདུལ་བ་རྒྱལ་མཚན།
		Sorokta	Zo rog ta	ཟོ་རོག་ཏ།
Speech of Reasoning	*Tarkabhāṣā*	*Tokgei Kyé*	Rtog ge'i skyed	རྟོག་གེའི་སྐྱེད།
	Sphuṭārtha	Drelba Dönsal	'Grel ba don gsal	འགྲེལ་བ་དོན་གསལ།
	śrāvaka	nyenthö	nyan thos	ཉན་ཐོས།
	Śrīparvata	Lhochok Palkyi Ri	Lho phyogs Dpal gyi Ri	ལྷོ་ཕྱོགས་དཔལ་གྱི་རི།
	Sugataśrī	Dewar Shekpai Pal	Bde bar Gshegs pa'i Dpal	བདེ་བར་གཤེགས་པའི་དཔལ།
	Sukhāvatī	Dewachen	Bde ba can	བདེ་བ་ཅན།
		Sukyi Nyima	Gzugs kyi Nyi ma	གཟུགས་ཀྱི་ཉི་མ།
		Sulphu	Zul phu	ཟུལ་ཕུ།
Summary of Suchness		*Denyi Düpa*	*De nyid 'dus pa*	དེ་ཉིད་འདུས་པ།
Summary of the Eight Branches of Medical Treatment		*Yenlak Drepaidu Dön*	*Yan lag brgyad pa'i bsdus don*	ཡན་ལག་བརྒྱད་པའི་བསྡུས་དོན།

English	Sanskrit	Phonetic Tibetan	Transliterated Tibetan	Tibetan (Uchen)
		Surkhang Shākya Drak	Zur khang ba ShAkya grags	ཟུར་ཁང་བ་ཤཱཀྱ་གྲགས།
Sūtra of Golden Light		*Dodé Serö Dampai Lung*	*Mdo sde gser 'od dam pa'i lung*	མདོ་སྡེ་གསེར་འོད་དམ་པའི་ལུང་།
	Suwinta	*Ming Drubpa*	*Ming sgrub pa*	མིང་སྒྲུབ་པ།
		Tanak	Rta nag	རྟ་ནག
		Takthok	Stag thog	སྟག་ཐོག
	Tārā	Drölma	Sgrol ma	སྒྲོལ་མ།
		Tarerong	Rta re rong	རྟ་རེ་རོང་།
		Taso Öchen	Rta so 'Od chen	རྟ་སོ་འོད་ཆེན།
	Tathāgata Bhadra	Tathāgata Bhadra	Ta thA ga ta bha dra	ཏ་ཐཱ་ག་ཏ་བྷ་དྲ།
Tathāgata King Proclaimer of Inexhaustible Melodies		Deshin Shekpa Drayang Misepa Drokpai Gyalpo	De bzhin Gshegs pa Sgra dbyangs mi zad pa sgrogs pa'i rgyal po	དེ་བཞིན་གཤེགས་པ་སྒྲ་དབྱངས་མི་ཟད་པ་སྒྲོགས་པའི་རྒྱལ་པོ།
		Terawa Jamgön	Te ra ba Byams mgon	ཏེ་ར་བ་བྱམས་མགོན།
		Thakar	Tha skar	ཐ་སྐར།
		Thangpé	Thang dpe	ཐང་དཔེ།
The Ten Different Medical Treatments		*Jeshung Chu*	*Dpyad gzhung bcu*	དཔྱད་གཞུང་བཅུ།

English	Sanskrit	Phonetic Tibetan	Transliterated Tibetan	Tibetan (Uchen)
three Hevajra tantras		Kyé Dorjé gyüsum	Kye rdo rje'i rgyud gsum	ཀྱེ་རྡོ་རྗེའི་རྒྱུད་གསུམ།
Three Unsullied Arali		*Nyokmé Arali*	*Rnyog med a ra li*	རྙོག་མེད་ཨ་ར་ལི།
		Thokcham Urma	Thog lcam 'Ur ma	ཐོག་ལྕམ་འུར་མ།
		Thokla Öchen	Thog la 'Od chen	ཐོག་ལ་འོད་ཆེན།
		Thoktsa Pawo	Thog tsha Dpa' bo	ཐོག་ཚ་དཔའ་བོ།
		Thupten Lhachen	Thub bstan lha chen	ཐུབ་བསྟན་ལྷ་ཆེན།
		Thupten Namgyal	Thub bstan rnam rgyal	ཐུབ་བསྟན་རྣམ་རྒྱལ།
		Thupten Yangpachen	Thub bstan yang pa can	ཐུབ་བསྟན་ཡངས་པ་ཅན།
	Tidenti	*Ching Drupa Tidenti*	*Byings sgrub pa Ti dan ti*	བྱིངས་སྒྲུབ་པ་ཏི་དན་ཏི།
		Tishrī Kunlo	Ti shrI Kun blo	ཏི་ཤྲཱི་ཀུན་བློ།
		Tokden Gyenpo	Rtogs ldan rgyan po	རྟོགས་ལྡན་རྒྱན་པོ།
		Toktsewa	Tog rtse ba	རྟོག་རྩེ་བ།
		Tönpa Lodrö Rabsal	Ston pa Blo gros rab gsal	སྟོན་པ་བློ་གྲོས་རབ་གསལ།
		Trang	'Phrang	འཕྲང་།
		Trang Drakmarwa	'Phrang Brag dmar ba	འཕྲང་བྲག་དམར་བ།
Treasury of Abhidharma	*Abhidharmakośa*	*Chö Ngönpa Dzö*	*Chos mngon pa mdzod*	ཆོས་མངོན་པ་མཛོད།
Treasury of Logic on Valid Cognition		*Tsema Rikter*	*Tshad ma rigs gter*	ཚད་མ་རིགས་གཏེར།

English	Sanskrit	Phonetic Tibetan	Transliterated Tibetan	Tibetan (Uchen)
Treasury of Words		*Tsikter*	*Tshig gter*	ཚིག་གཏེར།
Treatise on the Foundation of Yoga Practitioners	*Yogācārabhūmiśāstra*	*Sadé Nga*	*Sa sde lnga*	ས་སྡེ་ལྔ།
Treatise on the Objects of Cognition	*Alambanaparīkṣā*	*Mikpa Takpa*	*Dmigs pa brtag pa*	དམིགས་པ་བརྟག་པ།
Treatise on the Ultimate Continuum of the Mahāyāna	*Ratnagotravibhāga Mahāyānottaratantra Śāstra*	*Gyü Lama*	*Rgyud bla ma*	རྒྱུད་བླ་མ།
	Tripiṭaka	Denö sum	Sde snod gsum	སྡེ་སྣོད་གསུམ།
		Trisong Detsen	Khri srong lde btsan	ཁྲི་སྲོང་ལྡེ་བཙན།
		Trizé Lhalek	Khri mdzes lha legs	ཁྲི་མཛེས་ལྷ་ལེགས།
		Tsamorong	Tsha mo rong	ཚ་མོ་རོང་།
		Tsang	Gtsang	གཙང་།
		Tsang Barphuk	Gtsang Bar phug	གཙང་བར་ཕུག
		Tsarkha	Tshar kha	ཚར་ཁ།
		Tsarkhai Naljorpa	’Tshar kha’i Rnal ’byor ba	འཚར་ཁའི་རྣལ་འབྱོར་བ།
		Tsen	Btsan	བཙན།
		Tsezin	Tshe ’dzin	ཚེ་འཛིན།

English	Sanskrit	Phonetic Tibetan	Transliterated Tibetan	Tibetan (Uchen)
		Tsokgom Kunga Palsangpo	Tshogs sgom Kun dga' dpal bzang po	ཚོགས་སྒོམ་ཀུན་དགའ་དཔལ་བཟང་པོ།
		Tsomo Gyal	Mtsho mo rgyal	མཚོ་མོ་རྒྱལ།
		Tsurtön Shönu Sengé	Tshur ston Gzhon nu seng ge	ཚུར་སྟོན་གཞོན་ནུ་སེང་གེ
Twenty Thousand		*Nyitri*	*Nyi tri*	ཉི་ཁྲི།
Twenty Vows		*Dompa Nyishupa*	*Sdom pa nyi shu pa*	སྡོམ་པ་ཉི་ཤུ་པ།
		Umapa Sherab Bum	Dbu ma pa shes rab 'bum	དབུ་མ་པ་ཤེས་རབ་འབུམ།
Unification of the Buddha		*Sangyé Nyamjor*	*Sangs rgyas mnyam sbyor*	སངས་རྒྱས་མཉམ་སྦྱོར།
Unification of the Four Yoginis		*Naljorma Shi Khajor*	*Rnal 'byor ma bzhi'i kha sbyor*	རྣལ་འབྱོར་མ་བཞིའི་ཁ་སྦྱོར།
		Usé	Dbu se	དབུ་སེ།
	uṣṇīṣa	tsuktor	gtsug tor	གཙུག་ཏོར།
	Uṣṇīṣavijayā	Tsuktor Namgyalma	Gtsug tor rnam rgyal ma	གཙུག་ཏོར་རྣམ་རྒྱལ་མ།
		Utsé Nyingma	Dbu rtse Rnying ma	དབུ་རྩེ་རྙིང་མ།
		Ü Tsethang	Dbus Rtse thang	དབུས་རྩེ་ཐང་།
Uyghur		Yugur	Yu gur	ཡུ་གུར།
		Uyukpa	'U yug pa	འུ་ཡུག་པ།

English	Sanskrit	Phonetic Tibetan	Transliterated Tibetan	Tibetan (Uchen)
		Uyukpa Palgyi Gyaltsen	'U yug pa Dpal gyi rgyal mtshan	འུ་ཡུག་པ་དཔལ་གྱི་རྒྱལ་མཚན།
		Uyukpa Rikpai Sengé	'U yug pa Rig pa'i seng ge	འུ་ཡུག་པ་རིག་པའི་སེང་གེ
	Vādisiṃha	Mawai Sengé	Smra ba'i seng ge	སྨྲ་བའི་སེང་གེ
	Vaiśravaṇa	Namthösé	Rnam thos sras	རྣམ་ཐོས་སྲས།
Vajra Beneath the Earth	*Vajra Patala*	*Dorjé Sawo (Vajra Patala)*	*Rdo rje sa 'og (badzra pa ta la)*	རྡོ་རྗེ་ས་འོག ༼བཛྲ་པ་ཏ་ལ༽།
	Vajrabhairava	Dorjé Jikjé	Rdo rje 'jigs byed	རྡོ་རྗེ་འཇིགས་བྱེད།
	Vajra Ḍākinī	*Dorjé Khandro*	*Rdo rje mkha' 'gro*	རྡོ་རྗེ་མཁའ་འགྲོ།
	Vajradhāra	Dorjé Chang	Rdo rje 'chang	རྡོ་རྗེ་འཆང་།
	Vajra Gantipa	Dorjé Drilbu	*Rdo rje dril bu*	རྡོ་རྗེ་དྲིལ་བུ།
Vajragarbha Alankara Tantra		*Dorjé Nyingpo Gyen-kyi Gyü*	*Rdo rje snying po rgyan gyi rgyud*[5]	རྡོ་རྗེ་སྙིང་པོ་རྒྱན་གྱི་རྒྱུད།
Vajra Garland: The Commentary Tantra of Guhyasamāja		*Shegyü Dorjé Trengwa*	*Bshad rgyud rdo rje 'phreng ba*	བཤད་རྒྱུད་རྡོ་རྗེ་འཕྲེང་བ།
	Vajrakīlaya	Dorjé Phurba	Rdo rje Phur pa	རྡོ་རྗེ་ཕུར་པ།

5. "Rdo rje snying po rgyan gyi rgyud" seems to be a translation of two Kangyur texts: *Vajrahṛdaya-alaṃkāra-tantra* (Dege 451) and *Vajramaṇḍa-alaṃkāra-nāma-mahātantrarājā* (Dege 490), but I could not find a tantra named *Vajragarbha-alaṃkāra-tantra*.

English	Sanskrit	Phonetic Tibetan	Transliterated Tibetan	Tibetan (Uchen)
	Vajrapāṇi	Chakna Dorjé	Phyag na rdo rje	ཕྱག་ན་རྡོ་རྗེ།
	Vajrapañjara	Gur	Gur	གུར།
Vajra Verses		*Dorjé Tsik*	*Rdo rje tshig*	རྡོ་རྗེ་ཚིག
	Vajravidāraṇa	Dorjé Namjompa	Rdo rje Rnam 'joms pa	རྡོ་རྗེ་རྣམ་འཇོམས་པ།
	Vālmīki	Drokhar	Grog mkhar	གྲོག་མཁར།
	Varanasi	Waranasi	wA rA Na sI	ཝཱ་རཱ་ཎ་སཱི།
	Vasiṣṭha	Nejik	Gnas 'jig	གནས་འཇིག
	Vāsuki	Norgyé	Nor rgyas	ནོར་རྒྱས།
	Vasubandhu	Jiknyen	Dbyig gnyen	དབྱིག་གཉེན།
	Veda	*Rikjé*	*Rig byed*	རིག་བྱེད།
	Vedānta	Rikjé	Rig byed	རིག་བྱེད།
	vidyādhara	rikpa dzinpa	rig pa 'dzin pa	རིག་པ་འཛིན་པ།
	Vimalaśrī	Drima Mepai Pal	Dri ma Med pa'i dpal	དྲི་མ་མེད་པའི་དཔལ།
	Vinayamūla Sūtra	*Dulwa Dotsa*	*'Dul ba mdo rtsa*	འདུལ་བ་མདོ་རྩ།
	Virūpa	Birupa	Bir wa pa	བིར་ཝ་པ།
	Viṣṇu	Lha Chenpo	Lha chen po	ལྷ་ཆེན་པོ།
Vulture's Peak		Chagö Phungpo Ri	Bya rgod Phung po'i Ri	བྱ་རྒོད་ཕུང་པོའི་རི།
	Vyāsa	Gyepa	Rgyas pa	རྒྱས་པ།

English	Sanskrit	Phonetic Tibetan	Transliterated Tibetan	Tibetan (Uchen)
Wangchuk Tsöndrü from Ngonpa		Ngönpa Wangchuk Tsöndrü	Mngon ba Dbang phyug brtson 'grus	མངོན་པ་དབང་ཕྱུག་བརྩོན་འགྲུས།
Wati temple		Wati tsuklakhang	Wa ti'i Gtsug lag khang	ཝ་ཏིའི་གཙུག་ལག་ཁང་།
Well-Explained Reasoning	*Vyākhyāyukti*	*Chepai Tsé Namshé Rikpa*	*'Chad pa'i tshe nam bshad rigs pa*	འཆད་པའི་ཚེ་རྣམ་བཤད་རིགས་པ།
White Acala		Miyowa Karpo	Mi g.yo ba Dkar po	མི་གཡོ་བ་དཀར་པོ།
		Wönjo Darma	Dbon jo dar ma	དབོན་ཇོ་དར་མ།
Wrathful King		*Trowoi Gyalpoi Tokpaché*	*Khro bo'i rgyal po'i rtog pa che*	ཁྲོ་བོའི་རྒྱལ་པོའི་རྟོག་པ་ཆེ།
		Yachang	Ya changs	ཡ་ཆངས།
		Yadruk Silima	G.ya' 'brug Si li ma	གཡའ་འབྲུག་སི་ལི་མ།
		Yakdé Sönam Sangpo	G.yag sde bsod nams bzang po	གཡག་སྡེ་བསོད་ནམས་བཟང་པོ།
		Yalung	G.ya' lung	གཡའ་ལུང་།
		Yalung Chukyar	G.ya' lung Chu skyar	གཡའ་ལུང་ཆུ་སྐྱར།
	Yamāntaka	Shinjei Shé	Gshin rje'i gshed	གཤིན་རྗེའི་གཤེད།
	Yamāntaka Kṛṣṇaśaturā	*Dranak Jikor*	*Dgra nag 'jigs skor*	དགྲ་ནག་འཇིགས་སྐོར།
	Yamāntaka Tantra	*Shinjei Shedra Nakgi Gyü*	*Gshin rje'i gshed dgra nag gi rgyud*	གཤིན་རྗེའི་གཤེད་དགྲ་ནག་གི་རྒྱུད།

English	Sanskrit	Phonetic Tibetan	Transliterated Tibetan	Tibetan (Uchen)
		Yamatak Thengjuk	Ya ma stag Thengs 'jug	ཡ་མ་སྟག་ཐེངས་འཇུག
		Yangchen Gulgyen	*Dbyangs can mgul rgyan*	དབྱངས་ཅན་མགུལ་རྒྱན།
		Yapang Kyé	G.ya' spang Skyes	གཡའ་སྤང་སྐྱེས།
		Yarlungpa Jangchup Gyaltsen	Yar lung pa Byang chub rgyal mtshan	ཡར་ལུང་པ་བྱང་ཆུབ་རྒྱལ་མཚན།
		Yarlungpa Drakpa Gyaltsen	Yar lung pa Grags pa rgyal mtshan	ཡར་ལུང་པ་གྲགས་པ་རྒྱལ་མཚན།
		Yegen Pakshi	Ye rgan dpag shi	ཡེ་རྒན་དཔག་ཤི།
		Yogi Truma	Rnal 'byor pa phru ma	རྣལ་འབྱོར་པ་ཕྲུ་མ།
		Yönten Thayé	Yon tan Mtha' yas	ཡོན་ཏན་མཐའ་ཡས།
		Yuring	g.yu rings	གཡུ་རིངས།

Notes

1 Translated from *Sa pan rnam thar gsung sgros ma 'phags pa rin po ches mdzad pa la kha skong dang bcas* in *The Great Collection of the Lamdré Lobshé Teachings: Biographies of Masters, Volume 1* (*Gsung ngag la 'bras sbob bshad chen mo bla ma'i rnam thar skor - ka*), pp. 135–60. Printed by Sakya Dolma Phodrang, Dehradun U.A., India. Authorized by His Holiness the Forty-First Sakya Trichen. Edited by Khenchen Appey Rinpoche, 2008.
2 Sakya Paṇḍita's father's name was Palchen Öpo.
3 The *Commentary on Valid Cognition* (*Pramāṇavārttika*) and six other important texts by Dharmakīrti.
4 The second son of Ogodei Khan and grandson of Genghis Khan.
5 Hor is an epithet of Mongolia.
6 Translated from Sengé, Sönam (Bsod nams seng ge), *An Explanation Differentiating the Three Vows Clarifying the Intent of the Buddha's Scriptures* (*Sdom pa sum gyi rab tu dbye ba'i rnam bshad rgyal ba'i gsung rab kyi dgongs pa gsal ba zhes bya ba bzhugs so*), in *Collected Works of Kunkhyen Gorampa Sönam Sengé* (*Kun mkhyen go ram pa bsod nams seng ge bka' 'bum*), vol. *ta*, pp. 6–60. Published by Dzongsar Khamkye Lobling (Rdzong sar khams bye'i slob gling), India.
7 The four social gatherings is a set of virtues, like the six perfections. They are giving, kind speech, encouraging others to practice, and embodying a good example of practice yourself.
8 The two processes are creation and completion.
9 Although the text states that there were thirteen disciples, only twelve are listed in this and other editions of this biography.
10 Translated from the *Treasury of Amazing Sakya Biographies* (*Gdung rabs ngo mtshar bang mdzod*), published by Mi rigs dpe skrun khang in Beijing, 1986.
11 This section title is repeated from above in the original text.
12 A yojana is approximately thirteen kilometers.
13 Godan was the second son of Ogedei Khan and Toregene Khatun and a brother of Guyuk Khan. "Potholoyon" may be a title or secondary name.
14 Footnote in the original: "Forcefully not thinking of anything in the mind," "resting one's mind upon the mental continuum," and "pulling sluggishness and sleep inward."
15 Footnote in the original: King Indrabhūti stated: "By what the deluded call 'meditation,' the deluded attain delusion." Ārya Nāgārjuna stated: "If emptiness is incorrectly perceived, those with little wisdom degenerate. Without analyzing

discriminative wisdom, clinging to the dharma of space, and grasping nothingness, the experience of emptiness arises, by which objects of perception cease."

16 Footnote in the original: Not illuminating the movement of mind, naturally observing calm abiding due to excessive insight wisdom.

17 Footnote in the original: This means experience that arises without study and analysis of the Abhidharma and other sources, identifying that all phenomena are empty, like space and mind itself, and neither exist nor do not exist.

18 Footnote in original: Accumulating unwavering karma, which causes birth in formlessness.

19 Footnote in original: When abiding for a long period of time without remembering anything that is going on, while meditating in samādhi.

20 Footnote in original: Not having luminosity concerning the six sensory organs of the consciousness, such as the eye, etc.

21 Footnote in original: The *Ornament of the Mahāyāna Sūtras* states: "Therefore their body and mind are highly trained, their total familiarization is known as *the activities of awareness*."

22 Footnote in original: Āryadeva states: "Neither existent, nonexistent, nor existent and non-existent, nor neither. This is the tradition of the Middle Way, the exalted meaning that is beyond the four extremes."

23 Footnote in original: Master Buddhajana states: "Besides the movement of ordinary conceptual thought, there are no other shackles to this existence. The mind that overcomes that becomes nonconceptual in every aspect."

24 Footnote in original: *Avalokiteśvara White Lotus* states: "Suchness that transcends the most subtle particle of an atom, in the aspect of one able to perform *pra* (see the future on a fingernail), exalted in every aspect, Mahāmudrā is unchangeable bliss."

25 Arhats, prateykabuddhas, and buddhas.

26 Guyuk Khan was Godan Khan's older brother.

27 Divination based on a mirror or fingernail.

28 December 5, 1251, the Female (Iron) Pig Year.

29 Sakya Paṇḍita's relics were placed in a stupa on the grounds of the Emanation Temple.

30 Also known as Rinchen Gang Monastery, this is located in Sekshing village of Shigatsé.

Index

About the Authors

Drogön Chögyal Phakpa (Lodrö Gyaltsen) (1235–80) was the Seventh Sakya Trizin and fifth of the five founding masters of the Sakya order.

Although his religious name is Lodrö Gyaltsen, he is better known by his title, Drogön Chögyal Phakpa. Chögyal Phakpa was Sakya Paṇḍita's primary disciple, religious heir, and paternal nephew. He accompanied Sakya Paṇḍita on his travels to the Mongol court and participated in his activities there. He was at Sakya Paṇḍita's side to witness the miraculous nature of the great master's passing into parinirvana, described in vivid detail in this biography. Shortly thereafter, at the age of only nineteen, Chögyal Phakpa so impressed Emperor Kublai Khan that the khan designated him his personal religious master with the title of *tishri*, and gave him religious and secular authority over the three provinces of Tibet.

Gorampa Sönam Sengé (1429–89) was a great Sakya scholar, philosopher, and prolific author.

Gorampa Sönam Sengé wrote an impressive number of important commentaries on both sūtra and tantra, including the Middle Way, the Perfection of Wisdom, logic, Abhidharma, and the Vinaya. His explications of the Sakya view and rebuttals of its challengers still form the core of philosophical studies in Sakya and other monastic colleges today. The biography of Sakya Paṇḍita translated here appears in the introductory matter he wrote as a preface to his famous work *Classification of the Three Vows*.

Jamgön Ameshab (Ngawang Kunga Sönam) (1597–1659) was the Twenty-Seventh Sakya Trizin.

Although his religious name is Ngawang Kunga Sönam, he is better known by the respectful epithet Jamgön Ameshab due to his calm and dignified manner. Intensively trained in religious studies from childhood, he became throne holder of the Sakya order at the age of twenty-four. A prolific author of over thirty-five volumes of religious texts, he also played an important role as a peacekeeper and mediator between various warring states and factions during his time.

What to Read Next from Wisdom Publications

FREEING THE HEART AND MIND (3 VOLUMES)
His Holiness the Sakya Trichen

This trilogy is "required reading" for any Sakya practitioner, and will also be deeply inspiring for Buddhists of all traditions.

THE SAKYA SCHOOL OF TIBETAN BUDDHISM
Dhongthog Rinpoche
Translated by Sam Van Schaik

Since its 1976 publication in Tibetan, Dhongthog Rinpoche's history of the Sakya school of Tibetan Buddhism has been a key reference for specialists in Tibetan studies. Now English readers can consult it as well through Sam van Schaik's authoritative, fully annotated and accessible translation.

THE AMAZING TREASURY OF THE SAKYA LINEAGE, VOLUME 1
Ameshab Ngakwang Kunga Sönam
Translated and introduced by Khenpo Kunga Sherab
and Matthew W. King

"May the accounts of the holy lives preserved in this text inspire future generations of practitioners to follow in these great masters' footsteps, and may the future generations of the Khön Sakyapa continue to uphold the Buddhadharma for countless generations to come." —from the foreword by His Holiness the Sakya Trichen

Ornament to Beautify the Three Appearances
The Mahāyāna Preliminary Practices of the Sakya Lamdré Tradition
By Ngorchen Könchok Lhundrup
Translated by Cyrus Stearns
Foreword by His Holiness the Sakya Trichen

Ornament to Beautify the Three Appearances is the first book of a two-volume set of works written by Ngorchen Könchok Lhundrup (1497–1557) to explain the Lamdré teachings, the most important system of tantric theory and practice in the Sakya tradition of Tibetan Buddhism.

About Wisdom Publications

Wisdom Publications is the leading publisher of classic and contemporary Buddhist books and practical works on mindfulness. To learn more about us or to explore our other books, please visit our website at wisdom.org or contact us at the address below.

Wisdom Publications
132 Perry Street
New York, NY 10014 USA

We are a 501(c)(3) organization, and donations in support of our mission are tax deductible.

Wisdom Publications is affiliated with the Foundation for the Preservation of the Mahayana Tradition (FPMT).